QUESTIONS ANSWERED BY THIS BOOK

...... Who built the Great Pyramid?

...... Did Atlantis and Lemuria really exist?

...... Were some of the "gods" of antiquity really space visitors?

...... Who was the Pharaoh of the Exodus?

...... Who was the Pharaoh when Abraham was in Egypt?

...... Who was Pharaoh when Joseph ruled Egypt?

...... Did Solomon live in the sixteenth century B.C. instead of the tenth century B.C.?

...... Who was the Queen of Sheba?

...... Was Menelik the actual son of Solomon and Sheba?

...... Was a great stone ever "pushed" away from Christ's tomb?

...... Why did Mark leave Paul and Barnabas at Perga?

...... Was Peter ever really in Rome?

...... Where was the Last Supper celebrated?

...... Did the Garden of Gethsemane belong to Mary, mother of Mark?

...... Are there fantastic historical treasures which constitute a legacy for mankind hidden under some of the wonders of the world?

...... Was Akhnaton of Egypt later Simon Peter?

...... Was Joseph of the "coat of many colours" later Moses?

...... Are there hidden pyramids in North America?

...... What is the real meaning of the Aztec Calendar Stone?

...... Were the "Seven Cities of Cibola" myth or fact?

...... Is there a secret temple under the Sphinx?

...... Why did they say that the Pharaohs were descended from the "Sun"?

...... Was the Grand Canyon of Arizona caused by a great earthquake instead of gradual erosion?

...... Is there an ancient space ship buried under the Great Pyramid?

...... How did Moses cross the Red Sea?

...... Was there a curse on Tutankhamun's tomb?

...... Was the capstone of the Great Pyramid made of copper? And when will it be replaced?

...... What does the "blood" shed on the Cross really signify?

SECRET PLACES
OF THE LION

by
GEORGE HUNT
WILLIAMSON

Destiny Books New York

Destiny Books
377 Park Avenue South
New York, NY 10016

First Quality Paperback Edition 1983
Copyright © 1958 George Hunt Williamson

Library of Congress Cataloging in Publication Data
Williamson, George Hunt, 1926-
  Secret places of the lion.

  1. Occult sciences. I. Title.
BF1999.W564 1982   001.9   82-2374
ISBN 0-89281-039-4 (pbk.)   AACR2

Printed in the United States of America

Destiny Books is a division of Inner Traditions International, Ltd.

" Like as a *lion* that is greedy of his prey,
     and as it were a young *lion* lurking in *secret places.*"

PSALMS xvii: 12

Contents

Charts used as reference during the reading of this book

PROLOGUE

*W*HAT and *where* are the SECRET PLACES OF THE LION? History is rewritten in these pages in the light of translations from very ancient manuscripts preserved in the great library of one of the world's time-honoured mystery schools . . . a " lost city " high in the mountains of Peru. Few go there today, because only selected students of life trod the footworn path to its antediluvian gate.

In this city lives a master teacher . . . a survivor of the Elders, the great men who lived on earth when " giants " roamed the planet. One hundred and forty-four individuals work under this mentor, and some of them were formerly the " great " of earth.

Pharaohs . . . artists . . . saints . . . scientists . . . poets. Some of the " unknown " are there, too; those history forgot to record, but those who nevertheless shaped empires, kings, ideologies, and doctrines! The " crowned " and the " uncrowned " mingle here in fellowship.

It is the purpose of this work to show that the *race spirit* incarnated or ensouled itself into race leaders of the dim past . . . these leaders constitute the " Goodly Company." This band is composed of men and women from other worlds in time and space. They originally arrived on earth to assist mankind here in its long climb from "beasthood " to " godhood."

They migrated to earth—the " dark star " . . . planet of " sorrows "—about eighteen million years ago and have worked ceaselessly and tirelessly in their gigantic task of acting as the Creator's mentors to a backward, fallen race. They have come into life as Osiris . . . Apollo . . . Mercury . . . Thoth . . . the legendary gods of the ancients, and later incarnated as rulers of the people.

Baal, Bacchus, Moloch, and other false gods were nothing but pure earth deities, and always became the ruling hierarchy in the pantheon of gods after a " Golden Age " had gone out in a blood-bath. Great universal truth was brought to mankind through the instrumentality of beings from more enlightened worlds, and an age where " men talked with the angels " inevitably followed, only to decline and fall in decay when the mentorship was removed.

Examples of such periods would be the eclipse of truth that followed after the death of the great Pharaoh Amunhotep IV (Akhnaton), the first ruler in history to declare his belief in one God; and the veil that was thrown over the Word of the Infinite Father after the Crucifixion on Golgotha, when truth-seeking mankind was literally thrown to ravening beasts and clandestine councils handed down edicts which deprived man of God-given knowledge and truth!

The "Goodly Company "—the " Wanderers " who volunteer to come into earthly existence—time and time again have assisted mankind for thousands of years in all ages. They would declare universal wisdom and truth at a certain period of history when man had been prepared to receive it and then they would withdraw for a time to see what man would do with the new-found knowledge. Thus, the *rises* and *plateaux* of man's cultural history emerged.

During a hiatus of universal influx, man was ruled by powerful and aggressive earth spirits. Examples of such periods would be the decadent rule in colonies of the " Motherland " after the submergence of Lemuria and Atlantis; the idolatrous period of late dynastic Egypt; the perversion and licentiousness of Rome under the Caesars.

Legends of earth are rich in knowledge of the " Star People " ... the " Above People " ... the " Gods who came from the Sun or descended from Heaven to walk among mortals." Behind these so-called myths, which at first appear to be the imagining and fantasies of superstitious people, we find a logical answer to why man adored the immortals of Olympus and other fabled abodes of the great gods. We discover the startling truth behind the tales of the gods of classical mythology!

The ancient scribes and prophets spoke literal truth when they told later generations that *angels* and *gods* had taken on mortal flesh ... descended from their radiant heavenly homes ... to lift the physical, mental and spiritual level of humanity on the " dark star " in the Father's Cosmic House!

It is also the purpose of this work to show that there are fantastic historical treasures which constitute a great legacy for mankind hidden in secret chambers under some of the wonders of the world!

The "four corners" of the earth enclose timeless records that for millennia have been hidden from the eyes of seeking man. These priceless accounts of the struggles and intrigues of this planet are now coming to light—the SECRET PLACES OF THE LION are opening in the vibrations of a New Age!

The negative, opposing force which always intends to hold man back and keep him for ever in the dark chains of brutishness and beastliness has been behind the destruction of the great treasure-houses of remote antiquity. Examples would be the destruction of the Aton Tablets in Akhnaton's record sanctum by the evil Amun priesthood after the great Pharaoh's assassination; the burning of the Alexandrian library by fanatics in A.D. 389, the largest and most famous repository of antiquity, containing over seven hundred thousand volumes, comprising most of the literary treasures of the ancient world, an inestimable loss which brought about the "Dark Ages"; the total destruction of the Aztec libraries, where priceless codices were ravaged with fire and sword by Cortez in A.D. 1519 as he sacrificed untold treasures to greed and they were swallowed up in his incendiarism.

Certain secret orders have always managed to salvage or save universal truth, and on clay tablets, scrolls, and papyri they recorded the truth, so that future man might know . . . and in the *knowing*, the *truth* would make him free from the bondage of untold ages.

These records were hidden in tombs . . . secret chambers . . . caverns . . . temple ruins . . . catacombs . . . and every secret recess and tunnel was utilized. These records deal with the Most Ancient Wisdom and will be rediscovered in the years immediately ahead. These truths have been secreted away—then discovered, only to be buried again after they served their purpose of revealing that which was to be known during a particular age and time in man's spiritual development.

The author wishes to extend his appreciation to his wife for her encouragement; and to Brother Philip, O.A.,* of a monastery in the Peruvian mountains who worked tirelessly amidst Cyclopean masonry translating original, ancient records in the scriptorium there.

* Amethystine Order.

The *LION* is greedy of its *prey*, for the ancient records are well preserved and hidden—but they will be revealed soon. The young *LION* lurks in *secret places*—and these places will no longer be secret in the " Golden Age " now dawning. As far as the information in this work is concerned . . . " the memory of man runneth not to the contrary "!

This work is dedicated to all men everywhere that they may *understand*—blessed are their eyes for they shall see . . . blessed are their ears for they shall hear—when the seal of secrecy is broken, the " mystery of mysteries " revealed, and the SECRET PLACES OF THE LION are no more!

GEORGE HUNT WILLIAMSON

Chapter One

PREPARATION

T HE *WORD* was prepared. . . .
" In the beginning was the Word, and the *Word* was with
God, and the *Word* was God " (John i: 1). " Word " in its
first and original sense does not mean voice, sound, or speech. It
means: The Creation, according to divine laws, from the universal
creative *fluid*, in the " tomb," " cave," or manger of the earth of
that *Perfect One*, which has the power to spiritualize and regenerate
Adamic man. The Bible tells us that " Man does not live by bread
alone, but by every *Word* that proceedeth out of the mouth of
God."

Therefore, the " Word " . . . the Divine Creative Influx was
prepared on earth that man here might receive it in love and understanding . . . that he might ascend to higher spiritual knowledge
and wisdom because of this *preparation*.

To understand fully what " lion " means in its symbolic sense we
must search the ancient mysteries and the strange symbolism
associated with these mysteries known only to selected initiates.
" Lion " in the positive sense signifies divine truth in power! That
is why Christ is called " the lion of the tribe of Judah."

When the Prophet Daniel saw a winged lion emerge from the
sea, he saw the symbolic representation of a New Age in which
the Divine Truth of the Word sets out to conquer new spiritual
territory.

The " lion " denotes the fearlessness of one who is imbued with
Divine Truth . . . those who are in Divine Truths from the Word
are like lions, though they may have no more bodily strength than
a lamb.

Candidates who successfully passed the ancient Mithraic initiations were called " lions " and were marked upon their foreheads
with the Egyptian cross. Mithras himself is often pictured with the

head of a lion and two pairs of wings. The reference to the " Lion " and the " Grip of the Lion's Paw " in the Master Mason's degree have a strong Mithraic tinge and may easily have originated from this cult.

The sun rising over the back of the lion has always been considered symbolic of power and rulership. The Egyptian priests in many of their ceremonies wore the skins of lions, which were symbols of the great solar orb, owing to the fact that the sun is exalted, dignified, and most fortunately placed in the constellation of Leo the Lion. Among the Egyptians the sun's rays are often shown ending in human hands (Aton). Masons will find a connection between these hands and the well-known " Paw of the Lion " which raises all things to life with its grip.

Anciently the corona of the sun was shown in the form of a lion's mane, a subtle reminder of the fact that at one time the summer solstice took place in the sign of Leo, the Celestial Lion. Initiates of the Egyptian Mysteries were sometimes called lions or panthers. The lion was the emissary of the sun, symbolizing light, truth, and regeneration.

The lion is king of the animal family, and, like the head of each kingdom, is sacred to the sun, whose rays are symbolized by the lion's shaggy mane. The allegories perpetuated by the mysteries (such as the one to the effect that the lion opens the secret book) signify that the solar power opens the seed-pods, releasing the spiritual life within.

There was also a curious belief among the ancients that the lion sleeps with his eyes open, and for this reason the animal was chosen as a symbol of vigilance. The figure of a lion placed on either side of doors and gateways is an emblem of divine guardianship. Therefore lion figures were erected over buried treasure. For ages the feline family has been regarded with peculiar veneration. To the Egyptian priests the cat was symbolic of the magnetic forces of Nature, and they surrounded themselves with these animals for the sake of the astral fire which emanated from their bodies. Such animals were symbols of eternity, for when they sleep they curl up into a ball with their head and tail touching.

The lion symbolizes Secret Wisdom (King Solomon was often symbolized as a lion); to overcome this beast is to become a master of such wisdom. It will be remembered that Samson and Hercules both conquered the lion. The lion also represents one of the Four Corners of Creation.

When did the " lion " begin to lurk in the " secret places " of earth? To answer this we would have to go back to a time so remote in this planet's history that it would stagger the human mind. Man has been on earth far longer than he dare imagine.

The earliest records recorded the arrival of " radiant beings from heaven "; these spiritual creatures were the inhabitants of more majestic and enlightened worlds, but man's ignorance caused him to deify such visitors to the " dark red star "—planet of " sorrow and cataclysm."

Mercury, the Messenger of the Gods . . . Thoth, Scribe of the Gods . . . Apollo, God of Light . . . and all the other super-beings adored and deified were early mentors to the people of earth. Later, they became the culture-heroes of Lemuria and Atlantis. Man only remembered the great truth they had brought from out of the void. Later these beings incarnated, appeared, and lived as men among men.

Many thousand of years ago in the eastern section of the Mother-land Lemuria, in a land known as Telos, the first trade-ships arrived from the planet Hesperus (Venus). This land is now in the vicinity of the Grand Canyon of Arizona.

A prominent student of the mysteries, and historian of Mu, was exploring remote areas of the back country where observers reported they had seen great " Ships of Light " come down out of heaven in the night. The masters and teachers of the people were excited beyond belief and the great monolithic cities of ancient Mu were in utter confusion and the population was jubilant—they were rejoicing, for at last the " gods had come to dwell among mortals." This has been prophesied by sages for generations—and at last it had come to pass.

The prominent student was known as " Lady of the Sun " and had been commissioned by the ruling prince to locate the visitors and welcome them to the land of the children of men. The first thing discovered in the wilderness by the historian were strange footprints in the sand, not unlike those made by the Venusian who walked in the sand near Desert Centre, California, on November 20, 1952. (See: *Flying Saucers Have Landed.*)

The strange symbols in pictographic language told the story of the coming of the "Star People" to earth. The historian later interpreted this message to her people and it was known as the "Great Interpretation of the Day the Stars Fell."

The woman, who was the oldest and most revered historian, met the first space visitor to emerge from the craft. She learned he had been sent by the Elders of Hesperus to establish trade relations with the people of Mu ... to exchange ideas on science, art, literature, and universal truth. The Elders felt that the time had come when the people of earth were prepared for intense visitation from higher worlds. The earth people needed the wisdom and knowledge of their planetary neighbours—and they had proven their right to it by their way of life and their great love for the Infinite Father.

The first visitor's name was "Merk" (Marc, Marrk), and with his arrival the most advanced race on earth at the time began intercourse with the neighbour Hesperus. This lasted for a short period until evil priesthoods caused the almost total destruction of the Motherland and the greater part of her sank beneath the waves into the black depths.

The great historian spent much time with the visitors and accumulated many facts; facts which she organized into a set of records, preserved on the Lemurian "imperishable metal" tablets—tablets of "telonium." Many great truths were deduced from the careful and meditative study of these records, and the Light from other worlds in time and space made its way into the hearts and souls of the truth-seeking people of Mu.

"Merc" and the "Sun Lady" erected a memorial over the area where the first "Light Ships" had landed. It is still intact, although buried, and will be discovered in the years ahead. As Mu rises again from her resting-place and meets another dawn of a greater age this timeless monument will come to light in the present state of Arizona in America.

Finally, conditions due to storms, drastic terrain changes, and intense cosmic ray bombardment caused the ruling prince to call in the mentors from Hesperus. He asked for their advice. They told him to gather together all of his people who understood and attempted to live Universal Truth and follow the Great Path. The true followers of the Infinite Spirit were to gather at the giant monument that memorialized the coming of the Venusians, and they were then to enter great space ships for the migration to Venus. Those of the " Left-Hand Path " were to stay on earth to meet the imminent disaster of their own making.

The land of Telos was a great trade centre and the location of the most advanced scientific research amongst the Lemurians; for those of the Motherland had great slender craft that could go hundreds of miles out into space—but they could not traverse the space between the worlds! Later, the memory of *Telos* was incorporated into the mythological Roman deity of the Earth, Tellus, goddess of fertility.

The wise ruling prince led his people out of the great cities, where men had now become animals, only seeking to destroy and pillage. He led them as he was to lead others millennia later in another lifetime from Egypt across the Red Sea into the Wilderness. He brought them out of the land of darkness into the great open land of the pristine wilderness where the monument stood, and he told them that he would give them a sign that would for ever symbolize the fact that they had left earth and gone into the great ocean of space, for some day their descendants would return and a troubled world would recognize the meaning of the *Tree and the Serpent*!

" Merk," his companions and survivors of the last days of Mu, mounted up from the earth like great eagles and the " Ships of Light " took them to a new world. Telos, as the eastern section of Mu, was the only portion of the Motherland to stay above the angry waves that cried for the souls of the unjust!

" Lady of the Sun " and another historian, Mutan Mian, were the last of the *Remnant* to stay on Telos. They had elected to remain and place the valuable records of " imperishable metal "— " telonium " tablets—in Time Capsules to be put in and on the surface of Telos-Mu.

The ruling prince did not go into space with his people because he passed away from great age before the final exodus from doomed Mu. He had completed his mission and he passed in transition before reaching the promised land of Hesperus, millions of miles away in deep space.

Mutan Mian put the information on metal tablets, information concerning the fate of Mu, secrets of its great scientific knowledge, teleportation, invisibility, telepathy, and other vital knowledge that future man on earth would need in order to survive in a New Age yet unborn.

The facts were assembled and condensed by " Sun Lady," and Mian laboured furiously to complete the gigantic task. With the sinking of great land masses, earthquakes of monstrous intensity shook the earth; cities crumbled; mountains were levelled; valleys became mountain peaks. The air was full of debris and smoke from newly formed oceanic volcanoes. And a colossal tremor rent the earth and formed in a few seconds what is now known as the Grand Canyon of Arizona. It was not formed, as present-day science believes, by gradual erosion by a little river that could hardly eat its way through a field of corn, let alone a mountain of solid rock.

The winds were howling as if all the night gods were shrieking for vengeance as the two small solitary figures went about their task. Mian opened his account on the first tablet by saying: " These are the truths I, Mutan Mian, historian-scribe of Mu, realizing even more forcibly now, must pass on to future man, written on tablets that will be deposited in several places so that they may be found in some future time. These truths, in addition to a history of the great exodus I have observed, *must reach future man*! The telonium message plates will be distributed in the most likely places both *in* and *on* the surface of the remainder of Mu. I pray that the descendants of those few wild men [Indians] I have seen in the great forests, but have been unable to approach, may some day find these plates and have the sense to read them and heed their message. Some day, I have a feeling, they will be a race of men again. It is good seed they inherit, and they might be worth this effort in spite of the increasing cosmic ray activity. I pray that when they find these plates they will *understand*! "

The plates over which Mian and " Sun Lady " laboured so mightily have never been found. And judging from the information recorded by Plato, as received from Solon, it would seem that the telonium tablets were deposited about twelve thousand years ago. However, vast upheavals have occurred, such as the sinking of Atlantis, and the smashing down of the gates of the Pillars of Hercules which formed the Mediterranean Sea. Therefore some of the plates will never be discovered. Their hiding-places have been destroyed and rendered impossible of discovery. But, in the American South-West, the tablets left in Telos are safe and await rediscovery by men who will use their universal knowledge to build a world of peace in a New Age now dawning.

The fate of " Sun Lady " and Mutan Mian is not known, but they completed their appointed task and were reborn in future ages to assist the *future men* they had in mind when they created the tablets.

The destruction of Lemuria did not take place in a single day or even a year. It covered a period of several thousand years; for the beginning of Mu goes back some two hundred thousand years. But the final catastrophe which caused the submergence of nearly all of Lemuria occurred about twelve thousand years ago. The only land left above ground was part of California, Arizona, and other parts of the American South-West; Australia, and Easter Island.

Easter Island is the strange island in the south Pacific that contains gigantic monoliths and mysterious stone figures which science is at a loss to explain. The native population, which is very small, claim they know nothing of these figures. They are so huge and their construction so unique they could not have been made by savage, uncultured people. Easter Island is all that is left above water of a great Lemurian Holy Mountain—and the colossal figures belong to the culture of lost Mu.

Before the great civilization of Mu, there existed in the north Pacific a large continent known as *Adoma*. As it sank some five hundred thousand years ago, Lemuria rose in the south Pacific. A-Dom is a Lemurian word meaning " race of men from the red earth." It has come down to us today as " Adam."

The " T " or " TAU " cross, surmounted by a circle, is the Crux Ansata (Ankh) or the cross of life. It was the key to the mysteries of antiquity and gave rise to the more modern story of St. Peter's golden key to heaven. The Crux Ansata migrated to many parts of the earth from Lemuria and Atlantis. It was originally the great fertility symbol of the people of Adoma, because it employs the masculine " TAU " and a feminine oval.

The migration of the Ankh or Crux Ansata is proven by the fact that it is found all over the world amongst ancient civilizations. It was plainly sculptured upon the back of at least one of the great stone figures found on Easter Island. This figure was brought to London by a sailing ship and is now in the British Museum.

The Crux Ansata also has been found adorning the breasts of

statues and bas-reliefs at Palenque, Copan, and throughout Central America. This cross was always associated with *water*. Among the Babylonians it was the emblem of the water gods; among the Scandinavians of heaven and immortality; and among the Mayas of rejuvenation and freedom from physical suffering. In Egypt this cross signified immortality of the soul.

Many proofs can be given to show that Lemuria and Atlantis developed colonies all over the earth. But the migration of the Crux Ansata is given here as one point of proof because of its peculiar interest.

Lemuria transplanted its culture when it realized that eventual complete submergence would take place. They transplanted their culture both east and west. Vast hordes of people migrated westward—discovered the continent of Asia, populated Cambodia and Burma, pushed up into India and Tibet, and laid the basis for that racial development which was to come down into historic times as Chinese. They likewise crossed to the east coast of Africa and penetrated to the district now recognized as the source of the Nile.

They introduced Negroes into Africa apparently by their western migration, sending other Negroid peoples up into what are now the Philippines, and distributed what are called Oriental or Mongoloid peoples throughout Asia generally. There are indications that in their colonization of Africa those who had penetrated to the headwaters of the Nile came into conflict with the Atlantean peoples who had migrated from eastern Atlantis into the Mediterranean basin and established themselves in and around the delta of the Nile.

These two root races, from opposite sides of the earth, came into contact east of the Sudan, with a result that supplies many solutions to the mysteries of anthropology in connection with the entire Mesopotamian and Caspian areas.

The great colonization projects sent eastward by Mu went to South America, Central America—even to Atlantis—then Europe, the Mediterranean area, Egypt, etc.

One of the greatest of Lemurian colonies existed in what is now the dense jungle of the Brazilian Matto Grosso. In 1925, Col. P. H. Fawcett disappeared in this wilderness looking for the ruins of great cities incomparably older than those in Egypt. He had read in an ancient, decaying document (Manuscript No. 512, Archives of the Biblioteca Nacional, Rio de Janeiro, Brazil), that these fabled cities actually existed. They were reported in the 1700s by a Portuguese explorer, who claimed they were built of gigantic stones. There were beautiful temples of Grecian style, and in the centre of one city there was a plaza with a great, high stone statue of a naked youth holding a shield. On the base of this figure were curious hieroglyphics in an unknown language of a lost people. Both cities had been damaged by an earthquake, according to the Portuguese adventurer.

These cities were great cultural centres after the abandonment of the remainder of Mu about twelve thousand years ago. It must be remembered that not all of the Lemurian population left the earth for Hesperus. The inhabitants of the great colonies remained, but Telos was wholly abandoned, and this accounts for the great cultural hiatus in the American South-West!

Into the Matto Grosso culture, " S.in Lady," the ruling prince, and even " Merk " from Venus, later incarnated. " Merk " desired to return to earth and voluntarily assist in helping his fellow man on the " dark star."

Another colony of the Motherland Mu was the highly advanced Inca civilization. This was one of the outstanding colonies of South America. Their legends say that Divinity " parted the seas for their passage to their early home "—just as the Red Sea was parted for the passage of the Children of Israel thousands of years later.

Inca legends say that their great cities were constructed by bearded white men who came to South America long before the time of the Incas and established a settlement. The great roadways were ancient in the time of the Incas and were used by the Lemurians in early colonizing attempts.

The gigantic solid gold Inca Sun Disk was not of native Inca workmanship, but had been brought from Lemuria and was adored in temples for centuries in South America. It is said that when struck its peculiar vibrations could even cause earthquakes!

The Maya civilization of Central America was another great colony of Mu. It is claimed that a more correct pronounciation of " Mu " is " Mar," and the word Maya, pronounced as May-yar, meant Colony of Mar.

The Quiches, a branch of the Maya race, possessed a book now known as the *Popol Vuh*, in which we read that when their ancestors migrated to America the Creator parted the sea for their passage—again just as the Red Sea was later parted for the Israelites! It is known that colonists from Atlantis also influenced Maya culture; so here we find both Lemurians and Atlanteans mingling and helping to develop the high civilization of ancient Central America.

Itzamna was the personification of the *East* amongst the Mayas. He was said to have come in his *magic skiff* from the east across the waters. He performed miracles such as the curing of the sick by the laying on of hands; he possessed the power of reviving the dead. He invented writing and books. He is always connected with symbols of life and light; it is he who is connected with the Maya *tree of life*! After instructing the Maya people, it is said that Itzamna returned to a land beyond the waters to the east from whence he came.

Kukulcan was the personification of the *West* amongst the Mayas. It was claimed that he *arrived by way of the west* and reigned for a while in the present vicinity of Chichen-Itza. Later he returned to Mexico and was known in that country as *Quetzalcoatl*.

According to early Spanish chroniclers of Maya history, Itzamna arrived in the fourth Ahau of the Maya calendar (A.D. 219). The earliest-dated Maya stone yet discovered bears the date of 96 B.C., so the coming of Itzamna in the fourth Ahau could not possibly be accurate! It would be impossible for Itzamna, no matter how great, to have "founded" the Maya culture—the architecture, letters, language, writing, and religion in the early part of the third century A.D.—when we have positive evidence of that culture's existence in the same territory at least as early as 96 B.C.! It takes thousands of years to establish even a reasonably accurate calendar. How then could Itzamna invent the Maya calendar, which is almost perfect, and put it into use at the beginning of the third century A.D. when numerous tablets are in existence bearing undisputed dates of the Maya calendar at least three hundred years earlier?

The godlike attributes ascribed to Itzamna are identical with those assigned to other outstanding leaders of widely different periods. The Spanish chroniclers were very wrong! Itzamna, in order to be the "founder of the Maya culture and the first priest of their religion," must have arrived thousands of years before 96 B.C.! He came in a "magic boat or skiff"—he came from a great land to the *east*! Actually, *Itzamna* was a great Atlantean who attempted colonization of the natives of Central America! They deified him after he returned to Atlantis in his " magic boat " or slender airship.

Kukulcan was actually a teacher from Lemuria, who came from the *west*. So in the legends of the " gods of the east and west," we find the proof that both Mu and Atlantis colonized Central America and taught the native Maya people.

The Itzaes, the people taught by Kukulcan in the area of Chichen-Itza, wandered for *forty years*, as did the people led by Moses! Sacred origins recorded on both sides of the earth are identical—so much so that it is beyond belief that modern man will not accept the truth about Mu (Lemuria, Pan) and Atlantis (Poseid).

Plato tells us that the civilization of Atlantis disintegrated with the last major sinking of Atlantis in approximately 9600 B.C. If Lemuria completed its submergence about twelve thousand years ago (*ca.* 10000 B.C.), this would mean that the final destruction of the Atlanteans took place only a few hundred years later.

Some of the great souls of Mu and her colonies incarnated in Atlantis during her " final hour." These workers in the " Light " were *preparing the way* for the " Dawn " that was to come. These members of the " Goodly Company " wandered from one civilization to another—from one lifetime to another. They found themselves in many different civilizations, cultures, catastrophes, and developments, but it was all for the purpose of preparing mankind for the influx of great Universal Truth. This Truth dawned in all its glory and grandeur in Egypt when Akhnaton revealed the One God (Aton) to a sceptical, idolatrous world.

The people of the Motherland had known the One God . . . then fell from their high estate and destroyed themselves and their land. A dark age followed which continued until the " Dawn " in Egypt.

It is not the purpose of this work to go into great detail on Lemuria and Atlantis. Much has already been written on this subject, but several of the more interesting and unknown factors had to be brought out to show the great plan of *Preparation* being carried out over countless millennia.

An interesting sidelight on Atlantis is the story of the " dunce cap." The symbol remains today in the form of the conical dunce cap placed on the heads of our grandparents in the one-room schoolhouse when they displayed stupidity in the classroom. The ancient meaning has been lost, however.

The dunce cap is a cone and a cone is a great source of energy. On Atlantis a similar device was put on the heads of those who had suffered injuries to the brain through accidental causes and to others of a criminal nature. This device was actually an electronic instrument, and the outside cone was made of copper attached to other intricate controls. So we can see how it has come down to us in the present form and placed on the heads of those who are not so " bright." Everyone is familiar with the conical hat which is symbolic of the magician, whether of the white or black arts. And the peak-crowned conical hat of witches is known to every schoolchild.

The Mexican Queen of the Witches, Tlazolteotl, wears the cone hat just the same as the European witch. In a rock shelter on a hillside near the village of Cogul in Spain a remarkable wallpainting may be seen. It was executed by Aurignacian Cro-Magnon artists. This painting depicts a number of women wearing pointedcrown hats. This remarkable mural was possibly executed in the Biscayan area of Europe by people influenced by colonists arriving from Atlantis at least twenty-five thousand years ago!

Witchcraft with its cone hat was prevalent among the Cro-Magnons, the people of the Fortunate Islands and the Canary Islands, and the ancient races on the American continent. It appears very evident that this form of sorcery did not come to America by way of Asia. It is seen to have existed from the earliest times in both Europe and America.

During the last days of Atlantis the use of the conical device was perverted, and was used to stimulate and exhilarate the users to the point that they would indeed become " intoxicated " from the wrong use of a former beneficial instrument.

The Egyptian god Osiris wore the white cone-shaped crown of the south, and the Chippewa Indians of North America still produce great power and spiritual magic in cone-shaped wigwams that witnesses have seen shake with great force even though their supports were driven far into solid earth. These are all reminders of the once secret scientific knowledge of Atlantis and her use of cones of force to heal her mentally ill!

History records numerous instances of records being secreted away under threat of impending doom. And Atlantis was no exception to the rule. In the narrative given by Plato we read that the records of the Atlanteans were written on gold tablets " and deposited as memorials with their robes."

Thus Atlantis passed away with only memory and a few islands (Azores, St. Paul's, Ascension, Tristan da Cunha) that had been the peaks of mountains remaining. Survivors journeyed to Egypt, where a great civilization had already been founded in *ca.* 24000 B.C.

" And in that day shall there be an altar to the LORD in the midst of the land of Egypt, and a pillar at the border thereof to the LORD " (Isaiah xix: 19).

The Great Pyramid is situated exactly on the geographical centre between Upper and Lower Egypt. Thus it is " in the *midst* " of Egypt as a whole and " on the borders thereof," of both sections. The Great Pyramid is a fantastic encyclopaedia of physical science and astral lore. The science of numbers, weights, measures, astronomy, astrology, and the secret mysteries of physiology are symbolized in that incomparable monument.

The Pyramid—the " altar " in the midst of Egypt—was reared by great masters from Atlantis and its construction was supervised by men from other worlds. They possessed wisdom that enabled them to solve the mystery of mysteries . . . " The seed is the WORD of God."

At the present time there is no evidence to prove that the Great Pyramid (Pyramid of Khufu, or Cheops) was erected in the Fourth Dynasty. Its extraordinary characteristics, unlike any other pyramid, assign to it far more importance than a mere burial mound. If it was built at the beginning of so-called Egyptian history, then the stupendous work is a contradiction. The execution of so vast a project reflects very high engineering skill, as all scholars admit. The workmanship is of the most advanced order. All evidence points to the fact that an advanced culture existed in Egypt thousands of years prior to the historic period of that country!

It will be revealed—and no doubt within a comparatively short time now—that there are many secret chambers within the Great Pyramid and that its true entrance lies under the silent object that is like a lion and yet like a man—the Sphinx! It will not remain silent much longer. That celestial force which conquered the animal nature and resulted in a race of perfected human beings in a far distant "Golden Age" enabled them to build a monument that would withstand the wear and tear of the ages and be a beacon light for fellow travellers along the same Great Path, a path that is narrow and sharp as a razor's edge, a path filled with stones that bruise and cut the feet. As one persists, the stones become fewer— green, velvet grass and beautiful flowers spring up beside the way; the heart of the aspirant is cheered and strengthened, and he picks himself up again and yet again and goes on with eyes ever fixed on the flaming star in the distance.

The incomparable Great Pyramid shows us what was done in past ages, what is being done now, and what will be accomplished by future generations until all humanity shall kneel at the feet of God—Ultimate Perfection—for all of God's children . . . for we are *all* His.

In the King's Chamber, which occupies the highest position yet discovered in the Pyramid, there is a very unique object. It has been given many names from sarcophagus to corn-bin. It is really a " womb within a womb "—a sacred chalice—and represents the pineal gland within the head of every human being. This receptacle within the King's Chamber is for ever *uncovered*, waiting patiently for that precious treasure which will be revealed in the New Age.

The " sarcophagus " was not intended by its perfected builders to contain a *dead* body! The Pyramid was constructed over a natural magnetic anomaly, and its pyramidal, cone-like shape amplified this natural force, and the Pyramid became, literally, an instrument of great cosmic energy and force. That is why there is a strange atmosphere and temperature in the King's Chamber; a death-like cold that cuts to the marrow of the bone! And if the sarcophagus is struck, the sound emitted has no counterpart in any known musical scale! If anyone passed into the " valley of the shadow," which was death, he could be restored by merely being placed in the uncovered sarcophagus! Later, the force diminished in the Pyramid, and initiates were placed in the stone " coffin " in a symbolic gesture of its former, ancient meaning. It meant that the candidate to the mysteries was " brought into new life " . . . " ye must be born again."

Scientists have discovered a weak magnetic force still emanating from this gigantic structure, but it is no longer strong enough to perform its miracle of " from death into life."

The King's Chamber and the Queen's Chamber stand in the same relation to each other as do the pineal gland and the pituitary body, the King's Chamber being placed the highest, and likewise the pineal body. No trace of any lighting system has ever been found, for no system of lighting was needed. The perfected builders enjoyed full use of the All-Seeing Eye and were a light unto themselves—the radiance from the inner eye giving light to all that was within the temple.

Near the top of the Great Pyramid there is the most secret of chambers. It contains written records of all world civilizations—a legacy for mankind that cannot even be imagined by modern man! In the New Age, when the sign of the Son of Man has appeared in the heavens, *all* things will stand revealed. Once again in the course of the ages will mankind have reached the same goal which the builders of the Great Pyramid reached in that far remote age of at least twenty-six thousand years ago.

Here and there are found a few whose eyes are beginning to be cleared, whose material vision is being purified, whose brain cells are beginning to vibrate to that harmony which, to the Ancient Ones, was sweet and thrilling " music of the spheres." And when this " Golden Age " shall come, we too will be able to join in that great anthem of joy and sing the praises of the Most High . . . the God within us!

Humanity and its mentors have been wandering many, many years in the " wilderness," but the Promised Land, flowing with milk and honey, is very, very near. Soon the " Stone that the builders rejected will have become the head of the corner."

Egyptologists have attempted to identify the crude dabs of paint in the Pyramid as cartouches of King Cheops, but it is almost inconceivable that this great ruler would have permitted his royal name to suffer indignities, for the only hieroglyphics to be found within the Pyramid are a few builders' marks sealed up in the chambers of construction, and these were painted upon the stones *before* they were set in position. In a number of instances the marks were either inverted or disfigured by the operation of fitting the blocks together. Cheops would never have allowed such an act if he were the *true* builder of the Pyramid!

Sea-shells at the base of the Pyramid prove that it was constructed *before* a great flood! This theory is substantiated by the much abused Arabian traditions. Therefore the Pyramid was constructed before the great floods caused by the final submergence of Atlantis which caused walls of water to engulf coastal areas and some interiors. It dates *ca.* 24000 B.C. At this time the great Atlantean scientist, Thoth, came to Egypt to assist in the planning being conducted by space visitors. At the beginning of every new Cosmic Cycle (each lasting approximately twenty-six thousand years) a similar structure is built.

The Sphinx was built thousands of years later by the native workmen, for it is typically Egyptian. The true entrance to the Pyramid was later covered by the Sphinx—a SECRET PLACE OF THE LION. This was done to prevent intruders of a dark age from entering the sacred shrine. The passage leading to the King's Chamber, and other more secret rooms was sealed up thousands of years before the Christian Era; therefore those later admitted into the Pyramid mysteries received their initiations in subterranean galleries now unknown. Without such galleries there could have been no possible means of entering or leaving, since the single surface entrance was completely closed by the outer casing stones. Blocked by the mass of the Lion-Man Sphinx, the secret entrance will be opened in the years ahead.

The entrance to the temples under the Sphinx was formerly sealed with a bronze gate whose secret spring could only be operated by the high priest. It was guarded by public respect, and a sort of religious fear maintained its inviolability better than armed protection would have done. In the belly of the Sphinx were cut galleries leading to the subterranean part of the Great Pyramid. In these underground temples today exist records on clay tablets, tablets of precious metals, and rolls of papyri.

The capstone was a miniature pyramid itself, made of pure crystalline *copper*! This is the symbolic metal of Venus, and the symbol of Venus is the Crux Ansata (Ankh)—symbol of immortality. It is known that copper possesses a *dimensional quality* unknown in all other earth metals. It was this strange quality that qualified it for the position as capstone. The ancients said: " Copper is more *precious* than gold! "

From a great distance, any traveller entering Egypt would see a giant blazing triangle of white light reflected from the four sides of the Pyramid, and atop this was a flaming, shining torch, observed as the sun's rays turned the copper into dazzling golden light! This was the area where the *Preparation* was taking place for the revealing of the Aton to mankind. The Great Pyramid is the "House of the Hidden Places"—the first structure erected as a repository for those secret truths which are the certain foundation of all arts and sciences. Through the ancient, mystic passageways and chambers passed the illumined of antiquity. They entered the portals as *men* and came forth as *gods*.

The Pyramid was the place of the "second birth," the "womb of the mysteries." Tradition says that somewhere in its depths resided an unknown being called "The Dweller." He was a *lion-faced* master that few men ever saw.

Legends say that when man first arrived on earth, millions of years ago, he took beastly body—first that of the cat, and later the ape. The Great Sphinx of Egypt, showing the head of a man and the body of a lion, commemorates this stupendous transition far back in archaic time!

It has already been mentioned that Thoth, the Atlantean, aided in the building of the Pyramid. The prototypes of the later, inferior, and smaller pyramids were copies made by the Egyptians. Thoth placed secret records and his Twelve Emerald Tablets in the Pyramid. Later, during the chaotic reign of King Horemheb (1346-1322 B.C.), these tablets were removed and were sent to the Maya priests of Central America, who placed them beneath the altar of one of the great temples of the Sun God. After the conquest of the Mayas the cities were abandoned and the treasures of the temple forgotten.

Thoth also secreted other records and instruments of the Motherland Mu and Atlantis in the Pyramid. These records explain how the "Children of Light" dwelt amongst the ancients. These "Children of Light" are not as sons of men, except when they are in physical bodies. Evidently "spawn of a lower star" came to Atlantis and eventually caused its downfall.

Thoth tells in his records how he would "raise this *staff* and direct a ray of vibration." This obviously refers to the powerful *vril stick* used by many of the kings and ruling officials of Egypt in later years! Thoth incarnated in Egypt *ca*. 3000 B.C. in the Third Dynasty as Iemhotep, architect under King Zoser. He was later deified by the Egyptians as the god of science and medicine; he was identified with Thoth, Scribe of the Gods. And well he should be, for he *was* Thoth! His name as Iemhotep means " one who comes in peace." During the reign of Zoser, Iemhotep discovered the original vril sticks he had secreted in the Great Pyramid as Thoth. Iemhotep was deified because he brought to light the great power of the vril during his lifetime, and performed many miracles with its use.

Thoth says in his Emerald Tablets: " In the apex of the Pyramid set I the *crystal*, sending the ray into the ' Time-Space,' drawing the force from out of the ether. . . ." The *crystal* was the so-called capstone of crystalline copper! Thoth says that the Great Pyramid was patterned after the natural pyramid of earth force which burns eternally—therefore it will remain throughout the ages.

One of the Emerald Tablets says: " Far in a past time, lost in the space time, the *Children of Light* looked down on the world; seeing the children of men in their bondage, bound by the force that came from beyond; knew they that only by freedom of bondage could man ever rise from the earth to the sun. Down they descended and created bodies, taking the semblance of men as their own. The Masters of everything said after their forming: ' We are they who were formed from the space dust, partaking of life from the infinite All; living in the world as children of men, like and yet unlike the children of men.' "

Thoth knew that all men were essentially spiritual beings, for he said: " Man is a ' star ' bound to a body! Man is *space born*, a child of the stars. Man is a flame bound to a mountain! "

The builders of the Great Pyramid buried one of their great space ships near the structure. Its power was added to that of the monumental stone pyramid. Thoth mentions this when he says: " Deep neath the rocks was buried a space ship, waiting the time when man might be free . . . over the space ship shall be erected a marker in the form of a lion, yet like unto man."

All through the ages knowledge has existed; it has never been changed, even though it was buried in darkness . . . it has never been lost though forgotten by man.

The time is fast approaching when the secret wisdom shall again be the dominating religious and philosophical urge of the world. The doom of dogma shall sound; the secret room in the " House of the Hidden Places " shall be rediscovered. The chants of the illumined shall be heard once more in its timeless passageways, and all men seeking *Truth* shall find it!

The "Goodly Company" had travelled a long, hard path to Egypt, via Lemuria, Atlantis, and the colonies—but before the *Dawn* more and more *Preparation* had to be brought about by many lifetimes of labour in Light. To discuss all of the finer points of such lengthy service would be nearly impossible; therefore only those lifetimes that are well known historically will be dealt with in this work.

For instance, *ca.* 2000 B.C., Abraham, the progenitor of the Jews and first of the great patriarchs, and King Hammurabi of Babylonia were contemporaries. Abraham had set out from Ur in search of a land where he could build a nation free from idolatry. The king known as "Amraphel" in Genesis, Chapter xiv, is really Hammurabi, and Abraham knew him personally when he was in Ur.

Hammurabi's "Code of Laws" is a voice from the dust of Abraham's world. He had his scribes collect and codify the laws of his kingdom, and had these engraved on stones to be set up in the principal cities. These stones portrayed Hammurabi receiving the laws from the sun-god Shamash. The king was a great patron of learning, and his reign was a period of great literary activity. Is it strange, then, that Hammurabi, whose code of edicts resembles Israelitish legislation, later incarnated as Israel's first law-giver, Moses? Also, Hammurabi had lived on Mu as the *ruling prince* of the Exodus to Hesperus!

When Abraham journeyed on south from Bethel, he passed close to Jerusalem, where he visited with Shem (eldest of three sons of Noah). Shem was none other than the Priest-King of Salem (Jerusalem), Melchizedek! Ancient tradition says that Shem was a survivor of the Flood, still alive in Abraham's time—earth's oldest living man! Abraham had known Shem back in Babylonia.

On account of famine, Abraham journeyed on through the southland into Egypt, to sojourn there until the famine was over. The Pharaoh of Egypt at that time was Senusert II, of the Twelfth Dynasty. At Beni Hasan there is a sculpture depicting a visit of Asiatic Semitic traders to Pharaoh's court, as if it were an event of great importance. This is a record of Abraham's visit to Egypt!

When Sarah, wife of Abraham and mother of Isaac, died, she

was buried in the Cave of Machpelah, on the west slope of Hebron. A mosque, under Mohammedan control, is now built over this area. It contains stone tombs of Abraham, Isaac, Jacob, Sarah, Rebekah, and Leah. There is a circular opening into a cavern below which is the real Cave of Machpelah. It has been unentered for six hundred years! Writings of Abraham, Isaac, and Jacob will be discovered there and will cause world-wide theological protest and concern!

Now we come to the time of Israel's migration to Egypt—the time of Joseph of the " coat of many colours." This unusual coat was a badge of favouritism, indicating Jacob's intention to make Joseph heir to the Birthright. Joseph, though Jacob's eleventh son, was Rachel's first-born and Rachel was Jacob's best-loved wife; therefore Joseph was the favourite son. At seventeen, because of the jealousy of his brothers, Joseph was sold into Egypt. He was of unblemished character, unusually handsome, with an exceptional gift for leadership and ability to make the best of every unpleasant situation. Joseph was thirteen years in the house of Potiphar and prison. At thirty he became deputy ruler of all Egypt. He died at the age of one hundred and ten.

Now it came to pass that Joseph stood before Pharaoh during the seventeenth year of Apepa I (Apepa Aauserra or Apofis)—1761 B.C. The great period when the WORD was Prepared reached its apex in 1761 B.C., at the very moment Pharaoh proclaimed Joseph Shalit (viceroy) of all the Egyptians. It had taken thousands of years for this period to reach this point in its development—but only a moment after the pinnacle was reached. Joseph, who had been a slave, symbolized that lofty peak of spiritual attainment.

Apepa I ascended the throne and became Pharaoh of Egypt in 1777 B.C. (Fifteenth Dynasty). This great ruler later incarnated as Amunhotep III, father of Akhnaton!

The name "Joseph" means: "Whom Jehovah will add to; Jehovah shall increase; he shall increase progressively from perfection unto perfection"! And he did progress, for he had been Hammurabi and was later to lead his people out of Egypt, just as he had brought them into Egypt.

Pharaoh gave Joseph the name of " Zaphnath-paaneah " (Genesis xli: 45). It means: " God spoke and he came into life."

It should be mentioned here, although it will be dealt with in detail in a later chapter, that the intent of the Biblical writers demands a period of four hundred or four hundred and thirty years for the Sojourn of Israel in the land of Egypt. Therefore, if we can determine when the Sojourn *began*, we will be able to definitely fix the period of the later Exodus!

Stephen, *ca.* A.D. 33, told the Jewish Sanhedrin that the Sojourn lasted four hundred years. In Genesis xv: 13-14 we read: " ... Know of a surety that thy seed shall be a stranger in a land that is not theirs, and shall serve them; and they shall afflict them four hundred years ... and afterward shall they come out with great substance."

Exodus xii: 40: "Now the sojourning of the children of Israel, who dwelt in Egypt, *was* four hundred and thirty years."

Jacob, and all the brothers of Joseph with their families and flocks, descended into Egypt in 1752 B.C., the twenty-sixth year of Apepa I. From this date, taking the traditional four hundred and thirty years for the Sojourn, we get 1322 B.C. (the year Horemheb died) for the Exodus. If we take four hundred years for the Sojourn we come up with 1352 B.C., the time of young King Tutankhamun. We will show later why both dates are accurate for Israel's return home and we will show that there *never* really was a Pharaoh of the Exodus!

Joseph first served in the house of Potiphar, prince of the guards and priest of On. He was the officer of Pharaoh who had bought Joseph from the Midianites. The Potiphar of Genesis xxxvii: 36 and the Potipherah (Potiphera) of Genesis xli: 45 are one and the same entity.

Then Joseph was detained in custody, and afterwards made ruler of Egypt as Shalit. This symbolized the Master who later appeared as Christ, for it represented how the Lord progressively made the human in Himself divine. Joseph being sold into Egypt symbolized the same as the Lord's being sold by Judas Iscariot.

Joseph in Egypt symbolizes the word of the imagination in subconsciousness, or the involution of a high spiritual idea. Joseph in Egypt could be said to represent also our highest perception of Truth, dealing with the realm of forms and bringing it into a more orderly state.

Potiphar had a fair daughter named Asenath ("Dedicated to Neith") ... Joseph looked upon her often in her father's house.

Knowing this, Pharaoh gave him Asenath to wife. She became the mother of Ephraim and Manasseh. Asenath in an earlier lifetime had been the Lemurian historian, " Lady of the Sun "—Joseph had been the *ruling prince* of Mu. This time the two began an association that was to carry them through many lives and intrigues.

The " Tale of Two Brothers," on an ancient papyrus now in the British Museum, written in the reign of Seti II (1214–1210 B.C., Nineteenth Dynasty) has very close resemblance to the story of Joseph and Potiphar's wife. It was worked up from the real incident, which was recorded in the annals of the Egyptian court. There is proof of Joseph's sojourn recorded in ancient Egyptian documents, and there are even statues representing him as a scribe! These will be discovered in the years ahead. Some of them will be found in the Great Pyramid . . . in the temple under the Sphinx . . . and at Joseph's palace in On. (Joseph's palace was discovered by Sir Flinders Petrie in 1912.)

The Temple of On was built " for eternity " and was once the foremost temple of northern Egypt built on the Nile Delta. On was the Egyptian name of Heliopolis, being also called On-mehit (the " Northern On "), to distinguish it from the " Southern On." Joseph and Asenath spent much time in this temple—but it did not last " for eternity "; all that survives of this building of splendour, once in the charge of the high priest Potiphar, is a solitary shaft of red granite, the Obelisk of On erected by Senusert I (Sesostris, Twelfth Dynasty) before Abraham went into Egypt! But the work of Joseph and Asenath in Egypt *Prepared* the *WORD* of the Infinite Father " for eternity " amongst men. Remember, this was the *apex* of the *Preparation* period.

At this same time in Egypt, he who was to become King Tutankhamun of the Eighteenth Dynasty lived on the banks of the Nile in abject poverty. How the lives of men do change!—from an unknown waif on the banks of a sacred river, eating the refuse of Egypt, to a Pharaoh on the proudest throne on earth centuries later! But this waif has been " Merk " of the " Ships of Light " that came to ancient Mu in her darkest hour!

Many will ask: " Why is it that all these individuals always had such glorious incarnations? " But they were not always grand and Pharaonic! Others will say: " But if they had been kings and princes so many times, why was it necessary for them to become the lowest of society in other lifetimes?" Let us remember that what man on earth calls splendid and of high estate may not be that at all! As a king an individual might have been a monstrous tyrant; as a pauper he might have been a great leader amongst his own and may have shone as a light in the darkness of an age. Those considered " great " by history may not be so " great " in the eyes of the Almighty. And what of those history forgot to record—the thousands of men and women who have carried the torch of Truth down through the bloody centuries? A lifetime as a spiritual, humble man may have served a far greater purpose than a lifetime as a weak ruler.

The waif in the time of Joseph was brought to the Temple of On by Asenath many times and he was taught there. He later helped hide Joseph's records in the palace at On. His accomplishments for humanity were far greater then than they were centuries later when he sat on a throne and wore the fabulous " double crown " of Upper and Lower Egypt on his young head, for as Tutankhamun he was a poor ruler.

It came to pass that Jacob died and his body was taken back to Hebron for burial. As Joseph was dying he exacted an oath of his brothers (Exodus xiii: 19) that when Israel returned to Canaan, they would carry his bones with them. It is said that Moses four hundred years later carried Joseph's remains out of Egypt. But did he? We will see later!

God desired that Israel should be nurtured for a while in Egypt, the most advanced civilization of the day!

From Egypt of Joseph's time we pass over history to the reign of Ahmose I, founder of the Eighteenth Dynasty, 1580 B.C. Ahmose I is very significant, not only because he founded the greatest Egyptian dynasty, but because he was a *contemporary of David and his son*, Solomon! This statement will undoubtedly shock all Bible scholars! For it is assumed that King David reigned from 1010 B.C. until 970 B.C., and the date given for the accession of Solomon is 970 B.C. Solomon purportedly built his famous temple in 966 B.C.

However, ancient records from the Mystery School in the Andes, near Lake Titicaca, Peru, affirm something entirely different! We find that David and his great son Solomon lived between five and six hundred years earlier than commonly accepted.

To prove our point, let me quote one authority, a professor of Biblical archaeology, Dr. J. McKee Adams: " . . . Those were the halcyon days of David and Solomon when foreign potentates looked with respect toward Jerusalem. But, by a strange coincidence, from the surviving monuments of this period we get not the least intimation of either David or Solomon, and from this silence one might suppose that the Hebrew sovereigns *never* lived. On the other hand, such an inference would be wholly unjustified. We may be sure that the historical records of the Hebrews which deal with the outstanding achievements of David and Solomon were not manufactured, and that they may be accepted as authentic records of actual reigns."

Again Dr. Adams says: " . . . But scant records survive for this period of Biblical interest. Save for the narratives of the Old Testament the entire period, so far as it relates to the Hebrew people, would be almost *void*. At this juncture of world affairs the Hebrews had reached one of their ' blind spots ' in which they were either unknown or overlooked, usually the latter."

It is not a " strange coincidence " that we get no intimation of David or Solomon from the surviving monuments of *ca.* 1000 B.C.— because these noted rulers were kings centuries before! The " Hebrew sovereigns " lived all right, but at another time. The " historical records " of the Hebrews dealing with David and Solomon are not manufactured, but they are inaccurate in placing the period at *ca.* 1000 B.C. The Old Testament is the *only* source of information on these two kings; that is, if we vainly try to find them in the period traditionally assigned to them. However, if we look for them at the time of Ahmose I—1580 B.C.—we find ample evidence of their existence!

Dr. Immanuel Velikovsky, in his *Ages In Chaos*, discusses this very problem, and proves beyond the shadow of authoritative doubt that the time of David was that of Ahmose I, and the time of Solomon was that of the famous Queen Hatshepsut of Egypt; and the time of Thutmose III was that of Rehoboam, who was Solomon's son, and Jeroboam, his rival.

Dr. Velikovsky takes as a starting-point the simultaneity of physical catastrophes described in the Book of Exodus and in the Egyptian Papyrus Ipuwer. He shows that world history, as it really occurred, is entirely different from what we have been taught!

Does it seem likely that a king as renowed as Solomon would have been neglected in the history of his own period? . . . that his name or important happenings of his reign would go unheeded by his so-called " contemporaries." Of course not! However, no student of ancient history will see the slightest possibility of altering the history of the kings of Jerusalem by a single century, much less by six, without upsetting all established data and concepts. Either six hundred years disappeared from the history of the Jewish people or six hundred years were doubled in the history of Egypt and in the history of other peoples as well.

The mistake lies not with *history* but with the *historians*! And their fantastic and unheard-of error caused the histories of the ancient world to become " ages in chaos." But it is *not* the purpose of this work to debate this problem. Those interested in the pros and cons should read Dr. Velikovsky's book. The purpose here is to show that certain souls, not belonging to the planet Earth in the first place, arrived here to assist mankind in its struggle up from beasthood to godhood; and that these souls incarnated time and time again to accomplish this purpose. We are not concerned with *dates* as much as we are with *lives*; in other words, who was *who* and *why*! Also of concern here are the many hidden literary treasures of the ancient world and their present location which constitutes the SECRET PLACES OF THE LION!

A people called the Amu or Hyksos invaded Egypt after a great natural catastrophe, when the river " turned into blood " and the earth shook. They overran Egypt without any difficulty. They enslaved the Egyptians . . . destroyed valuable records and works of art . . . they murdered, burned, and ruled as Pharaohs with an iron hand and a savage brain.

The Amu or the Hyksos of Egypt and the Amalekites of the Hebrews and Arabs were not different peoples, but *one and the same* nation!

The negative or so-called evil force incarnated into the Hyksos people—the force which always fights Truth and universal knowledge! Later in Egypt this force was behind the evil Amun priesthood. It was the reason for the destruction of Mu and Atlantis by those of the " Left-Hand Path." Again it was responsible for the destruction of great records of Truth in the Old and New World. And the force is present today as the Anti-Christ—those who would keep the people of the world enslaved in ignorance; have them die by the thousand on a battlefield so that they might succeed in their conquests, their lust, their greed, and their plan for world domination.

King Saul carried on the war of liberation for Israel and Egypt, for the true Israelites and Egyptians had to be freed from the yoke of the Amalekites-Hyksos. And Saul performed the great deed of freeing the Near East from the terror of the cruel Hyksos. History, however, does not give him such credit. He was a strange man, an enigma in history. He loved David, yet was jealous of him. He was cursed by Samuel and went to his last battle with a premonition of his horrible fate. At this battle he and his son, Jonathan, were beheaded.

On the ruins of the fabulous Amalekite-Hyksos empire rose two kingdoms to freedom and great power: Judah and Egypt. The inheritance from the destruction of the Hyksos power was divided between them.

David was made king over all Israel. And in Egypt, Ahmose I ascended the throne—1580 B.C. (Eighteenth Dynasty).

David was short of stature, ruddy, of beautiful countenance, handsome, of immense physical strength and great personal attractiveness, a man of war, prudent in speech, very brave, very musical, and very religious. The name *David* means: beloved; loved; well beloved. David was a type of Christ, for his life was a forerunner of that of the more perfect man, Jesus, the Christ, who was of the house of David. David was a shepherd, not unlike Joseph before him, a keeper of the natural animal forces. David represents the Lord as to divine truth proceeding from His divine human. David had " stood before Pharaoh " in Egypt in 1761 B.C. as the viceroy Joseph. This time he followed the same reincarnational pattern. Joseph had been a slave—then became a ruler over Egypt. David had been a humble shepherd—then became ruler of the Israelites.

There has been vast confusion amongst historians as to who were the people of Israel, Judah, and Canaan! It will be difficult for students to accept the fact that David was living at the very same time the Israelites were still in the " house of bondage "—Egypt! How could he be King of Israel if the Israelites were still slaves in a foreign land and the Exodus was still centuries in the future!

Since David was a contemporary of Ahmose I, does that mean that he ruled over a Canaanite population? On the contrary, it must be remembered that when Jacob, his family, and flocks went into Egypt, their migration didn't include *every* inhabitant of Jacob's homeland. If we forget the terms *Israel* and *Canaan*, we find that the slaves in Egypt were a small segment of one group of people. Later this small segment returned to " Canaan," the land of promise. But the Israelites and the Canaanites were one and the same people. The people of Judah were also Israelites, but the term " Judah " came into effect at the time the kingdom of Israel was divided.

The so-called Canaanites were merely the people left behind when Jacob went into Egypt. Racially they were no different than Jacob, Joseph, and the other migrants who went to the south. All of these people should be called simply *Israelites*, whether they were in Egypt, Canaan, or Judah!

Joseph and Asenath prepared the way for the *Dawn* in Egypt; David and Bathsheba prepared the way for the coming of the Master or the *Fulfilment* in Israel.

The blackest spot in David's life occurred when he was lured by Bathsheba, wife of Uriah the Hittite. Bathsheba managed to bathe on her roof so that King David might gaze upon her incredible beauty—it was a temptation he could not resist. David, the " keeper of the natural animal forces," became dominated by these forces. David was guilty of adultery and virtual murder. His remorse made him a broken man. God forgave him, but pronounced the fearful sentence: " The sword shall never depart from thine house " (II Samuel xii: 10). David reaped exactly what he had sown, and more of it: a long, hard, and bitter harvest. His daughter Tamar was raped by her brother Amnon, who in turn was murdered by their brother Absalom. Absalom led a rebellion against his father David and was killed in the struggle. David's wives were violated in public, as he had secretly violated the wife of chivalrous Uriah. In his later years, David's glorious reign was clouded with unceasing troubles. Yet, this was the " man after God's own heart." David's reaction to his own sin showed him to be just that. Some of the Psalms, such as xxxii and li, were born of this bitter experience.

David was intensely human, impulsive, generous to a fault. He did some things that were very wrong, but he was heart and soul devoted to God and His ways. He always went directly to God in prayer, in thanks, or in praise.

It was part of the Great Plan that Bathsheba become the wife of David. She had been Asenath, wife of Joseph, and was destined to give birth to Solomon. As David united to Bathsheba brought forth Solomon, so love in its fulfilment, or completion, establishes peace.

The name Bathsheba means: seventh daughter; daughter of seven; measure of fullness (*Sheba* is the ancient form of a Hebrew oath, " swear by the seven," whereby one declared that the thing promised would be fulfilled). Later, her name was changed to Bathshua. This name has a more spiritual quality than Bathsheba. Where *sheba* signifies an oath of fulfilment, *shua* represents its accomplishment. She vowed, as the wife of Uriah, that she would have David as her husband. She achieved this goal; her oath was fulfilled and she went on to the accomplishment of her destiny in this particular age and incarnation.

Before David died, he remembered well the legend: " So long as the seed of Amalek exists, the face of God is, as it were, covered, and will only then come to view when the seed of Amalek shall have been exterminated." After centuries, we near the time when the " seed of all evil " shall be exterminated; for there shall be no war and man will be free at last—the " face of God " will be *uncovered*!

God made a convenant with David of an eternal dynasty. And he knew that some time the ungodly would end in final destruction of their own making.

Bethlehem was the birthplace of David and it was to be the birthplace of Jesus, the Christ. David prepared the vibration for that future event when a " star would shine in the east."

" Thou Bethlehem (city of David) . . . out of thee shall he come forth unto me that is to be ruler in Israel; whose goings forth are from of old, from everlasting. . . . He shall be great unto the ends of the earth " (Micah v: 2, 4).

" And when Hadad heard in Egypt that David slept with his fathers, and that Joab the captain of the host was dead, Hadad said to Pharaoh, Let me depart, that I may go to mine own country " (I Kings xi: 21).

King David and Joab had led the army against Moab, Amon,

Edom, and Aram (Syria). Edom's land was along the entire shore of the Red Sea, the greater part of Arabia. Joab remained six months in Edom (I Kings xi: 16) and smote " every male in Edom." Hadad, a child of royal blood, was among those who escaped from Midian and came to Paran; and " out of Paran they came to Egypt, unto Pharaoh, king of Egypt."

" And Hadad found great favour in the sight of Pharaoh, so that he gave him to wife the sister of his own wife, the sister of Tahpenes the queen " (I Kings xi: 19).

Who was this Queen Tahpenes? We know that the Pharaoh of David's time was Ahmose I (Eighteenth Dynasty). When we look at the ancient records to see if Ahmose has a queen by this name we find her name is actually preserved and read: Tanethap, Tenthape, or *Tahpenes*.

The sister of Tahpenes, wife of Hadad, bore him a son called Genubath and this young prince was weaned in Pharaoh's house and was in the royal household " among the sons of Pharaoh " (I Kings xi: 20).

Now when Hadad heard that David was dead, he wanted to go back to his own country and claim his princely birthright. Pharaoh had granted all of Hadad's requests because of his love for him, and could not understand why he wanted to leave Egypt where he was a powerful prince because of his marriage to the sister of the queen. But Hadad persisted in his desire to return home and become a ruler in his own right.

Hadad had been the waif of the Nile in the time of Joseph. He was " Merk " of the " Ships of Light," and he was to become Pharaoh himself later in the same dynasty (Eighteenth).

Hadad means: sharp; quick; majesty; glory; splendid; joyous. Another form of the name, Hadar, means: where one returns for rest; concealed inner chamber; hidden principle.

When Hadad was in Egypt he was known as Prince Hadar, brother-in-law of Pharaoh Ahmose I. And Hadad *rested* in Egypt; he was *concealed* in Egypt from his enemies!

Hadad took his wife and son and left Egypt. He became a great leader and ruled the Edomites, with his wife, sister of Tahpenes, and his son, Genubath, now a prince of Edom.

Now, a curious thing happened here—a rare pattern seldom duplicated in reincarnational history. David died *before* Genubath was born in Egypt. However, it was some time before Hadad heard of the death of David.

When David was on his death-bed, the Pharaoh Ahmose I was at the point of death from a sudden seizure. David passed away, but Pharaoh recovered. Yet the king of all Egypt was different after his illness . . . he became a " new " man; the " old " man was changed.

What happened was something that takes place only when an individual must immediately incarnate after death and must not start all over again as a child, but must take over an older body so as not to lose the years that would be taken up with childhood development. In other words, the individual has a job to do and must be an adult *at once* in order to do it.

David passed in transition (died), and while Ahmose was ill David's soul entered the body of the Pharaoh just as the ego that was Ahmose left that body! Therefore David immediately incarnated, but in an adult body! Some will say: " But that seems against all natural law! Why would God allow a soul to take over another's body? Wouldn't that constitute murder on the part of David if he forced Ahmose out of his own flesh? "

First of all, David didn't force Ahmose at all. The agreement was made *somewhere* and *some time* in the spiritual world between the two souls that the one would enter life at a certain time only to nourish and keep a body in good health so that the other might later continue in that same body and complete a duty.

So David became the first known man in history to actually be *contemporary with himself!*—because David and Ahmose I were contemporaries!

Genubath was not born until *after* the death of David. The ego that had been Ahmose I reincarnated as Genubath. Hadad prepared a body, by having a son, for the ego that had been Ahmose I, to take over! David became Ahmose I, and the former Ahmose I became Genubath! It is one of the most startling happenings of all time. David could not have become Genubath, because that would have meant starting over again as a child. However, the former Ahmose I could very well become Genubath because he went with his biological father, Hadad, and later was a great ruler of the Edomites.

No individual lost anything in this strange drama, except there was the most gigantic and wholesale "body-swapping" that had ever occurred before or since! Later, after Bathshua (Bathsheba) died, she took over the body of Queen Tahpenes when the latter passed away in Egypt.

It is necessary here to discuss the usually accepted chronology. Ahmose I ascended the throne in 1580 B.C. Most historians agree that he died in 1558 B.C. However, he did not die at this time, since we learn from ancient records that he reigned with Amunhotep I as co-regent, starting in 1560 B.C. After fifteen years, Amunhotep I died and Ahmose I continued as co-regent with Thutmose I. Ahmose I actually died in 1529 B.C. at the age of seventy-one and Queen Tahpenes died the same year at the age of fifty-six. Thutmose I then became complete ruler and was Pharaoh without a co-regent.

Of course, the original Ahmose I passed away and became Genubath in 1540 B.C. This was the same year that David died and Solomon became king. But David had then taken over the body of Ahmose I, and in that body lived until 1529 B.C. Bathshua (Bathsheba) lived after the death of David in Israel, but when she finally died she took over the body of Queen Tahpenes and lived in that body until the same year of 1529 B.C.

Historians have so confused the Israel and Egyptian chronology of this particular period that it is almost impossible to make sense out of it. They have placed David *after* the Exodus when he really reigned several hundred years *before* the Exodus took place! And they say Ahmose I reigned only twenty-two years instead of the actual fifty-one years!

One of the great proofs that Ahmose I lived longer than the accepted twenty-two years can be found in I Kings, Chapter xi. It is obvious, as we read there, that the ruler who was Pharaoh of Egypt when the child Hadad came there (I Kings xi: 17–18) is the *same* Pharaoh of the time when he left Egypt (I Kings xi: 21–22). If Ahmose I reigned only twenty-two years, the Pharaoh at the time Hadad returned to Edom would have been a *different ruler*! "Ages in chaos" is putting it mildly! The main thing to remember, however, is that these things did take place. The characters lived—the happenings are true. The dates and chronological arrangements were added years later, sometimes centuries later by those desiring merely to establish a chronology that

would fit their own preconceived ideas of history and what had
happened!

The two souls who had known existence as David and Bathsheba
became Ahmose I and Queen Tahpenes: founders of the greatest
Egyptian dynasty, the Eighteenth. They had laboured to prepare
the way for the Master in Israel and then they immediately returned
to life on earth to work again in Egypt and prepare the way for
King Akhnaton and the *Dawn*.

After David entered the body of Ahmose I, Hadad asked to leave
Egypt, not knowing that Pharaoh was now his former adversary,
David.

Hadad, in that incarnation, showed that back of the intellect,
back of every expression of intelligence or understanding, there
exists the *hidden principle* of all light, all wisdom, all knowledge—
God, Spirit.

The name Genubath means: theft; things stolen. The reason
why Hadad's son received this name is clear. Two earthly, human,
physical forms had been "stolen"; David took the body of
Ahmose I and, in turn, Ahmose I took the body (a "thing stolen")
that came about by the union of Hadad and his royal wife, sister
of Queen Tahpenes!

This tale of strange reincarnational patterns is the most intriguing
and sensational of the *Preparation* period! Although Hadad fled
into Egypt, he still faced the inevitable consequence of *karma*. He
paid for his abhorrence of Israel by giving his own flesh and blood
so that David might continue in life and become Ahmose I!

" And the Lord stirred up an adversary unto Solomon, Hadad
the Edomite: he was of the king's seed in Edom " (I Kings xi: 14).

So Hadad was an adversary of Solomon after he returned to
Edom and became King of Edom, as his forefathers before him.

When Solomon ascended the throne of his father, he consecrated
his life to the erection of a temple to God and a palace for the kings
of Israel. David's faithful friend, Hiram, King of Tyre, hearing that
a son of David sat upon the throne of Israel, sent messages of
congratulation and offers of assistance to the new ruler.

Solomon began the building of the Temple in the fourth year of
his reign and finished it in the eleventh year of his reign. When
Solomon was ordered to build the great Temple without the sound
of hammers, he could not cut the stones in the ordinary manner,

but by laying the magical stone called the *Shamir* against the side of the rock the stones instantly and noiselessly separated according to any desired pattern. This strange tale is recounted in the Talmud.

So, the Temple was put together without sound and without instruments, all its parts fitting exactly " without the hammer of contention, the axe of division, or any tool of mischief." In other words, it was built by the power of sound vibration that had been used thousands of years before by the master architects who erected the Great Pyramid and monolithic cities of South America.

The era of David and Solomon was the Golden Age of Hebrew history. David was a warrior. Solomon was a builder. David made the kingdom. Solomon built the Temple. Jerusalem was a magnificent city, and the Temple was the most costly and splendid building, beside the Great Pyramid, on earth. They came from the ends of the earth to hear Solomon's wisdom and see his glory.

God had told Solomon to ask what he would; Solomon asked for wisdom to govern his people. That pleased God, and God richly rewarded him, for all other things were added. Besides wisdom he possessed riches that would stagger the mind.

The name Solomon means: whole; entire; complete; integral; peace; concord; integrity; peaceful; pacific. David could not build the great Temple because he was a " man of war." When violent and resistant emotions hold sway in the mind, the turmoil is such as to prevent any permanent construction of the new body on the higher planes of consciousness. So we see the importance of cultivating peace instead of war, non-resistance instead of resistance, harmony and love instead of discord and hate.

Solomon represented the Lord, both as to his celestial and spiritual kingdom. Solomon's Temple represented heaven and the church. The Queen of Sheba, coming to Solomon in Jerusalem with exceeding great riches, with camels carrying spices, gold, and precious stones, represented the wisdom and intelligence which was added to the Lord in his natural man. Therefore, Solomon and Sheba *prepared* the way for the future plan that would eventually bring about the complete salvation of man on earth.

" And when the queen of Sheba heard of the fame of Solomon concerning the name of the LORD, she came to prove him with hard questions " (I Kings x: 1).

As we have already seen, *Sheba* means: seven; seventh daughter.

The Queen of Sheba then was " Queen of the Land of Seven or Seven Daughters." " Sheba " used here means Egypt, because Egypt was the seventh great colony of the Motherland. " Daughters of the Motherland " (Mu and Atlantis) represented the seven colonized areas of ancient times.

The Queen of Sheba was greatly impressed by what she saw while in Jerusalem. " And she said to the king, It was a true report that I heard in mine own land of thy acts and of thy wisdom. Howbeit I believed not the words, until I came, and mine eyes had seen it: and, behold, the half was not told me: thy wisdom and prosperity exceedeth the fame which I heard " (I Kings x: 6–7).

This great Queen of Sheba was, in reality, Queen Hatshepsut of Egypt! Both Hatshepsut and Solomon built great palaces and magnificent temples; both enriched their countries, not by war, but by peaceful enterprises; each possessed a fleet on the Red Sea and sent it on adventurous expeditions; the reigns of both were the glorious periods of Israel and Egypt.

Of Hatshepsut, it is written: " Thy name reaches as far as the circuit of heaven, the fame of Makere [Hatshepsut] encircles the sea," and " her fame has encompassed the Great Circle " (ocean).

" And all the kings of the earth sought the presence of Solomon " (II Chronicles ix: 23), and " all the earth sought to Solomon . . . " (I Kings x: 24).

These two great rulers had to meet—it was inevitable.

In the *Jewish Antiquities* of Josephus we find the story of the Queen of Sheba introduced by these words: " Now the woman who at that time ruled as Queen of Egypt and Ethiopia was thoroughly trained in wisdom and remarkable in other ways, and, when she heard of Solomon's virtue and understanding, was led to him by a strong desire to see him which arose from the things told daily about his country."

A great temple called " The Most Splendid of Splendours " at Deir el Bahari near Thebes in Egypt was built against a semicircular wall of cliffs. On the massive walls of this temple are engraved bas-reliefs describing the life and most important events of the reign of Queen Hatshepsut. One series, called the Punt reliefs, tells the story of a journey to the land of Punt or the Holy Land (Divine, God's Land). Punt was Palestine-Phoenicia, and the Divine Land or Holy Land was Jerusalem.

" And king Solomon gave unto the queen of Sheba all her desire, whatsoever she asked, besides that which Solomon gave her of his royal bounty. So she turned and went to her own country, she and her servants " (I Kings x: 13).

The " desire of the Queen of Sheba " is pictured on the walls of the temple of the Most Splendid. The many gifts are shown in the presentation scene, the scene of the loading for the return voyage, the scene of the counting and weighing after the return, and the scene of dedication to Amun.

The treasure brought by Hatshepsut (Sheba) from Jerusalem to Egypt was fantastic! The temple at Deir el Bahari did not follow the contemporary Egyptian style. After the return from Punt, Hatshepsut had the temple erected and it was copied from architectural styles she had seen while on her visit to Solomon. One authority has said: " It [the temple] is an exception and an accident in the architectural life of Egypt."

In the Temple of Hatshepsut will be found in the years ahead magnificent objects that were brought from Jerusalem as gifts of Solomon! In an undiscovered chamber, science will make one of the greatest discoveries of Egyptology! The many *lions* guarding this Temple of Splendours guard well a treasure that came from the Temple of God erected by Solomon himself!

Solomon knew Egypt well, before the visit of Hatshepsut, for he was married to an Egyptian princess who was his chief wife (I Kings ix: 16). This princess was a daughter of Thutmose I, as was Hatshepsut. So the chief wife of Solomon was the sister of the Queen of Sheba (Hatshepsut).

The Queen of Sheba returned from her visit pregnant with the royal seed of the King of Israel! Her son *Menelik*, born in Egypt, was born of her liaison with Solomon!

The Queen of Sheba was able to take back to Egypt the knowledge that there is a higher understanding or a brighter light that, when laid hold of by the body of consciousness, will transmute and lift that consciousness to incorruptible spiritual substance. This is the beginning of the process by which the mortal puts on immortality.

The great symbol of Solomon in his day was his marvellous throne. " Moreover the king made a great throne of ivory, and overlaid it with the best gold. The throne had six steps, and the top of the throne *was* round behind: and *there were* stays [hands] on either side on the place of the seat, and two lions stood beside the stays. And twelve lions stood there on the one side and on the other upon the six steps: there was not the like made in any kingdom " (I Kings x: 18–20).

The throne was so built as to represent truly the king's rule and the rule of everyone who is, with the Lord's help, king over his own heart. It also represents the Lord's own rule, who is the King of kings. The lions represent an element of rule . . . the power of the Lord, and the power received from the Lord to conquer and overcome evil . . . Solomon's throne and the guardian beasts— another of the SECRET PLACES OF THE LION!

Now Solomon's glorious reign was clouded by the fact that he was married to idolatrous women. But Solomon was permitted to institute idolatrous worship for the purpose that he might represent the Lord's kingdom or church with *all* the religions in the universal habitable world.

David represented the Lord about to come into the world, while Solomon represented the Lord after his coming. Therefore, since the Lord, after the glorification of His human, had power over heaven and Earth (Matthew xxviii: 18), Solomon had to appear in glory and magnificence, and was in wisdom above all the kings of the earth, and also built the Temple; and he moreover permitted and established the worship of many nations, by which were represented the various religions in the world. So we can see the reason why Solomon was permitted to establish idolatrous worship and to marry so many wives. The hidden meaning of " wife " in the Scriptures is " church "; and " concubine " means " religion."

It is written: " And king Solomon made two hundred targets of beaten gold . . . " " And he made three hundred shields of beaten gold . . . " (I Kings x: 16–17).

Solomon was a great artist; he designed most of the burnishings for his Temple of God. He was an alchemist, and manufactured by alchemical means the gold used in his Temple. The transmutation of base metals into gold was accomplished by " vibrations." Alchemy was more than a *speculative* art—it was also an *operative* art!

Later, in the Eighteenth Dynasty, Solomon was to incarnate as one of Egypt's greatest artists—an inspired youth who was to make a golden mask for a young, dead Pharaoh. It, too, was of " beaten gold "; and made by the alchemist's art!

" Moreover the king made a great throne of ivory, and overlaid it with the best gold " (I Kings x:18).

The throne that Solomon made was similar to the throne he was to make for King Tutankhamun years later when he entered life as a humble artist of Egypt. And he made it of the " best gold "— which was *transmuted gold*!

The sunset of Israel's Golden Age began in 1501 B.C. when " Solomon slept with his fathers, and was buried in the city of David his father: and Rehoboam his son reigned in his stead " (I Kings xi: 43).

In 1501 B.C. Thutmose III became co-regent with Hatshepsut. At first he played a very minor and subordinate role. When the great Egyptian queen died in 1480 B.C. he reigned alone and became the greatest of all conquering Pharaohs of the New Empire in Egypt.

Thutmose III was later to incarnate as the great sage Pythagoras of Crotona. In A.D. 1850 we find the same entity studying at Oxford in England. He left England and still resides at Shigatse in Tibet as the Master Koot Hoomi Lal Singh (Master K. H.).

When Thutmose III was a young prince he accompanied the Queen of Sheba (Hatshepsut) on her fabulous journey to Punt. He remembered well the fantastic treasure he had seen there, and what it meant to mankind.

In Hatshepsut's temple an inscription tells the story that a great statue of the Egyptian god Amon-Ra was erected in Jerusalem while the Queen of Sheba was there. This statue will be discovered soon, and will prove beyond any doubt that Hatshepsut actually visited Solomon!

Hadad, now back in his own land of Edom, had caused a great deal of difficulty for Solomon in the last years of the latter's reign. He stirred up Edom into a state of unrest, and he had powerful support. He was related by marriage to the House of Pharaoh, and the bearer of the double crown of Egypt favoured Hadad. Rezon was another adversary of Solomon and ruled in Damascus. Jeroboam was the third adversary. He had been made " ruler over all the charge of the house of Joseph " by Solomon, but he secretly plotted against his king and friend. When Solomon found this out, he sought to kill Jeroboam.

" . . . And Jeroboam arose, and fled into Egypt, unto Shishak king of Egypt, and was in Egypt until the death of Solomon " (I Kings xi: 40).

So Jeroboam went into Egypt, just as Hadad had done several decades before him.

Hadad's son, Genubath, was now vassal King of Edom. He is mentioned by name in the annals of Thutmose III as Prince of the vassal land of Edom paying tribute to Pharaoh. Genubath lived part of the time in Edom and part of the time was spent in the palace of Thutmose III.

The annals of Thutmose III read: " When his majesty arrived in Egypt the messengers of the *Genubatye* came bearing their tribute."

Historians cannot understand who the people of *Genubatye* were! They were, of course, the people of Genubath, their king, contemporary with Solomon's son, Rehoboam. Hadad was now dead, and so was his princess wife.

Pharaoh wanted Jeroboam to help him in his invasion of Palestine—the Holy Land. Jeroboam wanted to return to his own land, and said: " Let me go, and I will depart into my land." So Pharaoh rewarded him by giving him Princess Ano, the eldest sister of his own wife, Thelkemina. This is recorded in the Greek version of the Old Testament (Septuagint) made in Alexandria in Egypt in the third century before the present era.

Princess Ano gave a son to Jeroboam, and he was called Abijah. There is a canoptic jar in the Metropolitan Museum of Art in New York that bears the name of Princess Ano (Museum No. 10.130.1003). And the canoptic jar belongs to the period of Thutmose III! This is absolute proof that Thutmose III was a contemporary of Jeroboam and was the " Shishak " (Susakim) of the Bible. There was never before or after Thutmose III a " Princess Ano." Therefore the proof is ample that " Shishak " was not the Pharaoh Sheshonq (Sosenk, Shoshenk) of the Twenty-second Dynasty (945–745 B.C.). This was the dynasty of Northern Libyan stock.

Historians present Sheshonq as the scriptural " Shishak." In *Archaeology and the Religion of Israel*, W. F. Albright says: " . . . the date of Shishak's accession is dependent on Israelite chronology." Therefore, since the chronology is inaccurate, we find in the *correct* chronology ample evidence that Thutmose III was the Biblical

" Shishak "! (Sheshong was the Pharaoh So, who received tribute from Hoshea, last king of the northern realm (II Kings xvii: 4).)

Thutmose III, the great conqueror, had to obtain the priceless treasures of Solomon's Temple. But was it to rob and destroy, as historians believe? No! It was to obtain certain secret documents and other items so that they might be taken to Egypt and placed in the Great Pyramid and in other subterranean temples and hidden chambers. These treasures could not be allowed to fall into the hands of negative forces which abounded in the Holy Land since the death of wise Solomon!

These treasures, brought by Thutmose III from Palestine, are faithfully reproduced on a wall of the Karnak temple in Egypt! Identification of objects pictured in the temple with those described in the Books of Kings and Chronicles would be a matter of prolonged research and study.

On the walls of the tomb chambers of the officials of Thutmose III, the Palestine treasures are shown in the process of being transported to Egypt. The vizier or chief minister at this time was Rekhmire, most powerful, next to Pharaoh—and he had been Ahmose I when that royal body held the soul of David! The high priest under Thutmose III was Menkheperre-Seneb—and he had been Hadad the Edomite! The unusual tombs of these men are representative of this particular Egyptian period, just as the tomb of Tutankhamun is representative of his lifetime; and in that there is a *key*!

On his march northward, not to plunder but to *save* the treasures of Solomon's Temple from the vandals of a chaotic and strife-torn Israel, Thutmose III was one day going forth in a dazzling chariot of electrum (gold in amalgam with silver) when he spotted something in the sky which dared outshine the Pharaoh's splendid chariot.

In the Royal Annals of Thutmose III, in a much damaged manuscript, we read: " In the year 2, third month of winter, sixth hour of the day . . . the scribes of the House of Life found that a circle of fire was coming in the sky. They thought it had no head, and the breath of the mouth had a foul odour. Its body was one ' rod ' long and one ' rod ' large. It had no voice. Their hearts became confused through it and they laid themselves on their bellies.

" . . . Now after some days had passed over, Lo! those things were more numerous than anything. They were shining in the

sky more than the sun to the limits of the four supports of heaven.
. . . Powerful was the position of the *fire circles*. The army of the
king looked on and His Majesty was in the midst of it."

Thutmose III " was in the midst " of the " fire circles "! Obviously his entire march towards the Divine, Holy Land was closely
surveyed by ships from other worlds! The " fire circles " were the
" flying Saucers " of today! And men of other inhabited worlds,
belonging to the great Space Confederation, have ever been
interested in the development of the peoples of earth, and the
location of the SECRET PLACES OF THE LION!

Therefore we come to the conclusion of *Preparation*. . . .
Rehoboam, Solomon's son, was later to be Pharaoh Smenkhkare,
half-brother of Akhnaton. Jeroboam was to become the usurper of
thrones—Horemheb, last king of the Eighteenth Dynasty!

Through countless millennia the WORD had been *Prepared*: by
the Children of Light in Lemuria, Atlantis, the great colonies of the
Motherland, Egypt, and Israel. The men of earth were now ready
for the great day of " The Telling " when there would be a
New Dawn!

Chapter Two

DAWN

T HE *WORD* dawned. . . .
    The Eighteenth Dynasty, Egypt's Imperial Age, had begun
    with Ahmose I, a Theban princeling. Thutmose III had
salvaged the great treasures of Solomon's Temple in Israel. Now,
the heart of all mankind was ready to receive the WORD as it
dawned in Egypt as the blazing ATON. Aton's servant on earth was
to be Amunhotep IV, known to the world as Akhnaton, the
" heretic " Pharaoh.

Amunhotep II ascended the throne in 1447 B.C. and died in 1420
B.C. His son, Thutmose IV, succeeded him in 1420 B.C., and ruled
until 1412 B.C. This Thutmose and a Mitannian princess were the
parents of Amunhotep III (" The Magnificent "). Amunhotep II
(the Pharaoh who was buried with his famous bow which no
other man was strong enough to use) was the grandfather of
Amunhotep III.

After the seventh year of his reign (1405 B.C.), " The Magnificent "
never again led his armies out of Thebes, but spent the rest of his
life living in peace in his capital with his chief wife, the Great
Royal Wife, Queen Tiyi. Tiyi was the uncultured, outspoken
daughter of a commoner from Lower Egypt, but she had caught the
fancy of young Amunhotep III and he loved her more than any
other woman. Over the advice of his mentors, he made her the
greatest and most powerful woman in Egypt.

Another of his wives was his own half-sister, Sitamun, who was
jealous of Tiyi, and felt that she should be the Queen of Upper and
Lower Egypt because the royal blood of the Pharaohs flowed in
her veins. She was the mother of Smenkhkare (born 1390 B.C.),
the Princess Meriten, and young Tutankhaton (born 1370 B.C.).

Amunhotep III also dearly loved another wife, the Princess
Giluhepa. She had been given to him by King Shutarna, her father,

who was ruler of the Kingdom of Mitanni. She came to Thebes from her father's capital, Washshukanni on the upper Habur. She gave the Pharaoh a son, known throughout his life as Sinuhe (" he who stands alone "). He had been abandoned as an infant and set upon the water in a reed boat; to be adopted by Senmut, physician to the poor, and his wife, Kipa.

By Tiyi, Amunhotep III gave the world his successor, Amunhotep IV, who later changed his name to Akhnaton. Tiyi was also the mother of the " Magnificent " Pharaoh's youngest daughter, the Princess Beketamun.

The first suggestion of Aton's power in Egypt manifested itself with Thutmose IV, who was preparing the way for the *Dawn*. Amunhotep III and Queen Tiyi often sailed in their royal barge, which they called " The Aton Gleams."

The King was very concerned with the growing power of the Amun priesthood, and favoured the priests of the Heliopolitan sun god, Re (Ra). He was the first Egyptian monarch to be worshipped as a god *in his own lifetime*! He was looked upon as the sun god's earthly representative, and all his subjects believed he actually had a divine, solar origin. What does this mean? Actually, the rulers of this period of earth history were volunteers from other more enlightened worlds and came into physical existence on this planet only to help raise ignorant mankind to a higher understanding and perception of Divine Truth. Therefore they really did have other-worldly " solar " origins!

When the Crown Prince Amunhotep (Akhnaton) was twenty-one years of age he married the lovely Nefretiti, daughter of the powerful priest Ay. (She was not the daughter of Amunhotep III, as historians believe.) Her name meant " the-beautiful-woman-has-come." Her features have become famous through the sculptured head which was found by the German expedition at Akhetaton (known to the modern world as Tel-el-Amarna).

On the thirtieth anniversary of his reign (1382 B.C.), Amunhotep III appointed his son co-regent, and thereafter Amunhotep IV ruled Egypt jointly with his illustrious father.

During the first four years of the co-regency with his father the young Pharaoh ruled from the capital, Thebes. Then he began to build an entirely new capital city (1378 B.C.) on a virgin site, over two hundred miles down-river from Thebes. In the sixth year of the co-regency (1376 B.C.) he left the capital of his father and established himself in his new location, a holy city which he called Akhetaton (" The Horizon of the Disc ").

Here Amunhotep IV changed his name, which meant " Amun-is-satisfied," to Akhnaton (" It is well with the Aton "). He ordered that the name Amun be struck out of every tomb, temple, and monument on which it appeared throughout the length and breadth of Egypt. The inspired Pharaoh, who was later to incarnate as Peter, the " Big Fisherman," began his noble attempt to emancipate the human spirit. With a single stroke he wanted to replace the ancestral Egyptian religion of gross polytheism with a simpler, purer faith. He recognized and served only One God, symbolized by the Disc of the Sun (Aton).

He pitted his will against the religious inertia of the entire nation and the fanaticism and jealousy of the Amun priests in an effort to accomplish the will of the Divine Father he served. He succeeded in a sense, but later perished amid the ruin of his plans.

The human race on earth began millions of years ago with a belief in One God; then there was a rapid decline into polytheism and idolatry. Originally among all ancient races there was a universal belief in One Supreme God, so Akhnaton was not the *first monotheist*, as has been supposed by some authorities. But he did bring the Light of the One God back to the people of the world, after that Light had been hidden from man for thousands of years by negative or so-called " evil " forces.

The nobles of Egypt, their families, artists and poets, journeyed to Akhetaton and took up residence with Pharaoh in his new city. Overlooking the broad main street, known as " The King's Way," rose the official royal palace linked by a bridge with Akhnaton's house. Near by was the new, brilliant Temple of Aton. Where formerly there was only desolate, barren desert, gardens bloomed, enchanting with the flowers and rare trees which Akhnaton and Nefretiti loved.

In 1376 B.C. he declared full war on the ancient god Amun. His father, Amunhotep III, did not die in 1376 B.C., as historians believe, but lived until 1370 B.C. During the time after Akhnaton left Thebes for his new city (1376–1370 B.C.) Amunhotep III kept order in the ancient capital Thebes and subdued the great power of the Amun priesthood, until the worship of all other gods was forbidden. Osiris, Hathor, Ptah . . . the entire pantheon of lesser deities were swept away by the two rulers. Only Pharaoh would have dared such a revolutionary movement!

The demons and monsters who inhabited the Underworld of the gods were eliminated by royal proclamation from all Egypt. The reason historians place the death of Amunhotep III at 1376 B.C. is because that is the date he passes from historical reference. But it is not the date of his death, only the date when Akhnaton quit Thebes for the new holy city built on virgin soil. It had to be in a new area, uncontaminated by the vibrations of the evil Amun—the false god!

Accompanying the great religious revolution and revival was a drastic change in the traditional art of Egypt. All former conventions were abandoned, and artistic realism and humanism flourished in Akhetaton, and from there, the new capital of the world, Akhnaton poured out upon all mankind the new message of the One God. It was accomplished by converting the divine message into a new form of art, literature, and philosophy.

Akhnaton told other rulers, princes, and nobles of far-away lands that God (Aton) desired that His children should follow non-violence. He encouraged his contemporaries to be pacifists. Most of them laughed at him and called him *mad*! Because of this, they cleverly and secretly played on his beliefs, and would accept the Cross of Life (Ankh) when he sent it to them, but without his knowledge they began through warfare to destroy the outer fringe of the great Egyptian empire that had reached its military apex during the reign of Thutmose III.

Amunhotep III in Thebes sired Tutankhaton (Tutankhamun) just before he died in the spring of 1370 B.C. He never saw the young prince, who was born in the winter of the same year (December 9, 1370 B.C.). Smenkhkare, his brother, had been born of the same mother, Sitamun, in 1390 B.C., and was therefore twenty years older than the last child of " The Magnificent."

Throughout the entire history of the earth, the " Goodly Company " or the multitude of " Christ Souls " have incarnated in a *group* to fulfil the WORD and the Work—the Great Plan set down by the Creative Spirit. About Pharaoh Akhnaton in the new holy city gathered the greatest minds of the day, those who were to share with him the gigantic task of literally changing an entire world and its false teachings!

Pharaoh was addressed as "the King, the Ra, the Sun." This signified his position as leader of the "Goodly Company" of star-born beings dedicated to the salvation of a planet!

At this time other-worldly mentors incarnated as great rulers and leaders because mankind was in the consciousness of worshipping the king, the representative of their god in human, physical form on earth. The people knew him as the "Voice of God." Later in history mankind was subjected to the rule of the lesser souls, the "spawn of earth." These became the emperors of Rome and the cruel kings of vassal kingdoms.

The only temple allowed to continue in Thebes was the Temple of Isis, since it upheld the virginity of young maidens. Akhnaton desired that the young women of Egypt would fashion themselves after the precepts of modesty and innocence. But he removed the orgiastic nature of Isis worship, and instead of Isis being adored as a goddess her purity was stressed and she became a model for all young women to fashion themselves after. The only object of worship left in her temple was the symbol of Aton, the golden Disc of the Sun!

The Amun priests were very restless. Their temples had been violated, their idols shattered, their treasuries were empty. The wealth of Egypt and other nations flowed into Akhetaton, *not* Thebes. Evil priests and ideologies were dying, and their darkness was almost eliminated by the *New Dawn*; almost, but not quite. Just before Akhnaton's death, Amunism reared its ugly head once again and phoenix-like rose from the ashes of its ruin to the freshness of new life to live through another cycle of man's development. It still exists as the dominant and controlling force in the world today!

Akhnaton and the followers of Aton *did not worship the physical sun*, as some authorities believe! Each soul is like a single ray from the sun, and this celestial body symbolized Divine Love (Heat) and Divine Wisdom (Light). It was the visible, physical symbol in the world of the Creative Spirit, who, like the sun, quickens all with life.

The "Goodly Company" to this day carries the mark of the golden Sun Disc (Aton). On the foreheads of those who still serve, this symbol can be seen by those attuned to such consciousness.

It should be mentioned here that from the word "Aton" came

atonement (at–one–ment, at–tune–ment). From the word "Amun" the world derived *amen* and *a-mend-ment*. Atonism harmonized the entire creation so that man was ONE with his Creator. *Amunism* was a corrective discipline, for it attempted to amend and yet control human behaviour through false teachings.

In order to show the extreme importance of the individuals who surrounded Akhnaton at the royal court in Akhetaton, it is necessary to discuss several of the important and some of the lesser officials. Very little is known about anyone, except Pharaoh, and not much is known about him!

In later ages, these same workers in Light incarnated to continue the great work which had received so much impetus under Akhnaton.

There were two men at the court who shared the power as the most important and influential officials. One of these was Ay, chief priest, court chamberlain, and practically court everything else. He was a close personal friend of Pharaoh, and his wife Tyi was nurse to the royal wife, Nefretiti. This is logical, since Ay and Tyi were the parents of the beautiful Queen of Egypt!

In an earlier incarnation, Ay had been the high priest Phammon of Egypt. After he eventually served as a Pharaoh in his own right, succeeding young Tutankhamun, he left the earth vibration, never to return! At the present time, he lives in another dimension of time and space on a planet that revolves around the star-sun Capella in the constellation Auriga.

Ay worked diligently against the Amun priesthood and supported the Pharaoh in his demands that Amun be completely eradicated from the land.

The other official sharing power with the good Ay, was Maya, king's scribe, overseer of the treasury, and prime minister of Egypt. The two men worked closely together with Pharaoh. Maya had been Joseph of the "coat of many colours" and even now wore a similar garment of many bright and assorted colours to designate his high position as royal treasurer and scribe. This entity had been David, Ahmose I, and then the vizier Rekhmire under Thutmose III.

He had volunteered, as the others, to come down into flesh, time and time again, not for mere earthly glory and hollow acclaim, but wherever the *Work* would lead. Early in his career, when as a young man he served Amunhotep III, Maya discovered the records that he had left in the Great Pyramid when he was Joseph. Furthermore, he knew that he had been Joseph, son of Jacob! Maya was a man possessed of strange psychic gifts. One of these was the ability to recall certain past incarnations when it was important for him to do so! Before Maya left Egypt, during the reign of the commoner, Horemheb, he placed records under the Sphinx, and these read: "When future man reads what is written here he shall know that Joseph came again into the land of Egypt, sat on the right hand of Pharaoh, again he passed this way!"

Maya served in the scribe vibration, even as David and Joseph and Rekhmire had served. Maya was born in 1428 B.C. during the reign of Amunhotep II, and was a very young man when his lifetime friend, Amunhotep the " Magnificent," appointed him royal treasurer.

Now this Pharaoh's youngest full-sister was a fair child by the name of Ilipaamun (" Beloved Child of Amun "). This sister of Pharaoh had been Asenath, wife of Joseph. Even as Joseph saw her when she was the daughter of Potiphar, he looked upon her again at court and secretly desired her. However, Pharaoh knew this secret of Maya's heart and gave him Ilipaamun to wife. This was destined once again, because the two were to serve a great purpose in the *Dawn* of the WORD.

The first child born of this union was Tantahpe, who, as a babe, was dedicated in the Temple of Isis before this goddess had completely fallen from her high position in the pantheon of gods.

Another man close to the heart of the court at Akhetaton was Ahmose, a royal scribe and steward of the house. He had been Levi, son of Jacob and Leah; half-brother of Joseph in another lifetime. He was later to become Amos, a minor prophet of Judea.

Amenophis, son of Hapi, had been a great architect and adviser under Akhnaton's father and continued in this service to the court at Akhetaton. The records say: " . . . he found forms of mysteries for amulets and discovered magic names." He had been Thoth of Atlantis, and then Iemhotep, architect of King Zoser in the Third Dynasty. After his death, Iemhotep was deified, and so was Amenophis. As deified mortals, they stand almost alone in Egyptian history. (It is interesting, therefore, to note they were the same entity!) It was his duty under Akhnaton to secure the secret hiding-places for the Aton records, and his architectural skill produced fantastic results.

General Horemheb was head of the Egyptian army. He hated Akhnaton, for Pharaoh stood for peace and non-violence. Horemheb was the son of a cheese-maker and had risen to great power amongst the military faction because of his magnificent physique, his endurance as an athlete, and prowess as a great hunter. The army suffered under Akhnaton because there were no wars to be fought. The empire that Egypt had built over the centuries was fast crumbling. Horemheb knew that, even though it was far away from Akhetaton, on the fringes of Egyptian domination.

Horemheb longed for battle, to feel the heat of hand-to-hand combat and the blood of one's enemies on his strong hands. Generals were not popular at court, and especially this one, for Pharaoh said: " The sight of one so anxious to destroy his fellow man and so loath to take the Cross of Life fills me with disgust . . . he makes our sacred chambers smell of blood! "

Horemheb had been Jeroboam and was later to become a Roman emperor and a Spanish conqueror.

Huya was major-domo for Queen Tiyi, and supervised the preparation of records which the great queen completed after the death of her husband, the " Magnificent."

Mahu was the chief of police and was responsible for the protection of the temple and palace and of the holy city itself. His one desire was that the knowledge brought to the world through Akhnaton would " live eternally like the Aton."

Akhnaton's mother, Queen Tiyi, continued the work of her husband in Thebes and kept the Amun priests under control. She had been Hatshepsut in another lifetime, the queen who had herself portrayed as a man by many artists. Tiyi was the daughter of the commoner Yuya, and his wife, Thuyu. Yuya, since he was the father of the favourite wife of Pharaoh, was made provincial governor and master of the horse at the court of his son-in-law, Amunhotep III.

Sitamun was a half-sister of Amunhotep III, and therefore an aunt of Akhnaton. But she was also the second wife of the " Magnificent" Pharaoh. Sitamun bitterly resented the commoner Tiyi, for she was the rightful Queen of Egypt since she was of the House of the Amunhoteps and royal line.

The priests had informed the young Amunhotep III that "Hatshepsut, our great and good Queen, lives again in Lower Egypt, as daughter of Yuya." Through a divine oracle they had discerned that Hatshepsut was again in life. Amunhotep III knew that he had to find her, take her to be first royal wife, put her on the throne beside him, and fulfil his destiny with her.

Sitamun gave Pharaoh the child Smenkhkare, and later Tutankhaton (Tutankhamun), and a fair daughter named Meriten. But she took no interest in the children she bore her king and would have sent them down the river in reed boats had not Tiyi intervened in time. Sitamun wanted to become a channel of truth and spiritual wisdom, but she could not. However, her son, Tutankhaton, was to become a medium through which his father would speak again to the Egyptian world.

To the present day, Sitamun has had no children, but is now a great channel of truth in America.

But why did these people marry their own sisters, and so forth? The answer is an obvious one. This was before the Aton had been fully revealed to the world. The "Goodly Company" did not mix its vibrations with the "spawn of the earth." To do so would have meant a change in the pattern and a vibrational change would not have assisted in the coming of the *Dawn*. The practice is thought to be perverted today, but it was an entirely different thing then.

The bust that has been recorded by historians as that of Tiyi is actually that of Sitamun. Because she was of the royal blood, her portrait was used instead of Tiyi's on all State carvings, reproductions, and where the royal family was portrayed. She had the characteristic features of Egyptian nobility and the Amunhoteps. That is why her son, Tutankhaton, resembled her so much. (When the tomb of Tutankhamun was opened and the mummy unwrapped the striking resemblance between the so-called likeness of Tiyi and the young king was noticed. He also resembled Akhnaton, since they had the same father.)

Tutu was the minister of foreign affairs for Akhnaton. It was his duty to see that all correspondence from foreign rulers (Palestine, Syria, etc.) and officials was properly filed at the royal archives of Akhetaton. (About four hundred of these clay tablets were discovered in A.D. 1887 in the ruins of the Foreign Office at Tel-el-Amarna.)

Tutu had been Uriah the Hittite, the first husband of Bathsheba. He was later St. Clement of Rome.

Cato was Egypt's greatest artist, a master craftsman in stone, wood, and precious metals. Under his inspiration and direction the great art revolution took place under Akhnaton. This Master was to be born later as the famous Kungfutse (Confucius), Grand Master Mason and philosopher. He had been Cheops (Khufu), great king of the Fourth Dynasty.

Rahotep, the young son of Cato, was born in 1367 B.C. He became a greater artist than his illustrious father, even though he only lived to be seventeen years of age. He was a fine, sensitive young man; a channel for the powerful forces working with and through him. This youth had been none other than the great King Solomon, who was also an artist and alchemist. Rahotep later fashioned the golden mask for his boyhood friend, Tutankhamun. History has never known the identity of this artist.

Sinuhe was the court physician at Akhetaton, and one of Pharaoh's personal friends and advisers. He had been named " Sinuhe " (" He Stands Alone ") by his foster parents, Senmut, the physician to the poor, and his wife, Kipa. His actual name was Setymeramun, and he was the son of Princess Giluhepa of Mitanni and Amunhotep III. He was Akhnaton's half-brother, but Sinuhe did not know this until years later when he reigned for the brief period of one month. He had been put adrift in a reed boat after his birth and was found by Senmut, who adopted him and trained him to be a physician. He then entered the School of Life where he won recognition for his skill. He was later the physician Luke, one of the Four Evangelists.

Pharaoh Akhnaton was certainly not alone in the job he came to perform. The Infinite Father had hoped that man would grasp and understand the new Light of the *Dawn*, but he did not. Many followed their good Pharaoh, but the majority believed him to be a weakling. Behind his back he was called " Sister of Egypt." He was a small man, not over five feet five inches tall, and displayed feminine characteristics. He had a swollen belly and an elongated skull poised on an unusually long neck. History does not record it but he also had a deformity of one hand.

His physical peculiarities and attitude on non-violence and peace caused him to be looked upon with suspicious eyes. On one, occasion, when he was being carried through the streets on his throne, he waved to his people! The populace was shocked and some screamed in horror! Pharaoh—the Living God of Egypt—stepped down from his pedestal and became a human being. The people called after Akhnaton as he passed their way and shouted: " False Pharaoh—away with the false god! "

But, strange as it seems, Akhnaton was closer to God than any Pharaoh had been before him. Some of his people recognized this, but others only knew that their Pharaoh was no longer acting as Pharaoh should, according to the convention of tradition.

As time went on in Akhetaton, more and more people came to love Akhnaton. The Amun priesthood realized that if they were ever to regain any power whatsoever, they would have to strike quickly. They bargained with General Horemheb, who was ruling as Governor of Memphis, because they needed the strength of the army to achieve their purpose.

In 1365 B.C. Akhnaton's rule was strong because of the love of the people, but it was weak because of internal strife caused by the increasing power of Egypt's enemies. Pharaoh refused to fight a war, " holy " or otherwise. Horemheb tried to convince Akhnaton that he should fight for the sake of Aton if nothing else. But he was told that Aton is not a god of war and does not want his children to kill one another. Horemheb agreed with the Amun priests: Akhnaton had to be eliminated if Egypt's empire was to be saved. Another new threat were weapons of *iron* used by the Hittites. The Egyptian army only had spears and swords of copper.

Ay was the " Bearer of Pharaoh's Crook " in Thebes and ruled it as governor. Ay was very concerned over the state of affairs—the growing tension, and Horemheb's obvious pact with Amunism. But the priests did not want to put a cheese-maker's son on the proudest throne in the world. They hoped the surviving Amunhoteps could be persuaded to act as figure-heads for the priesthood. They knew the people would accept those of royal blood; but a cheese-maker's son for Pharaoh—never!

Akhnaton had seven beautiful daughters, not unlike the mythological seven daughters of Atlas who were pursued by Orion and transformed into a group of stars bearing the name of Pleiades. There was a Lost Pleiad or sister, because only six of the seven stars are visible to the naked eye. The seven daughters are found everywhere in legend: the seven daughters of the priest of Midian, and others.

Akhnaton and his daughters were being pursued by another evil force—Amunism. (*Orion* is mentioned in *Other Tongues—Other Flesh* as the symbol of negative, opposing force.) The oldest was Meritaton, the second was Maketaton, who was the first child of Akhnaton's to die. She was like the legendary Lost Pleiad, for she faded away, leaving the six. The physician Sinuhe attempted to save her life but she wasted away until Pharaoh could stand the sight no longer. Her death was one of the causes of his nervous collapse and mental unbalance just before he was murdered.

His third daughter was Ankhsenpaaton, and in an earlier lifetime she had been the sister of Queen Tahpenes and became the wife of Hadad. She did not marry her father Akhnaton as historians believe. She was only eight years old when she married Tutankhaton, who was the same age as she was.

An inscription was discovered at Hermopolis in 1938 which states: " The King's daughter, whom he loves, Ankhsenpaaton the younger, born of the King's daughter Ankhsenpaaton." How could Ankhsenpaaton have a child when she was eight years old? It is possible but not likely. This inscription will bear further investigation. It will be found that it means something very different. The translation should be: " The King's [Tutankhamun's] daughter, whom he loves, Ankhsenpaaton the younger, born of *a* [not *the*] King's daughter Ankhsenpaaton." The reference here is made to Tutankhamun, not Akhnaton, and it refers to the first child born to King Tutankhamun and his wife Ankhsenpaaton several years later.

Akhnaton quarrelled with Nefretiti in 1362 b.c. Previous to this, at the insistence of Nefretiti, Akhnaton had married Tutankhaton to his daughter Ankhsenpaaton. Queen Nefretiti knew what was coming; she also knew that Akhnaton was becoming unbalanced mentally. The death of his beloved daughter Maketaton had caused a great change in him, and the increasing pressure brought by the agitated Amun priests and Horemheb's lust for blood drove him to seek Aton, the One God of all men, in deep meditations and concentrations. He was not insane, but he was unbalanced; he was more in another world than he was in this one!

A great plan had been decided upon by the Aton priests and other-worldly (space) visitors who came to Akhetaton. Since it was now known that the world would not accept and was not yet ready for the *Greater Light*, a plan was devised that would make Akhnaton be remembered in the hearts of men for ever. Besides, a plot had been discovered and it was known that the priests of Amun intended to assassinate Pharaoh and other Atonists at prayer. Future generations would say: "Truly our Pharaoh Akhnaton was the chosen voice of Aton, for the One God himself as a blazing *disc* came close to earth and took our Pharaoh away as in a whirlwind that had no voice!"

The final plan was this: Nefretiti and Akhnaton would be praying in the beautiful Temple of Aton on the proposed day of assassination. The Amun priests planned to close the gates, destroy the Aton royalty, priests, priestesses, and worshippers, then step out of the temple as the new rulers of Egypt! Just as the Amun followers were about to strike, a great space craft would descend to the altar in front of the gigantic stone Cross of Life (Ankh). Its force field would hide the main body of the craft and it would only appear as a blazing disc, a "fire circle," like the ones observed by Thutmose III on his way to Israel. All the observers would be able to say was: "See, our Pharaoh has performed his duty; he has been the good god; now the Aton has been pleased and touches the earth in his radiant magnificence ... he takes our king with him in his golden chariot!" But the Atonists cancelled the plan because of Akhnaton's unstable condition. Instead, soldiers were disguised as Aton-worshippers and when the gates closed many of the Amun conspirators were taken captive instead. No blazing "Aton" descended for Akhnaton.

If such a plan had been put into action, historians would say: "Those superstitious Egyptians, they claim their insane, heretic Pharaoh went up to heaven in a golden chariot! The followers of this king and his Aton must have been mad!"

Nevertheless, the greatest climax of the Aton period would have been when "a great light came down and took away Pharaoh, never to be seen by mortal man again!" But Akhnaton's own ego and mental outlook prevented it. It was known that the world had rejected Atonism, yet many saw the Light for the first time because of Akhnaton's labour. The departure in the "fire circle" would have made the period indelible on men's minds. Yet, even without such a dramatic climax, the period has never been forgotten!

The Aton priests came to Queen Nefretiti and told her she would have to carry on because Pharaoh was in no position to do so. Daily he became weaker, mentally and physically. Sinuhe and all his knowledge could do nothing. Sedatives did not calm Pharaoh; he did not sleep, but wandered all day and night around the palace. He seemed desperately trying to find something—but what?

One night Sinuhe found him at a pool in the garden. When the physician asked him what bothered him, he said: " Sinuhe, my good friend, I desire only one thing before I die. . . ." Sinuhe said: " But sire, you shall not die, I . . . " Akhnaton retorted: " Physician, don't lie to a dying man, for I know that I have done what I had to do in this land. The Heavenly Father has not seen fit to continue the blessings of Aton on the people of this dark world. I symbolized him in paintings by showing the shining disc of the Aton always overhead, with its down-stretched rays, each terminating in a hand which seems to caress the entire world . . . even the whole of creation, Sinuhe."

Sinuhe looked into Pharaoh's eyes for a long, still moment and said: " What is it you seek, sire? " He looked at the physician as if it would be impossible to explain his deepest feelings, but he said: " My old friend, I said long ago that as my Father the Aton liveth, I would make Akhetaton the City of the Horizon of the Disc—on the very land we now sit on. And I have done that, but now that I know the end is near, I only pray that Aton will be satisfied! "

Nefretiti informed Pharaoh that she was to carry on the *Work* because of his ill health. This caused the temporary division between the two who were devoted to each other more than any other mortal mates. They were true *soul-mates* and the separation was a difficult one; but they never stopped loving each other. The necessity of the *Work* made it imperative that they be apart for a while.

Queen Nefretiti retired with young Tutankhaton and his child bride, Ankhsenpaaton, to a special palace in the northern part of Akhetaton, cut off from the city by a high wall. Akhnaton was left alone in his southern palace. Nefretiti knew that she had to work fast; she had to prepare the two children now in her charge to become the rulers of Egypt. They had to be told certain secrets, for

Nefretiti knew that the Amun priesthood would use them as tools on the throne.

Historians believe that Akhnaton tried to compromise with the Amun priests at Thebes and that Nefretiti may have been the fanatical force behind Atonism. They say she left him because he wanted to give the power back to Amun! But this is not true! Akhnaton served and loved Aton till the very end!

The same year that Nefretiti left Akhnaton (1362 B.C.), Pharaoh married his half-brother Smenkhkare to his oldest daughter Meritaton, and made Smenkhkare his co-regent, just as his own father, Amunhotep III, had made *him* co-regent during the latter years of his reign.

Akhnaton continued to live in Akhetaton, and Smenkhkare and his wife went to Thebes and ruled. The Amun priests hoped to use Smenkhkare as their figure-head. It would be easy to dispose of Pharaoh at Akhetaton; the city was already losing its population. Its beautiful gardens were withering for lack of proper care; everywhere there was the feeling of desolation and loneliness. The holy city was doomed, and everyone knew it.

Smenkhkare had been Rehoboam, son of Solomon, and was later Timothy, favourite disciple of Paul.

Smekhkare and his royal wife were playing a clever game, but, unfortunately, a losing one. They never intended to be anything but Atonists. In going to Thebes they hoped to learn the plans of the Amun priests by pretending to fall in with them and advocate the quick return of Amun to Egypt. Their true intentions were discovered and they were disposed of, but this came later.

Akhnaton's last proclamation as Pharaoh decreed that all men in Egypt would be hence forth *free men*; no longer would there be slaves, nobles, and class systems. All people would be equal and work together for their Infinite Father. On the day of this proclamation, Ay and Maya informed their king: " Sire, you have just torn the double crown from off your head; you are no longer Pharaoh by this act, but you are more: today you are truly Aton's chosen messenger! "

He who was to be born later as Judas Iscariot was a priest of Amun, and he secretly administered poison to Pharaoh Akhnaton. On the final night in the throne-room at Akhetaton, Horemheb was present to see that Pharaoh died. Others present were Ay,

Maya, Ahmose, Amenophis, Tutankhaton, and Sinuhe. Altogether there were seven, besides Pharaoh.

Akhnaton laid aside the red-and-white crown, for it was now too heavy for him, and he looked about the room. He was conscious of all present, yet there was a shining ecstasy in his countenance which made him seem apart.

Before the poison was administered Horemheb said: "Sire, come back to Thebes with me; renounce this Aton of yours; bow down to Amun, and I will see to it that you still wear the double crown. My army will support you!" This was Akhnaton's last chance to compromise with evil, and Horemheb wanted the record to state that he had given Pharaoh every opportunity to recant.

Akhnaton answered: "I have found that which I sought. Sinuhe knows of what I speak. I have had my vision . . . I saw Aton's face in a golden mist. . . ."

Horemheb whispered under his breath: "He's completely mad! I will not listen!" Ahmose responded: "Be quiet! He is still your Pharaoh."

The small, pitiful Akhnaton sat on his throne under the great symbol of Aton with the outstretched hand. He said: "I will live and die as Pharaoh. I came to bring a message to my people and from them to all the world. But Egypt has rejected the message of the great and kind Aton; the Aton that I saw as a boy in the blazing sun's rays. Not that the sun *is* Aton, but that the great light and heat from the solar orb symbolize Divine Love and Wisdom. The light and heat: one is love, the other wisdom.

"Man's eternal symbol of his Father's love and wisdom in the physical world is the Aton or Sun Disc. You, Horemheb, with your armies, you may tear all God's temples down stone by stone, and the Amun priests can destroy Aton's people. You can erase His name from the monuments, but in order to destroy Aton you must tear all the stars from the sky and pull down the skies themselves before you can destroy His Word.

"What care I," said Pharaoh, "if you ravage the temples of Aton and erect ancient Amun again? Aton's Kingdom is not made of material substance; it is Eternal!"

Horemheb, red with rage and disgust, said: "The only reality is that which we can see here and now; you, Pharaoh Akhnaton, speak in mad riddles; your illusions are insane. The only thing worth living for is gold, power, and battle. Your Aton is a weak, simple-minded god! I give you one more chance: although I do not agree with your ways, and I have told you that Egypt would fall unless Egypt retained her military strength, yet I will support with my army and my spear, and you shall come with me to Thebes and, if you bow down to Amun, I shall protect you and you shall be Pharaoh as you are now."

Akhnaton replied: "Horemheb, you are more mad than I, because I will not bow down to the false god. What care I what you do now in Egypt, for this night I have received the greater vision: I have seen Aton. He has told me the plan He has for man. Egypt has rejected the One God and in a future time yet unborn another land shall be the birthplace of Him who shall lead. It shall not be Egypt, but it shall be the Holy Land that our great and good Queen Hatshepsut visited and brought back a message of Light with her; a message that we have seen with our own eyes engraved in her secret chamber in the temple that she built.

" The world of men has rejected the Light. Let the dark priests bring back their ancient evil. The world has had its chance to do away with all the old systems of bondage. It came as Pharaoh, because only Pharaoh would dare attempt it—only Pharaoh could hope to accomplish it—and I failed. Yet, I see a greater plan now. All is not lost, for there will come a time when our labours will bear fruit. A generation yet to be born will know that I served well."

Horemheb now knew that Pharaoh could not be used for his selfish cause, and he secretly gave the signal for the poison to be brought in.

Pharaoh drank without even realizing it. All had their eyes on him, for he was suddenly bathed in a violet radiance; all saw it, except Horemheb.

In a voice now fully inspired, Pharaoh spoke over the sound of lightning and thunder outside: " My clarity of perception has wrought my undoing, for I have lived in a generation which has no concept of the simplicity of Truth. The world fears a mind which thinks more accurately than its own; such a mind it destroys in self-protection. To think is to be persecuted by those who do not understand; to have vision is to be hated by the visionless; to be wise is to be reviled by fools. Since the beginning of time itself men have laboured under the delusion that Truth could be destroyed by murdering those who sought to give it to the world. But the sublime verities of Aton are far beyond the reach of mortality and in every age are reborn in others who rise up to carry them forward again. My voice has been a weak and a small voice. But there shall be others and they will sing the glad song of freedom for all mankind to hear."

Akhnaton's words were now becoming faint and he slumped on the throne. Horemheb glanced at the double crown lying by itself on the table; it would need a new wearer shortly. He walked out of the throne-room and into the streets wet from the storm—shortly to be wet from blood—and he turned towards Memphis.

Pharaoh looked at his friends before him and said: "I have loved you, even as you have loved me. I go now to my Father Aton; my work is finished here in the land of Egypt . . . my heart has found peace, for, at last, the Solar Disc [Aton] is satisfied!" And Pharaoh died!

Later, gangs of workmen descended on the half-empty Akhetaton. Wherever they found the name and features of Akhnaton and Nefretiti in tombs, temples, and private houses, they obliterated them. The Temple of Aton was thrown down and buried.

Akhnaton had written: " There shall be made for me a sepulchre in the Orient Mountain; my burial shall be [made] therein in the multitude of jubilees which Aton my Father hath ordained for me; and the burial of the chief wife of the king, Nefretiti, shall be made therein in that multitude of years . . . [and the burial of] the king's daughter Meritaton shall be made in it in that multitude of years."

He gave orders that on his death he should be buried " in my sepulchre in the Eastern Mountain." There is a great *wadi* which interrupts a line of cliffs and which leads to the solitary Royal Tomb. There is no inscription above the entrance. A sloping passage and a steep flight of steps lead to the burial pit where a sarcophagus once lay. Beyond is a hall with reliefs showing the royal family worshipping the Aton. Opening from the top of the stairs are smaller tomb chambers which were made for Princess Maketaton, the first of the seven daughters to die.

Historians believe that the body found in the so-called Tomb of Queen Tiyi in the Royal Valley at Thebes was that of Akhnaton. From inscriptional and physiological evidence it can be established that this body, which is that of a man of not more than thirty, is the body of Smenkhkare.

No traces of the bodies of the royal couple (Nefretiti and Akhnaton) have ever been found. However, the corpse of a man which had been burned some time after mummification was discovered when the Royal Tomb was excavated. But this corpse was that of Sinuhe (Setymeramun), which had been deposited in the then empty Royal Tomb and later burned. The Amun priests burned the body of Akhnaton because they believed that once the mummy was destroyed all hope of survival by the royal owner vanished. Akhnaton's ashes were then strewed over the Nile, and the material substance of he who came to serve Egypt returned to her bosom from whence it came.

With Akhnaton dead, his co-regent Smenkhkare was now Pharaoh. But he and his wife, Meritaton, were fighting a losing mental battle with the Amun priesthood. With Akhnaton finally out of their way, they became drunk with power. They murdered nearly all the prominent Atonists. But they did not touch Ay and Maya. These two men were needed in Egypt for the secret knowledge they possessed, and the victorious priests were certain that they would both now follow Amun, since this false god was once again on the throne of the Egyptian pantheon of gods.

In order to save the knowledge that had been gathered during Akhnaton's lifetime, the small band of devoted Atonists decided to work in secret and in hidden chambers. Maya, as royal treasurer, possessed the secret of the Great Pyramid and Sphinx record chambers. If the Amun faction killed him, the secret would perish with him. This would never do, since they desired this knowledge for the depleted treasure houses of Amun. If they let him live, they hoped to eventually obtain the secret from him. His death would defeat them, but his life might serve them if they were patient!

Nefretiti stayed in her palace of retirement with young Tutankhaton and Ankhsenpaaton. Outside were the crowds, always anxious to plunder, whether it was a temple of Aton or one to Amun. But Nefretiti and her palace were not molested; no one of the royal blood would be openly murdered if they didn't interfere with the plans of Amunism.

Akhnaton had died in 1361 B.C. at the age of forty-seven.

Smenkhkare ascended the throne and ruled only nine months, until 1360 B.C.

The young son of Maya and Ilipaaton (Ilipaamun) was Ra, and he was in Thebes with Smenkhkare and Meritaton. The two young rulers had been entertained at a royal banquet and the priests poisoned them. Their secret planning with Nefretiti had been discovered, and the Amun priests knew that they could never use Smenkhkare as a Pharaoh who would serve Amun. So they decided to do away with him. However, something went wrong with the assassination attempt, and the King and Queen, taking Ra with them, went from the banquet hall to their chariot. Although poison had been given to them, it had not taken effect as soon as was hoped.

Although it was a long journey, they rode like the wind from Thebes towards Akhetaton. On the way they were ambushed and were clubbed to death, along with the young Ra.

Their bodies were left on the desert for beasts to devour, but were found by messengers of Nefretiti and were subsequently mummified, although the extremely mangled condition of Ra's body almost prevented mummification. Meritaton's remains were placed in the chamber prepared for her in her father's tomb.

Smenkhkare was buried in an insignificant tomb in the Royal Valley at Thebes, along with a few objects belonging to Queen Tiyi, and his body was therefore well hidden.

Horemheb and the priesthood from Thebes paid a visit to the dead city of Akhetaton and Nefretiti. They demanded that young Tutankhaton ("The Life of the Aton is Beautiful") change his name to Tutankhamun ("The Life of Amun is Beautiful"). Nefretiti knew that the young Pharaoh would be a puppet in the hands of the triumphant priests of Amun. But she knew too that he would fulfil an important mission as Pharaoh, a mission that the evil priests would never suspect. You see, Nefretiti knew that Tutankhaton was a "sensitive" or "psychic." Instructions could be channelled through him to the surviving Atonists for the work they had to complete quickly before they were all eliminated. It was only a matter of time, that they knew, but a short time was all that they needed to see to it that certain records were made safe and secure in the SECRET PLACES OF THE LION!

So the young heir to Egypt's throne became Tutankhamun and Ankhsenpaaton became Ankhsenamun. They were taken to Thebes and the double crown which had been so rudely torn from the heads of two recent rulers was placed on the young head of " Ratut " (Tutankhamun).

The priests still had to wait a little time for complete vengeance. The new Pharaoh was closely associated with the Aton heresy, and while he lived the memory of Akhnaton would not be openly scorned. Too many Egyptians still loved Akhnaton, and if the priests eliminated all the members of the House of Amunhotep it would cause civil war in Egypt, and that would, of course, destroy their new-found power also. They hated the royal family, but they hated anarchy more.

This period was an ugly struggle between powerful interests of Amunism and courtiers who used the royal children as pawns in their game of power. The young couple pretended, on the surface, to fall in with the new faction, but continued secretly as Atonists.

At this point Nefretiti disappears from history. In fact, she did disappear, for she left Egypt and went to a Mystery School in Tibet! Her fabulous beauty and great wealth never turned her head from the *Work*. She reported to the Masters and Adepts in India, Tibet, and even at Lake Titicaca, Peru, on the workings of Atonism and just how far the *Divine Experiment* had succeeded in Egypt.

Some day clay tablets will be discovered in the Mystery Schools, and these will prove to have been written by Nefretiti herself! But they were not *brought* to these areas from Egypt. If scientists ever examine the clay used in these tablets microscopically, they will find that the clay comes from the area in which the tablets were discovered, and not from Egypt!—definite proof that Nefretiti was actually a visitor to these places! Imagine! A history of Egypt and the world's first experiment in the Greater Light—preserved in Tibet!

These records will establish very important points. There is confusion in ancient dating today because the Amun priesthood deliberately changed dates on some monuments in order to destroy the logical occurrences of Akhnaton's reign. They wanted to be certain that Aton never had another *Dawn*!

Negative forces wanted to discourage future researchers so that little could be learned from the labours of Akhnaton. The job of the surviving Atonists, on the other hand, was to preserve the records for future man. Therefore Nefretiti placed the records in Tibet, India, and South America. Others placed the records in the very earth itself—the Truth had to remain!

Wherever Nefretiti journeyed, the outstretched arms of the Aton protected her: " The heiress, great in favour, lady of grace, sweet of love, Mistress of the South and North, fair of face, gay with the two plumes, beloved of the living Aton, the Chief Wife of the King, whom he loves, lady of the Two Lands, great of love, Nefretiti, living for ever and ever. . . ."

Maya and Ilipaamun (she had changed her original name to Ilipaaton—" Beloved Child of Aton "—during the reign of Akhnaton, and was now forced by new convention to change it back again) maintained a house at Thebes where they could be near Pharaoh. The old house of Maya at Akhetaton was practically abandoned except for certain meetings that were held there.

To Maya's house came the former close friends of Akhnaton, including his brother, the High Priest of Aton (later, the Emperor Justinian), and information from higher planes came to the little group of workers through Tutankhamun! Amunhotep III spoke through his youngest son as the latter was in a deep trance! Sitamun was never a channel in the sense she wanted to be, but she gave the world a son who was very much a medium for certain instructions that were desperately needed at this time!

At this time, two young men of a dark-skinned race were summoned by Amenophis (Iemhotep of another lifetime) to come to Egypt and serve Pharaoh Tutankhamun as bodyguards. At least, that was the apparent outward reason. But the real meaning behind their coming can be found in the fact that these youths were adepts of mental science. They were descended from an ancient, wise race that existed in Africa when Atlantis was in its prime. These strange people had not developed a very high culture from a materialistic point of view, but their mental development was astounding! They could stop armies by powerful thought-waves and mental vibrations!

The two young men, who were identical twin brothers, were the sons of a great White Magician, and were brought to Egypt to fulfil two purposes: first of all, they were to protect the Pharaoh so that no harm would come to him; secondly, and more important, they were to surround certain tombs, temples, and secret chambers with a peculiar vibrational thought-pattern that would endure through the ages and keep out all those of a frequency which opposed the area of the secreted records.

It should be mentioned here that immediately following the death of Akhnaton, the *Lesser Exodus* of the *Israelites* began. Because of political confusion and civil war, the Egyptians were not concerned with the Israelites. They didn't care whether they stayed or went. So, many left Egypt, along with some Egyptians who wished to escape the wrath of Amun, and thus the *Exodus* began. It continued over many years, however, with small groups and successive waves leaving at various opportune times. But there was a *Greater Exodus* to come, and we will speak of that when we come to *Revelation*.

Now Maya felt his position was secure, since he alone in the Two Lands of Egypt held the secret of the entrance to the treasure chambers under the Great Pyramid, the Sphinx, and Hatshepsut's Temple of Splendours. When the Pharaohs were taken to these chambers, even they were *blindfolded*! No one was to know the secret, except the royal treasurer!

Several thousand years before the Eighteenth Dynasty of Egypt, Maya had been the Ruling Prince of Lemuria, Ilipaamun had been " Lady of the Sun," and Tutankhamun had been " Merk." Here we find the same individuals working together once again.

Tutankhamun serves as a messenger once again as he delivers the message from higher planes. Maya leads his people again; and Ilipaamun serves as historian and record-keeper. At the house of Maya many, many records were written by all those gathered on clay tablets and papyri.

These records have not yet come to the attention of archaeological investigation, but they will soon. They speak of the coming of Space People to Egypt, of the early Pharaohs as men of other worlds (planets) who incarnated on earth to bring certain Light to mankind, and of the true purpose for Akhnaton's life and labour. Even records brought from other inhabited planets are there!

Shortly after the work was being conducted in Maya's residence, Princess Meriten, daughter of Amunhotep III and Sitamun, was murdered by robbers at Akhetaton. She was at the studio of her lover, the great artist Thotmes, the oldest son of Cato. Thotmes was the sculptor who made the world-famous painted limestone bust of Queen Nefretiti, the brown sandstone head of the same gracious lady, several heads and masks of Akhnaton himself, and other splendid works.

Bek and Auta, the brothers of Thotmes, had been murdered in Thebes the night Pharaoh Akhnaton died in Akhetaton. And now the two lovers, Thotmes and Meriten, were hurriedly burying the famous bust of Nefretiti, which was eventually discovered centuries later by the German expedition during excavations at Tel-el-Amarna. They were surprised by vandals and killed.

Meriten was an artist herself and a student of ancient symbology. She had been in charge of the decorations in the temple of Aton at Akhetaton. Meriten is in life today and is still carrying the message of the Infinite Father brought to man in the language of symbolism!

Maya had made a visit to the secret Pyramidal subterranean chambers and brought an ancient vril stick to Tutankhamun. This was further protection for the boy king. Existing statues of him show him holding strange " rods."

Also at that time, Maya brought out two of the crystal balls originally brought by visitors from outer space during the building of the Great Pyramid. These objects were not solid crystal, but were made up of *nine sections*, fitted and locked together to form a globe or ball. As light passed through them, it was changed in a most unusual manner and the past and future could be partially ascertained in the ball. However, a certain amount of mental control was needed by the user during the period of concentration using the crystal ball.

These balls were used telepathically as a screen and for time-scanners. Their existence was not known by the Amun priests. However, it wouldn't have done them any good, because these objects could never be used for a negative purpose! Several of these crystal balls are still under the Sphinx! Nostradamus had one of them, and deduced many things from its use!

The orb and sceptre of later rulers had their origin in the crystal ball and vril stick—ancient symbols of power!

Tantahpe was the daughter of Maya and Ilipaamun. She had been dedicated to Isis as a child and was now a priestess of Isis. However, as stated before, the cult had undergone drastic changes whereby Isis was not worshipped as a goddess but was venerated as the symbol of female purity and innocence. The virgins dedicated in her former temple were similar to the later Roman vestal virgins, and served in the temple of Aton at Akhetaton.

Tantahpe had met her lover outside the temple and had disgraced her sacred office. She was later in life Miriam, the sister of Moses, and in the present age was born of American parents in the town of Tantah, Egypt. Here was the vibration of her former name, *Tantah*pe!

Now that Amun was reigning supreme again, Isis was installed once again as a great goddess. Tantahpe had to decide whether or not to stay with Isis in her new role under Amun or stay with Aton. She would not be held in disgrace in the revamped Isis cult, since virginity was not a requirement for the women who served there with the sistrum.

When her younger brother, Ra, had perished with Pharaoh Smenkhkare in the royal chariot, she decided she would soon leave the service of Isis and go to her lover, make him her husband and work with him. He was an Atonist who worked closely with her father, Maya.

Rahotep, son of Cato, had been Solomon and Queen Tiyi had been Hatshepsut. Therefore there was a great attraction between these two and the young artist made many sketches of the great queen when he was at her palace. She assisted him in every way she could in the furtherance of his inherent artistic talent. Rahotep lived in the house of Maya, and Maya was like a second father to him. Since this youth had the same name as the murdered son Ra, he was welcome to fill his place and memory. So again we find David (Maya) and Solomon (Rahotep) working together!

Tutankhamun reigned for nine years, and his conduct during his brief reign had not been such as altogether to please the priesthood of Amun, for his name, like that of Akhnaton, was later omitted from the king-lists, and Horemheb erased his name on every possible opportunity, which shows that the youth struggled against the malignity of the priests.

Tutankhamun assisted in writing and depositing the Aton records; then when his purpose in that lifetime was fulfilled it was ordained that he return to his Father Aton.

Pharaoh "Ratut," his queen, and their young friend and

constant companion Rahotep, often went hunting in the Theban neighbourhood. In those days the great morass attracted and harboured large quantities of game. The marshes provided the boy king with all kinds of wildfowl. The desert afforded a varied field for the skill of the royal sportsman, who hunted in his chariot. Bulls, lions, gazelles, and hares were his favourite game.

One day in the spring of 1350 B.C., when Pharaoh was nineteen years of age, he was on a hunting trip with his devoted wife and Rahotep. He came in from the hunt, riding vigorously into camp in his chariot, which prominently displayed the royal golden solar-hawk on its poles. "Ratut's" name was incorporated on the solar disc fixed on the head of the hawk. Since the Pharaohs were looked upon as the sun-god's earthly representatives, it is obvious that this device symbolized Ratut's "solar" (space) origin!

The young ruler had slain a lion this day, aided by his *slughi* hound, and he was excited; excited as any teen-ager would be over such a conquest. However, these hunting expeditions on the desert were not all that they appeared to be. It was partially for relaxation, true, but it was also to get away from teeming Thebes and be able to meet with certain visitors and officials without being under the suspicious eyes of the Amun priests!

However, "Ratut" was betrayed, and the evil priesthood finally knew the guarded secret that had been well kept for nine years. Poison was placed in the drinking water near Pharaoh's tent. "Ratut" was thirsty from the hot, desert ride in the open chariot and asked his friend, Rahotep, to procure him a drink. Therefore his best friend killed him innocently without even knowing it. Here was *Hadad* and *Solomon* of a former age, working out their karma together.

The priests believed that if they removed the "psychic" channel from the hated Aton meetings, they could force Ay and Maya to their will. They especially desired the knowledge that only Maya in all the land of Egypt knew!

When Pharaoh realized he had been poisoned and betrayed, he had Rahotep summon Queen Ankhsenamun. Before he passed into transition, he looked at his beloved queen, and his dearest friend, Ra: "Today I killed a powerful lion with my spear, and is this not symbolic of the fact that I have aided in the making of the SECRET PLACES OF THE LION? We children of Aton have 'killed' the lion and hid him from the view of the profane. I know that even as I am now pictured on my chariot as a human-headed lion, I shall in centuries yet to be born be symbolized as the *Winged Lion* [Mark, the Evangelist].

" As I pass from this existence to a better, I remember well the words of my brother Akhnaton. Strange I should remember them at all, for as a child I could not memorize the Hymn to the Aton, composed by good Akhnaton, but now I recall the words. . . .

" ' Thou risest beautifully in the horizon of heaven, O living Aton who creates Life! . . . How manifold are thy works! They are hidden from the face of man, O sole God, Like unto whom there is none other. . . . How excellent are thy plans, thou Lord of Eternity! . . . Thou art in my heart . . . the earth exists in thy hand . . . when thou risest man lives; when thou settest man dies.'

" I have served my Father Aton; I have lived on Truth—for me Aton is not setting; therefore I cannot die! For me Aton is but rising, and I shall live on, not here in this shabby dream world of earth, but in Aton's Kingdom until it is time for me to pass this way again and serve—serve until that day when all our serving shall have come to an end, an end that is but a *beginning* for all men of earth!

" O, Father Aton, hold me in thy hand. . . ." With these words, Pharaoh died.

Centuries later, workmen in their excavations discovered a vigorous sketch near the entrance of Tutankhamun's tomb. It was on a flake of limestone, and represents the young king, aided by his hound, slaying a lion with a spear. It had been drawn by Rahotep as he contemplated the sad end of Pharaoh and the words spoken that day. He drew it while working on Tutankhamun's tomb with his father Cato, and had been in a meditative mood while so doing; then he tossed it down by the entrance, where it was to be found many hundreds of years later!

After the assassination of Tutankhamun, Ay and Maya debated who should take up the double crown and become Pharaoh. Ay did not want to be Pharaoh and asked Maya to ascend the throne, but Maya could not, for he was still the royal treasurer and, as such, had to remain free of official pressure. Besides, Maya was married, and any successor to Tutankhamun would have to marry the young heiress Ankhsenamun in order to legitimize his claim to the throne! Since Ay's wife Tyi was already dead, it was decided that he would ceremonially marry the widowed Queen—a marriage in *name only*, for Ay was a very elderly man and the Queen was still but a child!

Ankhsenamun did not understand this, and sent a letter to the Hittite King Shubbuliliuma in which she said: "My husband is dead; I have no male children; your sons are said to be grown up; if to me one of your sons you give, and he will be my husband and king, he will be a help; send him accordingly, and thereafter I will make him my husband. I send gifts."

Time was short, for she had only seventy days, the time taken for the embalming and burial of her husband's body.

The Hittite king waited too long to decide, and when he finally dispatched his youngest son it was too late. Maya and Ahmose met the prince before he entered Thebes, and explained that Ay was now Pharaoh in the land of Egypt because of his marriage to the Queen. The prince returned home bitter and sad; to have been a Hittite and King of Egypt at the same time—this would have been the supreme attainment!

King Tutankhamun was laid to rest in his small tomb on April 23, 1350 B.C.

The funeral arrangements had been costly and were well prepared and supervised. Never before had a successor to the throne actually personally supervised the construction and decoration of the tomb of his predecessor. But Ay and Maya wanted certain objects to be sealed up with Tutankhamun. It was for a record; a proof that Aton still lived in Egypt. The Amun priests did not care, for they had eliminated their source of contention—the channel "Ratut"!

Ankhsenamun was beside herself with grief, for put to rest with her husband in his tomb were the remains of two of her children by "Ratut." One of these children had formerly been the murdered wife of Smenkhkare, Meritaton. She almost immediately reincarnated as one of the children of Tutankhamun and his queen. The other child had once been Genubath, son of Hadad the Edomite!

Why did these children die so young? It was to give the young rulers a saddening experience, if indeed they needed it, for their life was not too happy under the existing conditions brought about by Amunism. They served Aton, but they hardly led a normal, young life.

Now the King and Queen had a third child that did not die. She was known as Ankhsenpaaton the younger, and lived in the house of Maya as an adopted daughter to protect her from the priests.

Maya chose young Rahotep to be the artist that would fashion the beaten and burnished golden portrait mask of " Ratut." This youth had designed the magnificent golden throne later discovered in the tomb by Howard Carter. Its legs, fashioned in feline form, were surmounted by lions' heads, fascinating in their strength and simplicity. The chief glory of the throne was the panel of the back. The scene depicted here shows one of the halls of the palace. The King sits in an unconventional attitude upon a cushioned throne, his arm thrown carelessly across its back. Before him stands the slim figure of the Queen, gently anointing her husband's shoulder and collar with perfume. It was a simple composition, but Rahotep had faithfully reproduced his two dear friends as he saw them— living, loving, and serving in strife-torn Egypt!

Above the King and Queen on the back panel of the throne Rahotep pictured the Aton with the outstretched arms gently caressing the royal pair.

Historians cannot understand why an object like the throne, which bore such manifest signs of Aton heresy upon it, would be publicly buried in this stronghold of Amun faith! Why did Tutankhamun still sit on an Aton throne when the very name of the *One God* had been forbidden nine years previously? It is true that the cartouches were changed on the throne, but not all of them. In some of them the Aton element was erased, and the Amun form substituted, but in others the Aton remains unchallenged.

The attempt made to change *some* of the names was enough to appease the Theban priests, and, after all, the throne was now being buried with the young ruler who, as he grew more into manhood, became a threat to their security. They were afraid that he might cause a holy, religious war and return Aton to his rightful place in Egypt. This way they were burying this threat, now very much dead—burying him and all the symbols of his accursed faith!

So Rahotep, the artist, created a throne not unlike the one he designed when he was the great Solomon!

Rahotep created in imperishable metal a beautiful portrait of his dead friend and king. It was made of the " best " gold—*transmuted* gold! And the artist was being used as a channel himself to perfect and complete this effigy mask, which is more than just a mask— much more!

Maya had taken Rahotep's father, Cato, to the secret chambers many times, blindfolded, until they were safe within the treasure rooms. Cato, being a great artist, interpreted many things for Maya, things of artistic worth. Cato learned the art of transmutation from these hidden documents and passed on the knowledge to his son. Rahotep worked under the direct guidance of a deceased Aton priest-artist. This mentor was later to be John the Beloved, and, later still, the incomparable Leonardo da Vinci!

All preparations having been made, the body of young Tutank- hamun was placed upon a lion-shaped bier, within a shrine resting upon a sledge. This was drawn by courtiers to the tomb in the Theban Valley. Over the dead king, Ilipaamun and the women of the court placed festoons of garlands.

Four lesser nobles and General Horemheb preceded the sledge; then followed Sinuhe and Maya together, and behind them Ahmose and Amenophis. Ay, as the new king, and his queen Ankhsenamun were already at the tomb preparing for the last rites. Besides, Ankhsenamun was weak and ill; she could not have gone with the body on its journey to the tomb.

So " Ratut " was brought to his tomb on this spring night in 1350 B.C. The funeral rites were presided over by King Ay. Maya placed an offering in the tomb showing the King reclining on a *lion*. Maya inscribed it with his name and an appropriate farewell message. Finally, the gathered group of nobles, present to pay final homage to Pharaoh, began to pass out of the tomb. The last three individuals in the tomb were Rahotep, Horemheb, and Ankhsen- amun. The Queen was required by custom to be left alone with her deceased mate, and be the final one to bid him farewell.

Now, Rahotep's strength had been depleted because of the great concentration needed to complete the mask and other funeral equipment. Being used as a channel while conceiving the trans- muted mask was too much for this frail youth. Besides, the ordeal of seeing his friend die, and realizing he unknowingly caused this death (although innocent of any crime), was far too much for one so young. The entire Amun period was one of the cruellest man has ever experienced!

Rahotep left the tomb with General Horemheb, and, once outside, he fainted on the steps. It was thought the boy had died, because there was no perceptible pulse. But he was only in a trance condition—a coma brought on by his deep concentration and exhausting work. The others were no longer at the tomb entrance, and Horemheb very quickly had Rahotep buried on the spot. The General later informed Cato, when asked the whereabouts of his son: " Ra, thy son, perished at the tomb. The sight of his dead friend and Pharaoh was too much for the boy. I was forced to bury him at once; it would have been his wish."

Cato retorted: " But he wasn't mummified! "

Horemheb quickly answered: " But think of it, Cato, he doesn't need mummification; he is now buried near the tomb of a Pharaoh —he shall enjoy the eternal pleasures of a god in the other life."

Cato in his grief replied sarcastically: " Thank you, General, for your kindness and consideration; you always have the happiness of the people on your heart! "

Yet Cato knew that Rahotep would perish shortly after the supreme achievement of the golden mask; this was his purpose in life, and his duty was now fulfilled.

Outside the tomb several groups of slaves had been put to death by the priests, as was the custom of Amunism, to ensure the Pharaoh servants in the after-life. With these groups were the identical twins of the dark-skinned race of wizards! They desired to die at this time, for they had also completed their duty in Egypt. They were to protect Tutankhamun for his purpose of being a channel, and now they wished to die so that the Amun priests would never learn their secrets and powers they had brought with them from their strange land!

Inside the tomb, Ankhsenamun was paying her final tribute and visit with her young husband. She was trying to remember, in her girlish way, if all had been properly arranged as " Ratut " would have wanted it. She had always worried over him, her gentle and sensitive king. Did he have his favourite bow when he went hunting with Rahotep? Or was he dressed properly? These things were of great concern to her always, for she was very devoted, since he was her only true love.

She had seen to it that he carried with him to his tomb the rare iron dagger with the gold haft and knob of rock crystal which had been given to him at Akhetaton by the Hittite ambassador when he was only seven years old. His favourite bow was in the tomb also.

Ankhsenamun thought of their brief reign and of their only happiness—their love and their service to Aton. She thought of the two children who rested in the same tomb—the little ones who never hardly lived at all.

She had a farewell offering; not more gold, for the chamber was dazzling with the precious metal, but an offering that would please "Ratut." Upon the brow of his effigy, as he lay in his quartzite sarcophagus, she placed a tiny wreath of flowers. Among all that regal splendour and royal magnificence there was nothing so beautiful as these flowers!

Ankhsenamun was in the burial chamber for the last time, and with her own fingers she gently drew over her husband the shrouds beneath which he was to rest undisturbed for over three thousand years.

She turned to go, and, in a final gesture of affection and grief, she placed beside the entrance to the ante-chamber a bouquet of delicate wild flowers. Then she mounted the sixteen steps to the outside, where she beheld the heavens where Aton is Lord. She knew that " Ratut " had once come from one of the stars (Hesperus) in that sky. She knew too that some time in the far distant future she would meet her king again.

Before turning towards Thebes, where she was now Queen with Pharaoh Ay, she said: " Oh, Aton, until you ordain we meet again, spread thy eternal wings over Ratut as the Imperishable Stars."

The father of Nefretiti only reigned four years (1350–1346 B.C.), and Ankhsenamun never recovered from her illness and died of a broken heart in 1348 B.C.

The tomb was entered a few years after the burial by robbers, but two of them were caught in the act and subsequently died because of the vibration which had been placed around the tomb by the magician twins just before they perished in front of it. One robber had escaped, but died shortly afterwards. He had taken the solid gold statuette from its pedestal in the small golden shrine. This statuette has never been found, but it was a beautiful representation of Tutankhamun's father, Amunhotep III. It had been inscribed: "To my unborn son, whom I have not yet seen."

The proof that the robbers were caught in the act is the fact that a precious bundle of solid gold rings was left in the tomb—the last thing a thief would be likely to forget!

Maya and other officials removed all written documents from the tomb and resealed it after the robbery, and buried the entire entrance to the tomb so that it might be completely hid from view. And they were successful, for no hand touched the seals upon the door until Howard Carter made his world-famous discovery in 1922!

The written documents removed by Maya gave a complete history of the dead king and told of his true parentage. That he was truly the son of Amunhotep III can be proven by the cartouche on a magnificent red granite lion now in the British Museum (Gebel Barkal lion). This lion bears the cartouche of Tutankhamun, who expressly states that he is "the restorer of the monument of his father, Amunhotep."

The Pharaohs were not buried in splendour just to satisfy vain glory or pride; it was to preserve literal "Time Capsules" for future man. The symbols of Atonism years after it was forbidden, found in Tutankhamun's tomb, prove that the youth was an Atonist to the end. It has been said that once he returned to Thebes from Akhetaton, he restored the monuments and temples of the old gods and Amun. But Tutankhamun's long security in his tomb was not due to the fact that Amun protected the King because he acknowledged the false god's triumph over the religious revival of Akhnaton. "Ratut" actually did not reconstruct Amun's sanctuaries and re-endow his temples, but the priests did it in Tutankhamun's name!

The Pharaohs of the early Eighteenth Dynasty decided to use the Valley of the Tombs of the Kings for burial purposes. Its loneliness and comparative inaccessibility recommended it for the tombs that were to be record chambers, not just the luxurious apartments of dead kings! The valley was the ideal place for carrying out the experiment of a new method of concealment for the royal burials.

Information was placed in these tombs, and Tutankhamun's was better preserved because of the so-called "curse." Actually, it was a "blessing" and *not* a "curse" that was placed on the tomb. It was a "blessing" to ensure Divine protection and also to ensure a certain vibrational frequency that would endure until it was time for the information within the tomb to be released to mankind.

By the time the twentieth-century archaeologist—formerly Horemheb—had returned to this tomb, the force field had diminished until it was almost non-effective. Nevertheless, it still proved fatal to several of the excavators and scientists who entered the tomb. Lord Carnarvon had once been a high priest of Amun; now he had to return to life and make possible this discovery. The archaeologist himself had to return also to the very tomb he once stood inside of. By revealing the contents of the tomb to the world he paid in part for his action in turning his back on Aton!

So Ay ruled for only four years, and then, fearing that he would be poisoned, he literally starved himself to death.

Sinuhe, since he was a son of Amunhotep III, became Pharaoh and reigned for one short month as King Setymeramun. He was then buried in Akhnaton's empty royal tomb, and later the mummy was burned.

The cheese-maker's son, Horemheb—the blood-spattered soldier of Egypt—became Pharaoh. He ruled from 1346 B.C. to 1322 B.C., and was the last Pharaoh of the Eighteenth Dynasty. He married Princess Beketamun, which legitimized his succession to the throne.

Horemheb usurped the throne and started a blood-bath that ended only in his own death in 1322 B.C. It was he who chased a group of Israelites leaving Egypt in another wave of the *Lesser Exodus*, and because of this historians later confused his cruel acts with the so-called " Pharaoh of the Oppression " and " Pharaoh of the Exodus." However, Horemheb was not drowned in any Red Sea. But he hacked names from monuments; he didn't have any love for Aton, Amun, or any other gods—he adored only himself, Horemheb. He did everything in his power to see to it that only he would be remembered in Egypt. He is remembered, but not for that which he wished!

Mankind had seen for a short time the *Greater Light*, but, as always, after the Light dimmed terror overtook the world. Then when the last vestiges of Atonism had been removed, including the *Workers*, that Light went out in Egypt, and was not seen again on earth for centuries. With Horemheb the Light went out like a sputtering candle, and with it the Eighteenth Dynasty fell.

Maya, Ilipaamun, Tantahpe, Ankhsenpaaton the Younger, and all the rest of the followers and labourers who served Akhnaton and Aton perished at the hand of Horemheb. Maya was an old man of ninety years when he and all the others were beheaded in the most cruel fashion! Cato too was there in the house of Maya when this happened and he met the same end.

The Atonists had told the world that man did not need priests to act as intermediaries with the One God, for Aton was the God of all people and therefore accessible to *all*!

The man on the Nile could talk with God as well as Pharaoh. The Gospel brought by Akhnaton was the forerunner of the Gospel of Jesus the Christ! Akhnaton *spoke* of Universal Truth and the Master Jesus *proved* the same Truth by performing Divine Miracles!

If the world had accepted the *Greater Light* from Akhnaton and the other members of the " Goodly Company " Egypt would have later produced the greatest Pharaoh of them all, for the Christ-Spirit would have incarnated as Pharaoh Sananda! But the experiment failed, for the time being!

The *Dawn* had come to earth—and is not always the *Dawn* glorious? The golden rays of Father Aton shone on the dust of earth and touched the dark hearts of men, and mankind had a glimpse into the " pool of knowing "; they disturbed its surface (reflective knowing) when Pharaoh Akhnaton brought Aton to the period of the *Dawn*.

The *WORD* had been *Prepared*—the *WORD* had *Dawned*; now it was time for the *Revelation*. . . .

Chapter Three

REVELATION

T HE *WORD* was revealed. . . .
The Nineteenth Dynasty in Egypt was founded by
Ramses I in 1322 B.C. after the death of King Horemheb,
the usurper of the throne and a cheese-maker's son. Ramses I had
been the brother of Maya and head Aton priest, but was murdered
by the Amun priests during the reign of Tutankhamun. He incarnated almost at once as Ramses I, but reigned only one short year.

In 1321 B.C. Seti I ascended the throne and began to prepare the
way for the move back to the Holy City (Jerusalem). This will
sound strange to individuals familiar with accepted Biblical theories.
However, the Pharaohs who attempted to serve Aton (One God)
after Akhnaton introduced Him to the world, were not the cause
of " bondage " in Egypt; this was the work of Amunism under the
evil priesthood.

The experiment to bring in the Greater Light during the reign
of Akhnaton had failed—Egypt would have no Pharaoh Sananda,
and the world of men would have to wait until a night in Bethlehem
before the opportunity came once again for man to accept the
Light! For centuries various men, inspired of God, had incarnated
both in Israel and Egypt. It had not been decided just where the
experiment would finally succeed.

It had not succeeded with Abraham; then Joseph prepared the
way for it to take place in Egypt, but this also failed. David and
Solomon had not succeeded in Jerusalem, and Thutmose III removed
the treasures and secret documents from the Holy City and brought
them into Egypt for safe keeping. This was to prepare for Akhnaton
and his great labour. The " Goodly Company " by this time was
bolder in its attempts. Mankind was getting *Prepared* in slow but
continuous doses! Joseph became Maya and more preparation in
Egypt took place, but again the Light did not completely dominate

the world and its people. The entity that was to be known to the world as Moses had to come into life to remove secrets from Egypt and lead his people back to the Holy Land. This set the stage for the appearance of the Great Master, Jesus, the Christ. But he did not enter the world scene as Pharaoh; he came to man amidst the humblest of surroundings.

The Plan was literally carried back and forth between Israel and Egypt for generations and generations; it never really took root, for it would grow and flourish a short time and then wither and die. Finally, Israel was able to produce just the right circumstances for the appearance of He who rules this Solar System—second only to the Infinite Father.

"And there went a man of the house of Levi, and took to wife a daughter of Levi. And the women conceived, and bare a son: and when she saw him that he was a goodly child, she hid him three months. And when she could not longer hide him, she took for him an ark of bulrushes, and daubed it with slime and with pitch, and put the child therein; and she laid it in the flags by the river's brink. And his sister [Miriam] stood afar off, to wit what would be done to him. And the daughter of Pharaoh [Seti I] came down to wash herself at the river; and her maidens walked along by the river's side; and when she saw the ark among the flags, she sent her maid to fetch it. And when she had opened it, she saw the child: and, behold, the babe wept. And she had compassion on him, and said, This is one of the Hebrews' children " (Exodus ii: 1-6).

Miriam was the oldest sister of Moses. She had been Tantahpe in her former lifetime. We find the former father-daughter (Maya-Tantahpe) relationship, now changed to a brother-sister relationship (Moses-Miriam). Miriam came from behind her hiding-place, and asked the princess if she should bring a nurse. Of course, Moses' real mother was brought. When the child was able to eat solid food he was brought to the royal palace, and his mother kissed him good-bye. With that kiss all his Hebrew associations were severed. The princess adopted him as her own son, and he began his long career as a possible heir apparent to the throne of Egypt.

This child was named Seti-Meshu when adopted by the princess. *Meshu* means " the son of," or " drawn or rescued from the water." Therefore the name has two meanings: " the son of Seti " and " the one who was rescued from the water."

Moses symbolizes a progressive or *drawing-out* process, which works from within outward; as applied to the universe, the upward trend of all things—the evolutionary law. Involution always precedes evolution. *Joseph* in Egypt portrays the *involution* of a high spiritual idea.

Joseph led the Israelites *into* Egypt; Moses led them *out* of Egypt. And they were one and the same entity!

Moses represents the Lord as to the Divine Law, which is the WORD. He also represents Divine and Scientific Truth. Moses in another lifetime had also been the great law-giver, Hammurabi.

The princess who adopted Moses had been Meritaton, the oldest daughter of Akhnaton. Then she had incarnated as the young daughter of Tutankhamun who was buried in his tomb with him. Now she was the daughter of Pharaoh Seti I. This ruler had been Smenkhkare, the husband of Meritaton! So we find the former husband-wife combination (Smenkhkare-Meritaton) back in life in the Nineteenth Dynasty as father-daughter (Seti I - princess who adopted Moses).

One day, when Moses was a small child, he came to Pharaoh bearing a small golden image. Seti I couldn't believe his eyes! The image could have come from only one place! the secret Pyramidal chambers! And knowledge of the hidden entrance had died with Maya in 1338 B.C. Even as a mere child, Moses knew he had been Maya, and recalled the lost entrance to the Great Pyramid and other structures!

This is why a Hebrew child was held in such high esteem in Egypt. How can Bible scholars reconcile the fact that Moses was a member of a supposed " hated " race in Egypt and also loved by a princess of the ruling race and taken into the very palace itself? They will say: " Oh, but she loved the child and her father gave in to her whim." That is absurd, to say the least! An Egyptian princess would have been repelled by the sight of the " untouchable " Hebrew child. She would have chosen a waif of Egyptian blood for her adopted son before she would have chosen a Hebrew!

It is obvious that the account as given in Exodus and elsewhere is inaccurately reported. The Pharaohs were not as cruel as we are led to believe; neither were the Israelites in " bondage " because of Pharaoh. The only true " bondage " was caused by the teachings of the false god, Amun. It is the same today; many world leaders are inherently good men, but they, too, are ruled by the firm hand of *Amun*!

The mantle of Maya, the " coat of many colours," was taken up by young Prince Moses, and he alone in Egypt could once again lead Pharaoh, blindfolded, to the subterranean rooms and temples of antiquity!

Moses and Crown Prince Ramses (Ramses II) were like Jonathan and David. In fact, they had been these individuals and loved each other dearly. They were raised in the palace together; they shared each other's clothes, games, pleasures, and sorrows. This Ramses had been none other than Amunhotep III, the " Magnificent " Pharaoh, in his previous earthly existence!

Moses had been born in 1313 B.C., during the eighth year of the reign of Seti I. Ramses II was somewhat older than Moses and looked after him as an older " brother " would. The two knew that they had an important mission to complete in Egypt. They were both very much aware of *who* and *what* they were!

When Prince Moses was thirteen years old, Pharaoh died (1300 B.C.), and Crown Prince Ramses ascended the throne. The days of childhood were over, although both were still in their teens. They had to work quickly and secretly in order to prepare Moses so that he might remove the family records of Abraham, Isaac, and Jacob that had been carried to Egypt generations before. Original records were left under the Great Pyramid and Sphinx, but Moses made accurate copies of those he would need to take with him when he led his people out of Egypt to the "Promised Land" where the Christ would eventually be born.

Moses had a private tutor at all times, and also attended the great schools of the land. He studied art, literature, science, law, theology, music, military art and science, naval instruction, mineralogy, and many other things.

Some Bible students believe that Ramses II was the " Pharaoh of the Oppression " and his son, Meneptah, the " Pharaoh of the Exodus." However, this is not accurate.

" And it came to pass in process of time, that the king of Egypt died: and the children of Israel sighed by reason of the bondage . . . " (Exodus ii: 23).

The " king of Egypt " that died was not Ramses II, but the reference relates to the death of Seti I in 1300 B.C. The later historians knew that a " king of Egypt " had died, but they didn't know when it had really taken place. Therefore, we find mention of it at the end of Chapter ii in Exodus. No definite time is assigned to the death of the king, only that he died " in process of time." So there was no so-called " Pharaoh of the Oppression." At least, not as historians picture it. If we can assign that name to any Pharaoh, we would find that it fits Horemheb, who was not only a persecutor and an oppressor of Hebrews but also of Egyptians!

Historians knew a " king died " and they knew that there had been great persecution at a certain period (Horemheb). Historians of a still later date took these same ideas and came up with Ramses II as the " king who died " and also the " oppressor." This is another example of " ages in chaos."

In the first year of his reign, the young Ramses II married Nefretari (" Beautiful Companion "). This woman, who had great influence with her husband and was his favourite wife, had been none other than Queen Tiyi of the Eighteenth Dynasty. So we find the former husband-wife team (Amunhotep III - Tiyi) return-ing to life as husband-wife again (Ramses II - Nefretari). Tiyi had great influence with her husband, and now as Nefretari she had the same influence—the pattern repeats and repeats and repeats!

Ramses II had another wife by the name of Ist-nofret. She had been his wife, Sitamun, at the time he was Amunhotep III. This time she again gave him sons who were channels of Truth, but she was not a channel, except in her giving to the world men who would act in such a capacity.

Nefretari gave Ramses II his ninth son, Seti, and another son by the name of Anub-er-rekhu. This Seti had been the mentor-artist of a spiritual plane who inspired and guided the young artist Rahotep who fashioned the golden mask of Tutankhamun!

Ist-nofret gave Ramses II his second son, Ramses, his fourth son, Khaemweset, and his thirteenth son, Meneptah. She also gave him his eldest and favourite daughter, Bant-Anat.

The fourth and favourite son of Ramses II, Prince Setne-Khaem-weset (known to his father as Senti-Khaem), had been Sinuhe, and was later to be the physician Luke. He would have succeeded to the throne, but died after he celebrated the thirty-seventh anni-versary of the accession of his father, Ramses II (1263 B.C.).

Prince Setne-Khaemweset was a famous wizard prince and,

(Amunism) is now associated with free, winged thoughts (Zipporah). However, these thoughts are limited, because the name means " *little* bird." Fear is losing some of its power over the soul, however, and the preparations for the *Final Exodus* are prospering in Midian.

"And she bare him a son, and he called his name Gershom . . . " (Exodus ii: 22). Gershom had been Rahotep, the young artist, son of Cato. So the former relationship of father - adopted son (Maya-Rahotep) was now one of father - eldest son (Moses-Gershom). Rahotep had so loved Maya that he came back as a real son in this, his next lifetime. Moses' other son, Eliezer, had been his son Ra when he was Maya, the young Ra who had been murdered in the royal chariot with Pharaoh Smenkhkare and Queen Meritaton.

Aaron means: "illumined; enlightener; mountaineer (very lofty)." This entity had also been "Merk" of the "Ships of Light" on Lemuria. Once again he was the "messenger," the "enlightener." He later married Elisheba (Elisabeth), his second wife, and she bore him Nadab and other sons. Nadab had been Genubath when Aaron was Hadad; and he was the young son of Tutankhamun who was buried with the boy king in his tomb.

Elisheba had been Bathsheba, wife of David, and, later, Ilipaamun, the wife of Maya. Elisheba means: "a worshipper of God; God of the *seven*." So this entity was carrying the same vibration of *sheba*.

"Merk" and "Lady of the Sun" from Lemuria were now husband and wife (Aaron - second wife Elisheba).

Now for forty years Moses lived the life of a shepherd—not unlike the life he had led as Joseph and later as the shepherd David! The centre of the Midianite country, where Moses sojourned, was on the east shore of the Gulf of Akaba. The Midianites controlled the rich pasture-lands around Sinai, and Moses' forty years there carried him over the whole region. During this time, Moses wrote the Book of Job.

One day in Midian, while Moses watched over the flock of Jethro, his father-in-law, the "angel of the Lord appeared unto him in a flame of fire out of the midst of a bush: and he looked, and, behold, the bush burned with fire, and the bush was not consumed" (Exodus iii: 2).

Moses couldn't understand why the bush wasn't burning, since it was surrounded with flames! The Biblical account says that God called Moses by name, and Moses answered.

Then God commanded: " Draw not nigh hither: put off thy shoes from off thy feet, for the place whereon thou standest is holy ground " (Exodus iii: 5).

It is obvious that this was no ordinary " fire," but a magnetic force field that didn't burn the bush, but did give the appearance of real " flames " (like the aurora). That is why Moses was instructed to take off his shoes. It was necessary, for the contact to be made, that Moses remove his shoes and allow his body to directly touch the earth!

In Chapter iii of Exodus we find that there were three separate beings who spoke from out of the bush. First of all, in Verse 2: " And the *angel of the Lord* appeared unto him in a flame of fire. . . ." Then in Verse 4: " And when the *Lord* saw . . . " And finally, in Verse 4: " . . . *God* called unto him out of the midst of the bush. . . ."

Now the " angel of the Lord " was a messenger of the Lord, or a being (man) whose soul was winged. Here we have direct reference to the fact that Moses was instructed by a space visitor to return to Egypt. The visitor told Moses that " . . . ye shall serve God upon this mountain " when you bring your people forth from out of Egypt (Exodus iii: 12).

When Moses and Aaron (for Aaron went up to meet Moses) came down from Mount Horeb, a messenger from Pharaoh was awaiting them at the home of Jethro, priest of Midian. The messenger said: " My lord, Seti-Meshu [Moses], the great and good god, ruler of Upper and Lower Egypt . . . Pharaoh, commands that I give unto you this Cross of Life [Ankh], and inform you that he has spoken to the ' angel of the Lord ' in a flaming ' fire circle ' in the garden of the royal palace. Pharaoh says that it is now time for you to return as you vowed."

The " flame " seen by Pharaoh Ramses II in Egypt and by Moses on Mount Horeb signifies divine good of love shining forth by truth, which is of the Divine Law. " Horeb " also means " solitude." This signifies that we have to go into the solitude of the inner mind and lead our flock of thoughts to the back of the wilderness, where dwells the Exalted One, the divine I AM, whose kingdom is good judgment.

When Moses had been on the mountain, the *voice* had told him that "I will stretch out my hand, and smite Egypt with all my wonders . . ." (Exodus iii: 20).

Moses knew that the Amun priests would not even allow Pharaoh the power to release his people, and they would never allow an exodus if they knew the real purpose behind it. If they knew that valuable ancient records were leaving the Land of the Nile they would have staged a mass murder at once!

" And Moses answered and said, But, behold, they will not believe me, nor hearken unto my voice . . ." (Exodus iv: 1).

The *voice* asked Moses what he had in his hand, and Moses said, "I hold a rod." Moses was commanded to cast this rod on the ground; he did so, and it became a *serpent*. ". . . it became a serpent; and Moses fled from before it " (Exodus iv: 3).

When Moses put his hand forth, the *serpent* became a rod again. A rod signifies power and Divine Spiritual Truth: ". . . thy rod and they staff they comfort me " (Psalms xxiii: 4). The "rod and staff" signify the Divine Truth and Good to which belongs power.

A *serpent* also is symbolic of a vortex, or vortical currents and force! When Moses cast or turned his rod down (a rod he brought with him from Egypt), the power of the ancient vril stick (rod) was activated by the field of the "flame" in the bush, and it turned into a *serpent* (vortex of force). The *voice* told Moses to "Put forth thine hand, and take it by the tail " (Exodus iv: 4). When Moses raised it to its normal position again, using the small device at the base (tail) of the vril rod, the power was shut off, and the rod became inactive, or changed from a *serpent* to a rod again.

Moses was to show miracles and wonders upon his return to Egypt in order to convince Amunism of his powers and to enable him to carry out his plan for the Exodus—not only an exodus of people, but of recondite and ancient knowledge in the form of records!

Moses had told the *voice* " . . . I am slow of speech, and of a slow tongue " (Exodus iv: 10). But the *voice* in the "flames" told him, "Is not Aaron the Levite thy brother? I know that he can speak well. And also, behold, he cometh forth to meet thee: and when he seeth thee, he will be glad in his heart " (Exodus iv: 14).

Now Aaron was three years older than Moses, and he felt he should go to meet his brother on Mount Horeb. " And the Lord said to Aaron, Go into the wilderness to meet Moses. And he went, and met him in the mount of God, and kissed him " (Exodus iv: 27).

Moses told Aaron the words he had heard from the " flames " and the wonders they were to perform in Egypt. So the two brothers came down from the mount and met the messenger of Pharaoh. They then " gathered together all the elders of the children of Israel " (Exodus iv: 29).

Aaron is of the vibration of the " messenger ": as " Merk " he brought a message to Lemuria from Hesperus (Venus), and as Tutankhamun he was a " messenger " between the " worlds." Now " Aaron spake all the words which the Lord had spoken unto Moses, and did the signs in the sight of the people. And the people believed . . . " (Exodus iv: 30–31).

The rod that Moses had carried with him to the top of Mount Horeb was an inactive vril that he had discovered in the SECRET PLACES OF THE LION, while a prince at the court of Seti I. It came from the same place as the golden image which Moses had shown to Pharaoh Seti when he was a child! On Mount Horeb, the space craft hovering there had activated the vril rod or stick once again by magnetic affinity. Then Moses had Aaron demonstrate the power of the rod, because Moses' older brother was the more eloquent!

Aaron and Moses then journeyed to ancient Memphis in Egypt. Ramses II was overjoyed at seeing his dear friend. He said: " Seti-Meshu, my brother of my heart; we have done our work well, and Aton [One God] has brought us together again for the final work of my lifetime and the beginning of the final hour for you! "

Moses had brought Zipporah with him, and his two sons, into Egypt. " And Moses took his wife and his sons, and set them upon an ass, and he returned to the land of Egypt: and Moses took the rod of God in his hand " (Exodus iv: 20).

" And thou shalt take this rod in thine hand, wherewith thou shalt do signs " (Exodus iv: 17). Moses informed Ramses II that he had learned how to use the ancient instruments of *serpent* (vortex: a coiled serpent) power that were in the subterranean chambers of Egypt. Previously, as a child, he had recalled the location of these chambers, but he still did not know how to use what he did find. Now he possessed that knowledge!

Now wherever the Holy Bible says, " Pharaoh said this or that," or " Pharaoh commanded such and such," it does not refer specifically to Ramses II. Remember, the controlling factor behind the throne was Amunism. Therefore it was the Amun priesthood that Moses and Aaron performed for with their new-found powers and instruments.

" And Pharaoh commanded the same day the taskmasters of the people, and their officers, saying, Ye shall no more give the people straw to make brick, as heretofore: let them go and gather straw for themselves " (Exodus v: 6–7).

Therefore the Biblical records tells us that " Pharaoh " was insolent, and ordered the taskmasters to lay heavier burdens on the Israelites, requiring them to make the same number of bricks and yet gather their own straw. Remember, again it was not Pharaoh that commanded these things, but the *real power* behind him, the power that literally put words in his mouth!

In 1883 Naville and in 1908 Kyle found at the city of Pithom the lower courses of brick filled with good *chopped straw*, the middle courses with *less straw*, and that was stubble plucked up by the root; and the upper courses of brick were of *pure clay*, having *no straw* whatsoever. This is an amazing confirmation of the Exodus account!

The Israelites in Egypt had helped to build two cities for Ramses II. " Therefore they did set over them taskmasters to afflict them with their burdens. And they built for Pharaoh treasure cities, Pithom and Raamses " (Exodus i: 11).

The " treasure cities " had been built by Ramses II while Moses was in Midian for forty years. This was part of the work that Ramses II said he would perform while separated from Moses. The " treasure [store] cities " of Pithom and Raamses contained secret hiding-places where certain documents and other valuables would be placed by Moses after his return to Egypt. He would remove that which was needed from the SECRET PLACES OF THE LION, and bring it quietly to Pithom and Raamses, where it would be packed and prepared for the long journey.

The *voice* on Mount Horeb had said to Moses: " And I will give this people favour in the sight of the Egyptians: and it shall come to pass, that, when ye go, ye shall not go empty " (Exodus iii: 21).

Moses, Aaron, and all the others would not " go empty," for they had a mission to perform.

Moses and Aaron came to the royal palace, where Ramses II had assembled the head Amun priests.

"Thou shalt speak all that I command thee: and Aaron thy brother shall speak unto Pharaoh [the power behind Ramses II], that he send the children of Israel out of his [Amun's] land' (Exodus vii: 2).

At this time Moses was eighty years old, and Aaron was eighty-three years old (Exodus vii: 7).

"Then Pharaoh also called the wise men and the sorcerers: now the magicians of Egypt . . . " (Exodus vii: 11).

The Amun priests demanded a miracle, so Aaron took the rod and cast it before them. It turned into a *serpent*. The priests cast down their rods (magician's wands), and they turned into *serpents*— but Aaron's rod swallowed up their rods. Moses and Aaron had the greater power: the power of Aton (One God) (Exodus vii: 9, 11–12).

However, Amunism would not heed the words of Moses when he said, "Let my people go!"

The Ten Plagues had to come to Egypt; for if they hadn't, an exodus would have been impossible. Since the Light had failed with Akhnaton's unsuccessful experiment, it was now imperative that certain objects and knowledge be returned to the Holy City in Israel! *There had to be an exodus!*

Two of the head Amun priests who opposed Moses were Jannes and Jambres (II Timothy iii: 8). They were men who "resist the truth: men of corrupt minds, reprobate concerning the faith."

The Bible mentions over and over again that Moses was commanded by the Lord to "Take thy rod [lift it up], and stretch out thine hand upon Egypt."

Through the power of the vril rod came the Ten Plagues. They lasted nearly a year: waters of the sacred Nile turned to blood; frogs swarmed out of the Nile across the land; lice appeared on man and beast; swarms of flies covered the people, the ground, the houses; murrain hit the cattle and they died in vast quantities; boils came to man and beast, and then the hail came. Locusts came in vast clouds, reposed at night on the ground in layers to a depth of four or five inches. If they were mashed, the smell would be unbearable. Then came horrible darkness; there was midnight darkness over all of Egypt for three days. Even the sun, the physical visible symbol of Aton (One God) was blackened and taken from the view of man! Even today in Egypt when the sun doesn't shine the people consider it an ill omen.

The miracles that had been planned for the time of Akhnaton were now manifest throughout Upper and Lower Egypt! This was the time of the *Revelation*!

The Ten Plagues were actually very symbolic. Frogs were produced from the Nile because the waters in the land of Amun symbolized "falses" of doctrine upon which the reasonings of Amunism were founded. Locusts in Egypt symbolized "falses" in the extremes, which consume the truths and goods of man.

By these miracles both Israel and Egypt knew that Aton (One God) was the true and Supreme Creator; it showed Amun to be a false god. While the priests imitated some of the plagues, they did not have the Greater Light or Power.

Now the Holy Bible says that Pharaoh's heart was "hardened," sometimes by God, and sometimes by the stubbornness of the ruler himself. However, again this refers to the unyielding priests of Amun. Nineteen times it is declared that Pharaoh's heart was "hardened." Eleven times God did it; three times Pharaoh did it himself; and in five cases it is only announced as being done.

So the Amun priests were "hardened" against Moses and the idea of letting his people go. Yet there is another strange fact. Ramses II actually suffered from a disease called atheroma. His son, Meneptah, also suffered from this disease or "hardening." (In 1909 Meneptah's mummified heart was sent to the Royal College of Surgeons and Dr. Shattock reported that it really was "hardened" —from the disease atheroma.) The "hardening" was an ageing process which we know as arteriosclerosis, and not an act of God.

At last, after nearly a year (ten months), the crisis was at hand. Jannes and Jambres acknowledged defeat. The blow fell with such a crushing effect that Amunism yielded and Israel departed. They departed with treasures and jewels of Egypt. A large part of Egypt's wealth was transferred to Israel and some of it was later used in the construction of the Tabernacle! But the outward appearance of wealth and "jewels of silver, and jewels of gold, and raiment" was to hide the real treasures—the manuscripts and secret documents brought from the secret store-rooms in Pithom and Raamses in the final hour. If the Amun priests saw all this elaborate display of treasure on the " sons and upon the daughters " of Israel, they would not look deeper, nor would they suspect the nature of hidden things! (Exodus iii: 22; xii: 35.)

"And the Lord said unto Moses, Yet will I bring one plague more upon Pharaoh, and upon Egypt; afterwards he will let you go . . ." (Exodus xi: 1).

"And all the firstborn in the land of Egypt shall die, from the firstborn of Pharaoh that sitteth upon his throne, even unto the firstborn of the maidservant that is behind the mill; and all the firstborn of beasts" (Exodus xi: 5).

What is actually meant by " firstborn "? What could actually happen that would destroy *only* the " firstborn "? A plague couldn't do it, neither would any natural catastrophe. And it certainly wouldn't be God waving a wand and suddenly causing the " firstborn " to perish! " The firstborn " actually stands for some other word! In the Book of Exodus we read: " And thou shalt say unto Pharaoh, Thus said the Lord, Israel is my son, even my firstborn . . . if thou refuse to let him go, behold, I will slay thy son, even thy firstborn " (Exodus iv: 22-23).

The above scripture should be read: " Thus saith the Lord, Israel is my son, even my *chosen* . . . if thou refuse to let him go, behold, I will slay thy son, even thy *chosen*."

So we see the " firstborn " actually means " chosen." The confusion on the part of Bible scholars when attempting to explain the Tenth Plague (death of " firstborn ") arises from the similarity of the words used. " Israel, my *firstborn*," is Israel *bekhori*. " Israel, my *chosen*," is Israel *bechiri* (bechori).

"And it came to pass, that at midnight the Lord smote all the firstborn [chosen] in the land of Egypt, from the firstborn of Pharaoh that sat on his throne unto the firstborn of the captive that was in the dungeon; and all the firstborn of cattle" (Exodus xii: 29).

The " firstborn "—the select, the flower of Egypt—died in a great natural catastrophe. The planet then existing between Mars and Jupiter was called *Lucifer*, and Amun (the false god) ruled this planet. That is to say that negative forces had gained complete control over it, and it destroyed itself by thermonuclear power. The destruction of Lucifer and its moon, Malona, is fully discussed in the book *Other Tongues—Other Flesh*.

This was not the planet Car (where we obtain our word " *car-rion* "), for it had destroyed itself several million years ago. Lucifer was the only planet to go through such destruction in our solar system. Many planets have been eliminated from Creation because it is true that too great a preponderance of evil eventually destroys itself!

There was never a night like this before in history, and possibly it will never be equalled, for the very heavens themselves shook with violence from the shattered planet Lucifer. The " Morning Star " was no more.

Now Pharaoh and Moses were informed by the *voices* in the " flames " (or space visitors) that the reason the great " Day Star " had suddenly vanished was because it had destroyed itself; they were warned that great " hail " (meteor showers) would strike the earth.

It was decided that this was the psychological time for the *Fina Exodus*! The space visitors told Moses the exact time calculated for the Tenth Plague (devastating meteor showers), which would undoubtedly kill the " firstborn " (chosen). The result of the earth's field being unbalanced by the shower would cause gigantic earthquakes. The setting was perfect! With such destruction going on, the priesthood of Amun would hardly find time, or even be interested in the Israelites' departure! They would be too busy saving their lives!

How ironic, but not coincidental, that an evil planet announced its horrible end like an exploding star in some vast corner of the universe on the same night that Moses led his people and the fabulous treasures out of Egypt to the " Promised Land " where the Work would begin for the *Fulfilment*!

" And Pharaoh rose up in the night, he, and all his servants, and all the Egyptians; and there was a great cry in Egypt . . . " (Exodus xii: 30).

Those fleeing the earthquake were killed by the meteors, and those who sought shelter from the great shower of hail-like stones were destroyed by the force of the earthquake. Houses were smashed, and fell in on strong and weak alike. Temples were levelled; and the tombs were opened up, the dead bodies exposed and plundered by those who must steal no matter what is happening!

Pharaoh "called for Moses and Aaron by night and said, Rise

up, and get you forth from among my people, both ye and the children of Israel; and go, serve the Lord, as ye have said " (Exodus xii: 31).

Moses and Aaron came to the royal palace to see Ramses II just before the great structure crumbled into ruin. Pharaoh said: " Dear ones of my own heart; this is the night for which we have prayed and waited many decades—it has not come too soon. I will gather men from the ranks of those I trust, and we shall follow you shortly to Pihahiroth [Pi-ha-Khiroth]. I will inform the evil priests that I am leading an army that will destroy you. This will satisfy them, for when this chaos is over, and the madness of this night is forgotten, they will seek your death, that you may depend on! Go now! I pray that I may soon once again look upon your faces, although my task is completed."

The three men embraced for a moment, then separated. Pharaoh went to prepare his chariot, horses, and men. Moses and Aaron went into the streets outside the palace. The groaning throughout the land was unbearable—" mingled with lamentations." The other plagues had driven the population from the country into the cities, and now they were in the worst possible area to be when an earthquake strikes!

People were smashed on the pavement of dark and ruined streets; prisoners tore each other to shreds as they fought frantically to get free of landslides that had buried them alive in their pits and dungeons.

The ground continued to contract in violent spasms; the Nile flooded the land; the government collapsed under the strain of great disaster; the mob ruled in the streets—women were violated, children crushed under heavy feet; plunderers searched the city; everywhere people were dying.

According to the tradition of the Haggadah (non-legal part of Jewish traditional literature) the majority of the population of Egypt was killed during the horror of the Tenth and Final Plague (nine-tenths according to certain ancient records)!

" Evil fell upon the earth . . . the earth was in a great affliction."

After Moses and Aaron had left Pharaoh, and the King himself had gone out to make ready his men, the royal palace crumbled, half of it falling into a great gap in the earth caused by an earthshock.

Crown Prince Seti, ninth son of Ramses II and heir apparent, was killed as the gigantic walls fell in on him. The second son, Ramses, had died early, as did Khaemweset and all the others. Even the tenth, eleventh, and twelfth sons had died in infancy. This left only Seti and Meneptah (ninth and thirteenth sons respectively). Prince Seti had been the spiritual mentor of Rahotep the artist in another lifetime. He was later born as the " Beloved " follower of the Master Jesus.

The death of this prince was the outward reason for the changing of the scriptural text. Because it was remembered that Pharaoh's son (not his firstborn, but the surviving heir apparent) and heir died that night, the word *bekhori* (firstborn) replaced the word *bechiri* (chosen). Historians were confused over the death of the " chosen " throughout all the land of Egypt and the death of Pharaoh's heir (" firstborn "). Therefore the words were interchanged and became hopelessly mixed up in later documents.

As Moses and Aaron departed from the terror of the city behind them, Moses happened upon the tomb of Joseph. And a legend is preserved in the Haggadah that during the last night, when Egypt was smitten, the coffin of Joseph was found lying upon the ground, lifted from its grave.

" And Moses took the bones of Joseph with him: for he [Joseph] had straitly sworn the children of Israel, saying, God will surely visit you; and ye shall carry up my bones away hence with you " (Exodus xiii: 19).

But Joseph's sarcophagus was empty! What is meant by " bones "? This is an indication that when Joseph told his brethren that his " bones " would be removed when the children of Israel left Egypt he realized that he would be in life at that time (Moses). It also shows that when Moses left Egypt, the " bones " of Joseph were, in a sense, going with him. After all, he (Moses) had been Joseph in another lifetime. Joseph's " bones " belonged to Moses in a symbolic sense, and vice versa!

But " bones " mean much more! *Bones* signify " falses " and *sepulchres* signify evils. When Joseph's tomb was opened by the earthquake and his sarcophagus revealed, it symbolized the destruction of the false god Amun in Egypt. As Amun had waged a holy war on Aton (One God) during the reign of good Akhnaton, now Aton was triumphant as the Israelites and the treasures of Aton's secret temples and shrines left Egypt. On the night that evil fell upon the earth, evil priests paid karma, and paid dearly: " For I will pass through the land of Egypt this night . . . against all the gods of Egypt I will execute judgment: I *am* the Lord " (Exodus xii: 12).

After this night, Egypt was never the same again; her glory that had reached its apex in the Eighteenth Dynasty at Akhetaton was gone for ever. The Government and rulers were ever afterwards weak and uninspired. A country will become great and endure in direct proportion to the amount of Light it allows to enter its national life. Amunism had snuffed out the Light and therefore they snuffed out Egypt—it was no longer needed for the *Plan*.

Sepulchres were opened; evils were revealed! By taking out the " bones " of Joseph, we find that Moses was taking out the " falses " of Joseph! This means that all the mistakes made by the entity when he was Joseph were paid for completely by succeeding lifetimes, culminating with the labours of Moses. The " bones " were removed—the " falses " were gone; they existed no more!

It is true: Joseph's coffin was empty! He had departed from earthly existence in another manner! Moses removed certain records from the tomb as SECRET PLACES OF THE LION were revealed this night; just as they will *all* be revealed in days to come, in much the same manner—earthquake, pestilence, destruction, and the will of God!

" And the children of Israel journeyed from Rameses to Succoth, about six hundred thousand on foot that were men, besides children. And a mixed multitude went up also with them; and flocks, and herds, even very much cattle " (Exodus xii: 37-38).

Rameses was one of the cities in Goshen, Egypt, that had been built by the Israelites for Ramses II. The other store-city was Pithom. When these cities were excavated it was found that the rooms were made *down* into the surface of the earth—they were literally store-cities, or treasure-cities, built to house the objects that would finally be taken by Moses and his people out of Egypt.

The inscriptions on the monuments of the site of the city of Ramses tell plainly that the builder of the city was Ramses II, or Ramses the Great. Also a temple of Ramses II was found there. The title " the Great " is interesting, since the same entity had been called Amunhotep the " Magnificent " in an earlier existence!

Some authorities believe that Ramses was not the actual builder of the city, but had placed his cartouche or "autograph" on a city that had been built by one of his predecessors. However, this is not the case.

Critics also believe that the Land of Goshen never existed! But two papyri maps of Egypt have been found which show that Egypt was laid out in twenty or twenty-one nomes, or counties, or units for local administration. On both maps is the nome "Land of Goshen."

The collapse of the great temples, the dead and wounded in the debris, the destruction of the monstrous statues of false gods inspired dread, terror, and horror. Therefore many Egyptians also went with the Israelites. It was " a mixed multitude." And all the Hebrews did not go with Moses; some stayed in Egypt! When Joseph and Jacob went down into Egypt, all their people didn't go, for some stayed home. This time the same thing happened: all the Israelites did not leave in the *Final Exodus!*

Moses and Aaron went to the city of Rameses (Raamses, Ramses) and gathered up that which had been prepared for their long journey. They then went to Pithom, a few miles to the east. They left the two cities not a moment too soon, for their walls fell and were partly swallowed by the earth. Many Israelites perished when this happened.

Moses led his people through " the way of the wilderness of the Red Sea " and they marched five in a rank. The people rejoiced and sang. This was the day of deliverance from the land of " bondage " (Amunism).

" And the Lord went before them by day in a pillar of a cloud, to lead them the way; and by night in a pillar of fire, to give them light; to go by day and night; He took not away the pillar of the cloud by day, nor the pillar of fire by night, from before the people " (Exodus xiii: 21–22).

A gigantic space ship led the Israelites out of Egypt! The " pillar of a cloud " was the force field, and at night this magnetic field appeared as a " pillar of fire." That is exactly how space ships are observed today. Their force fields cause them to become fiery and spectacularly brilliant at night.

Egyptian papyrus records state: " Behold, the fire has *mounted up on high.* Its burning goes forth against the enemies of the land."

Space visitors were surveying and watching the route taken by Moses and the Israelites as they were returning the Light and the Word of God (Aton) to Israel. They had done this very same thing when Thutmose III marched towards Jerusalem to obtain the treasures of Solomon's Temple of God. That is why so-called "saucers" are here today—they are the *Guardians* of the SECRET PLACES OF THE LION!

Now, Pi-ha-Khiroth was on the road from ancient Memphis to Pisoped. When the Israelites beheld Pharaoh and his army coming after them, "they lifted up their eyes . . . and they were sore afraid" (Exodus xiv: 10).

Ramses II had an appointment with destiny; he hoped that by deceiving the Amun priests into thinking he was going to kill the fleeing Israelites he would actually be able to give them safe escort out of Egypt! Many of the Israelites did not understand this; all they knew was that their former taskmasters were pursuing them. Moses and Aaron and a select inner group knew the real meaning of the exodus, but many thousands of Hebrews did not know the meaning. Is this not true, even today? Certain inspired men lead people, but how many of the people know *why* they are being led at all?

Moses again heard the same *voice* he had heard in the "flames." It commanded him to tell the Israelites to go forward into the Red Sea! " . . . lift thou up thy rod, and stretch out thíne hand over the sea, and divide it: and the children of Israel shall go on dry ground through the midst of the sea " (Exodus xiv: 16).

" And the angel of God, which went before the camp of Israel, removed and went behind them; and the pillar of the cloud went from before their face, and stood behind them: And it came between the camp of the Egyptians and the camp of Israel . . . " (Exodus xiv: 19–20).

" And Moses stretched out his hand over the sea; and the Lord caused the sea to go *back* by a strong east wind all that night, and made the sea dry *land*, and the waters were divided. And the children of Israel went into the midst of the sea upon the dry *ground*: and the waters *were* a wall unto them on their right hand, and on their left. And the Egyptians pursued, and went in after them to the midst of the sea, even all Pharaoh's horses, his chariots, and his horsemen " (Exodus xiv: 21–23).

Now many of those who Pharaoh trusted were secretly serving Amun, and they came up with their chariots to destroy the Israelites. However, it came to pass that " the Lord looked unto the host of the Egyptians through the pillar of fire and of the cloud, and troubled the host of the Egyptians, And took off their chariot wheels, that they drave them heavily [or, and made them go heavily] . . . " (Exodus xiv: 24–25).

The force field from the craft stationed above actually held back the group (made chariot wheels heavy) that was trying to run down Moses and his people. By the time this part of the army was in the midst of the sea, between the walls of parted water, the entire area was surrounded by a vortex.

" And the Lord said unto Moses, Stretch out thine hand over the sea, that the waters may come again upon the Egyptians, upon their chariots and upon their horsemen " (Exodus xiv: 26).

And Moses did as he was commanded and the sea returned to where it had been before the crossing (the vicinity of the present city of Suez), and the Egyptians were overthrown in the midst of the sea.

" And the waters returned, and covered the chariots, and the horsemen, and all the host of Pharaoh that came into the sea after them; there remained not so much as one of them " (Exodus xiv: 28).

Now the Bible doesn't say that all the pursuing Egyptians were killed. It says that " all the host of Pharaoh that came into the sea *after them* " were killed. In other words, only those who dared chase the Israelites and follow them into the midst of the sea were actually destroyed. Those who stayed on the shore with Pharaoh were *not* killed.

The force field of the space craft had parted the Red Sea. " And with the blast of thy nostrils the waters were gathered together . . . " (Exodus xv: 8).

" For the horse of Pharaoh went in with his chariots and with his horsemen into the sea, and the Lord brought again the waters of the sea upon them . . . " (Exodus xv: 19).

However, the Book of Exodus nowhere states that Pharaoh himself was drowned! If he had been, his body would probably have been washed up and duly mummified. (Certain authorities say that the body of the " Pharaoh of the Exodus " will never be found because he perished in the Red Sea. This is absurd, because if he was washed ashore his remains would have been mummified.)

Many of the drowned Egyptians were washed ashore. " . . . and Israel saw the Egyptians dead upon the sea shore " (Exodus xiv: 30).

The Egyptian Papyrus Ipuwer (vii: 1–2) says that Pharaoh was lost under very unusual circumstances " that have never happened before." Now surely this indicates that Pharaoh was not drowned. After all, drowning had happened many times before; it was common in Egypt.

What were the strange circumstances " that had never happened before "?

Certain ancient records call the place of the crossing of the Red Sea the " Place of the Whirlpool " and also say that his majesty (Pharaoh) leapt into the so-called " Place of the Whirlpool."

These papyri records go on to state: " Pharaoh was *thrown* by a great force, *thrown* by the whirlpool high in the air . . . he surely departed to heaven . . . he was no longer with his horse, and he departed from his army."

The " whirlpool " was the vortex of force which surrounded the area of the crossing. Pharaoh Ramses II was taken up bodily by the space craft and " departed to heaven." His men didn't see the waves engulf him; they saw his horse go on into the water after Pharaoh had been removed from the animal, and they saw him rise as if " thrown by a great force . . . thrown by the whirlpool [vortex] high in the air."

" . . . the horse of Pharaoh went in with his chariots . . . into the s:a," but Ramses II himself did *not* go into the sea. He was taken aboard the space ship and returned to the ruins of his royal palace (Exodus xv: 19).

When the Amun priests found that Ramses II was still in the capital city they couldn't believe their eyes. Had he not gone out with the army to bring back the slaves and destroy those who refused to return? They said, " Surely this is magic, or has Pharaoh deceived us? Perhaps his love for Seti-Meshu [Moses] is too deep; greater than his love for the gods of Egypt. He is therefore a false Pharaoh and not fit to rule the Two Kingdoms."

They set upon him and killed him. Ramses II, whose name means " son of the sun; born of the sun," died amidst the ruin of his palace and beside the body of Crown Prince Seti, who had been killed by the collapse of the building during the earthquake. And he was truly "born of the sun," as are all those who serve as members of the "Goodly Company" working always for the Greater Light of Aton (One God).

The new Pharaoh was to be Meneptah, thirteenth son of Ramses II, the only surviving member of the House of Ramses. He had followed his father after the latter had pursued the fleeing Israelites.

In the 1860s, in el-Arish, a town on the border between Egypt and Palestine, a shrine of black granite inscribed with hieroglyphics all over its surface was discovered. An inscription on this shrine relates that a son of the Pharaoh who "leapt into the Place of the Whirlpool" set out to locate his father. However, all who accompanied the prince were killed by a terrible blast, and the prince sustained burns before he returned from this expedition to seek his father, who he was afraid had perished.

Those who had accompanied Meneptah were officials of Amun, who went with him to see that Ramses II carried out their plan to bring back or kill the fleeing Israelites. The force field of the space craft surrounded this group and the members were "killed by a terrible blast." Only Meneptah survived the power of the magnetic field, and even he "sustained burns."

When Meneptah returned to the capital he discovered the body of his father, Ramses II, and that of his brother, Seti, which had been pulled from the ruins. The priests came, bowed before him, and put the red-and-white double crown on his head. He was now Pharaoh over all the Land of Egypt.

This Meneptah was later to incarnate as Saul of Tarsus who was struck by a great light, even as Meneptah was on the side of the road as he sought his father!

In the Ramesseum at Thebes in 1896 a black granite stele was discovered on which Amunhotep III had described his building operations at Thebes. This stele was usurped by Meneptah, who engraved on the back of it his Song of Triumph over the Libyans and other people. The song contains the only direct reference to the Children of Israel which has yet been found on an Egyptian monument!

The discovery has brought more confusion into modern conceptions of the *Oppression* and *Exodus* of Israel than any other factor.

The King Meneptah speaks of his triumph over his enemies:

" Wasted is Tehenu [a tribe on the Libyan border of Egypt],
The Hittite land is pacified,
Plundered is the Canaan, with every evil,
Carried off is Askalon,
Seized upon is Gezer;
Yenoam is made as a thing not existing,
Israel is desolated, her seed is not,
Palestine has become a defenceless widow for Egypt."

This song has been taken to imply that by this time the Israelites
were in Palestine, and consequently that the Exodus had taken
place considerably earlier; but it can also be argued that it refers to
some portions of the Hebrew race which had remained in Palestine
when the family of Jacob went down into Egypt.

However, we must state here that Meneptah was not the
" Pharaoh of the Exodus," and his father, Ramses II, was not the
" Pharaoh of the Oppression." If we *must* have a " Pharaoh of the
Exodus " we have to list two rulers: Akhnaton and Ramses II.
This is because there was no particular date for any one exodus.

Pharaoh Akhnaton had freed all men before he was murdered,
and many of the Israelites left Egypt at that time during the chaos
that followed with the priests fighting a holy war so that Amun
would be restored. That was the beginning of an exodus, and we
should call it the *Lesser Exodus.* The entire Exodus therefore covered
a period of many years, with successive waves of Israelites leaving at
different opportune times.

In connection with the above, it is interesting to note that if we
take the date 1761 B.C. (the year when Joseph stood before Pharaoh)
and the date 1361 B.C. (the year Akhnaton died) and subtract one
from the other we get the number 400!

Most authorities agree that the Sojourn of Israel in the Land of
Egypt was four hundred years! Some say it was four hundred and
thirty years (Exodus xii: 40). However, we must determine *when*
the Sojourn began.

In *Preparation*, we took the date 1752 B.C. (the year Jacob descended
into Egypt), and then took the traditional four hundred and thirty
years for the Sojourn. From this we get 1322 B.C. (the year
Horemheb died). If we took four hundred years for the Sojourn
we come up with 1352 B.C., the time of Tutankhamun!

Now, let us take the year that Joseph stood before Pharaoh—1761
B.C. It seems more logical to take this date, since Joseph was Hebrew
and the Sojourn should be dated from his appearance in Egypt (1761
B.C.) and not the date of Jacob's descent several years later.

Using four hundred years for the Sojourn, we get 1361 B.C., as
shown above. This was the year Akhnaton died. This is very
accurate, because the first Israelites did leave Egypt immediately
after the death of Akhnaton!

Now if we use the Biblical four hundred and thirty years for the
Sojourn and the 1761 B.C. date—subtract one from the other—we
come up with 1331 B.C. This was during the reign of Horemheb!

No matter what date we use for the beginning of the Sojourn
(either 1761 B.C. or 1752 B.C.) and no matter whether we use four hundred or four hundred and thirty years for the length of the Sojourn,
we come up with a correct answer! We get either Akhnaton,
Tutankhamun, or Horemheb for "Pharaoh of the Exodus"!

Of course, they all fit the title, since we have already shown
that the Exodus was in successive waves over many years.

If we must have a "Pharaoh of the Oppression," it would be
Horemheb, for he persecuted his own people as well as Hebrews.
But it must be remembered that the Hebrews were not persecuted
in Egypt because of their race, but because they were Atonists
(believed in One God). Besides, the Hebrews were not a *pure*
race by any means. They were mixed with the blood of Egyptians,
Persians, Babylonians, Midianites, and many, many other peoples.

Therefore, from the evidence, we obtain the following:

Akhnaton	"Pharaoh of the *Lesser* Exodus."
Smenkhkare ⎫	
Tutankhamun ⎬	(Pharaohs when successive waves of
Ay ⎪	small groups of Israelites left
Setymeramun ⎭	Egypt.)
Horemheb	"Pharaoh of the Oppression."
Ramses I ⎫	(Pharaohs when successive waves of
Seti I ⎭	small groups of Israelites left
	Egypt.)
Ramses II	"Pharaoh of the *Greater* Exodus."
Meneptah	"Pharaoh of the Post-Exodus period
	in Egypt."

At midnight on April 6–7, 1233 B.C., the Final or Greater Exodus had taken place. Egypt would no longer be used in an experiment with the Great Light.

From Joseph to Moses the *Work* had gone forward; now a new *Plan* was put into effect.

" And Moses said unto the people, Remember this day, in which ye came out from Egypt, out of the house of bondage; for by strength of hand the LORD brought you out from this place . . . " (Exodus xiii: 3).

A " Song of Deliverance " was in order: " And Miriam the prophetess, the sister of Aaron [and Moses], took a timbrel in her hand; and all the women went out after her with timbrels and with dances " (Exodus xv: 20).

This Miriam had been Tantahpe, daughter of Maya. She who once worshipped with the sistrum now performed with the timbrel, and said to the Israelites: " Sing ye to the Lord, for he hath triumphed gloriously."

The deliverance out of Egypt is similar to what the deliverance of God's people will be at the time of the " Golden Dawn." The redeemed will sing praises to their Creator through endless ages of eternity.

A little over one month out of Egypt, the people began complaining about the hardships of wilderness life. They were hungry and asked Moses and Aaron for food.

The great space craft was still high above . . . hovering . . . watching. As Aaron spoke to the multitude, " they looked toward the wilderness, and, behold, the glory of the Lord appeared in the cloud " (Exodus xvi: 10).

Quail then came in immense flocks, flying low. And manna was found which fell with the dew each night.

" . . . it was like coriander seed, white; and the taste of it was like wafers made with honey " (Exodus xvi: 31).

" And they gathered it every morning, every man according to his eating: and when the sun waxed hot, it melted " (Exodus xvi: 21).

This "manna" is not unlike the so-called " angel's hair " that has been observed many times falling from the sky after space craft have been sighted in a certain vicinity. Both substances are white, and " melt " in the sun or in the warm palm of a human hand.

" Manna " was created in the force field of the space craft hovering above. The people received it from " heaven " for forty years, until they crossed the Jordan, when it ceased as suddenly as it began. The coming of the " manna " was a forerunner of the Christ, who said, " I am the *bread* of life " (John vi: 31-35).

" And the Lord said unto Moses, Go on before the people, and take with thee of the elders of Israel; and thy rod, wherewith thou smotest the river, take in thine hand, and go " (Exodus xvii: 5).

Shortly before this, Moses had made the bitter waters of Marah sweet (Exodus xv: 25). Now, in Rephidim, he produces water out of a rock. Later he was to perform a similar miracle at Meribah (Numbers xx: 1-13).

The *voice* told Moses to smite a rock and that water would gush forth from it. Moses obeyed, and the people drank and were thirsty no more. Again we see the power of the ancient vril stick in action!

Hur, son of Caleb, was the man who, with Aaron, held up Moses' hands so that Joshua and the Israelites defeated the Amalekites (Exodus xvii: 10-13). Hur was a very influential man, trusted and loved by Moses, who was his brother-in-law, since Hur was the husband of Miriam. Hur had been the scribe Ahmose at the court of Akhnaton. So we find the former relationship of scribe-friend (Ahmose-Tantahpe) returning as husband-wife (Hur-Miriam).

Hur means: white; brilliant; noble; liberty; hollowed out; subterranean hole; cavern. And Hur today conducts the Work of Aton (One God) in a desert cavern of the earth!

Moses spoke to the head of his army, Joshua, son of Nun. This oshua had formerly lived as Tutu, foreign minister under Akhnaton.

Moses told Joshua to choose good fighting men to fight the Amalekites, for, the next day, he (Moses) would stand on the top of the hill with the rod (vril) of God in his hand.

" So Joshua did as Moses had said to him, and fought with Amalek: and Moses, Aaron, and Hur went up to the top of the hill. And it came to pass, when Moses held up his hand, that Israel prevailed: and when he let down his hand, Amalek prevailed " (Exodus xvii: 10-11).

On top of the hill Moses represented Divine Truth proceeding immediately from the Lord; Aaron represented Divine Truth immediately proceeding from the Lord; and Hur, Divine Truth again immediately proceeding; thus they are truths in successive order.

" But Moses' hands were heavy; and they took a stone, and put it under him, and he sat thereon; and Aaron and Hur stayed up his hands . . . and his hands were steady until the going down of the sun " (Exodus xvii: 12).

Would God give victory to the Israelites in a bloody battle just because Moses managed to keep his hands up in the air? Of course not! The idea makes the Creator appear idiotic! But we find some very significant facts in the story. First of all, Moses again had " the rod of God " with him, and when he " held up his hand " the power of the vril was utilized. When he " let down his hand " the power was shut off! Now Aaron and Hur "took a stone, and put it under " Moses. A *stone* in the supreme sense signifies the Lord and His spiritual kingdom or the truth of faith. It also means the Lord as to the Divine Truth of the Word, and natural truths.

The " stone " being placed under Moses represents the fact that the " Lord was with him." It means that Moses' *foundation* was of Divine Truth, and therefore he had been given the knowledge of the ancient instruments and power.

" In the third month, when the children of Israel were gone forth out of the land of Egypt, the same day came they into the wilderness of Sinai. For they were departed from Rephidim, and were come to the desert of Sinai . . . there Israel camped before the mount " (Exodus xix: 1–2).

The peninsula of Sinai was named for the Babylonian moon-god, Sin. It was known for its mines of copper, iron, ochre, and precious stones. Long before the days of Abraham the kings of the East had made a road around the north and west fringes of the Arabian Desert to the Sinai region.

The mountain peak, known as Mount Sinai, where Israel received the Law, is located towards the south point of the peninsula. It is an " isolated mass of rock, rising abruptly from the plain, in awful grandeur." On the north-west side is a plain, two miles long, one half-mile wide, where Israel camped.

The northern part of the mountain chain was called Horeb, and the southern Sinai. The Children of Israel went from Rephidim to Sinai, or Horeb, the mount where the *voice* had first revealed itself to Moses in the "burning" bush. Later, in this same area, Moses received the Ten Commandments.

This area, and especially Mount Sinai (Horeb), was one of the SECRET PLACES OF THE LION! Forty miles to the north-west, in the Valley of the Caves, there is a sculpture on smooth rock. It is four hundred feet above the mines. Here Pharaoh Semerkhet of the First Dynasty had himself portrayed slaying the defeated King of Sinai. There are two hundred and fifty inscriptions of later kings. Ten miles north of this Valley of the Caves is an ancient temple of Hathor, where Sir Flinders Petrie discovered the oldest known alphabetic writing. Mount Sinai (Horeb) itself contains subterranean chambers of unbelievably fantastic age!

"And Moses went up unto God, and the Lord called unto him out of the mountain . . ." (Exodus xix: 3).

God, the Lord, or the *voice* called unto Moses "*out of the mountain* [Sinai, Horeb]"! Something must have been *inside* the mountain!

Then the *voice* said to Moses: ". . . I bare you on eagles' wings, and brought you unto myself" (Exodus xix: 4).

The "eagles' wings" refer to the giant space craft above!

The Israelites were at Mount Sinai (Horeb) about eleven months. "And the Lord said unto Moses, Lo, I come unto thee in a thick cloud . . ." (Exodus xix: 9).

Moses was to prepare the people for the coming event to take place on Mount Sinai (Horeb). ". . . the Lord will come down in the sight of all the people upon mount Sinai" (Exodus xix: 11).

Moses was to set bounds around the area, telling the people: ". . . go not up into the mount, or touch the border of it: whosoever toucheth the mount shall be surely put to death . . ." (Exodus xix: 12).

"And it came to pass on the third day in the morning, that there were thunders and lightnings, and a thick cloud upon the mount, and the voice of the trumpet exceeding loud . . ." (Exodus xix: 16).

"And mount Sinai was altogether on a smoke, because the Lord descended upon it in fire . . . the whole mount quaked greatly" (Exodus xix: 18).

The "voice of the trumpet" became louder and louder, and Moses went to the top of Mount Sinai, and when he spoke, the *voice* answered:

" . . . Go down, charge the people, lest they break through unto the Lord to gaze, and many of them perish " (Exodus xix: 21).

It is obvious that the great space craft that had been following the Israelites since they had left Egypt now had descended in a " cloud " and in " fire " on top of the mount. A *voice* spoke to all assembled, and the Ten Commandments were given.

Five hundred years later Elijah, at the same mountain, was given a hint that God's Work on the earth would be accomplished, not by fire and earthquake, but by the " still small voice " of a later prophet.

The mountain (Sinai, Horeb) symbolizes in us a high place in consciousness where we come into conscious communion with the Divine.

Moses received the Law on two tablets fashioned from divine sapphire. It is said that this sacred stone was formed of " heavenly dew." When he came down from the mount, he found that Aaron, his brother, had built a Golden Calf for the people.

Now Aaron did not want to build this idol for the people, which was similar in every way to the Sacred Bull (Apis) of Egypt. The fact that the Israelites wanted this Golden Calf signifies the false states of thought (idols) that man builds into his consciousness when he perceives the Truth but does not carry his spiritual ideals into execution, choosing instead to let his thoughts function in a lower plane of consciousness.

When Moses saw the idol, he knew that the people were not yet ready or worthy to receive the sapphire tablets; therefore he destroyed them, so that the great mysteries would not be violated by those of little understanding.

It has already been stated that very few of the Israelites knew the real meaning behind the Exodus. And many of them, including the Egyptians in the group, desired to worship their old gods of Amunism again. Therefore, the Golden Calf or Apis was constructed. The people were afraid of the great " fire circle " on Mount Sinai (Horeb) and believed that Moses had been destroyed in the " flames " on top of the mountain.

Many were afraid and reverted to faith in their ancient gods. The people knew that great power was being manifested, but they did not wish to investigate such power and chose instead to remain on a lower plane of spiritual consciousness.

Aaron had allowed the idol to be constructed because he knew
that the people did not understand the Plan, and, besides, the
purpose of the Exodus had been served: the Fulfilment would come
about in the " Promised Land." The treasures of millennia would
be safely deposited in the new land; there would be an Ark and a
Tabernacle!

Now after the first two tablets were broken by Moses, ". . . the
Lord said . . . Hew thee two tablets of stone like unto [similar to]
the first . . . " (Exodus xxxiv: 1).

So Moses had broken the original sapphire tablets because he
knew that the people were not yet ready for the eternal verities of
the " Mystery of Mysteries." Now he substituted two tablets of
rough stone, into the surface of which he cut ten ancient letters.
These were somewhat different from the original tablets, for they
revealed only temporal truths. Thus the ancient wisdom returned
again to " heaven " in the great space craft; only a shadow of the
Greater Light and Truth was left with the children of the Ten Tribes.

On the original sapphire tablets there were *Twelve Commandments*
instead of *Ten*! The Lost Two Commandments were to remain
hidden until man was ready to receive them. To this day they have
not yet been revealed to mankind!

Moses did indeed " hew two tablets of stone like unto the first,"
and he went up to the top of Mount Sinai (Horeb)—" And the
Lord descended in the cloud, and stood with him there . . . "
(Exodus xxxiv: 5).

When Moses came down from the mount, his " face shone "
(Exodus xxxiv: 29–35), and he had to put on a veil to hide his face,
for Aaron and the others were afraid to come near him because of
the light round about him. He was charged with a force field that
made him appear luminous to all. Later, Jesus' face " did shine as
the sun " when he was transfigured (Matthew xvii: 2).

" But when Moses went in before the Lord to speak with him,
he took the vail off, until he came out . . . " (Exodus xxxiv: 34).

Moses shielded his face and the force about him from the multitude, but exposed it before the " Lord " or *voice*!

The second set of tablets, now of rough stone, were kept for
centuries in the Ark of the Covenant. Some believe they were
eventually destroyed in the Babylonian Captivity; however, they
were not lost. and some day will be found!

A special hereditary order of men was now created to keep a semblance of Aton (One God) worship amongst the Israelites; although the Greater Light could not be theirs because they were not yet ready for it, a less spiritual worship was set up, based on pagan ritualism, that nevertheless was symbolic in its sacrifices, ceremonies, vestments, etc.

Aaron and his sons were to be the priests of this order. The Levitical priesthood was divinely ordained as mediator between Aton (One God) and the Hebrew nation in the ministry of animal sacrifices. Such sacrifices would not have been necessary if the knowledge of the sapphire tablets had been revealed. Priests would not have been necessary either. But man was not ready to meet his Creator in Divine Truth and Full Understanding! Animal sacrifices were no longer needed after the master Jesus brought in the *Fulfilment*—and priests will be done away with in the " Golden Dawn " now approaching! Mankind will go to the Infinite Father himself—no mediators or rituals will be necessary. Actually, they have never really been necessary, but man has believed they were, and until his understanding increases he has to be bound by dogmas, creeds, rituals, and authoritative mediators in the long, flowing robes of *Amun*!

This highly symbolic form of worship was of a low spiritual order, that is true, but it prevented the Israelites from reverting completely into calf or bull (Apis) worship. Even so, many Israelites continued in this form of Amunism! Blood-smeared altars and burning flesh is obnoxious to Aton (One God), but if it is for his glorification it is a far sweeter smell than the perfumed incense of Amun's altars and shrines! For God knew that eventually man would learn from his rituals and grow into the Greater Light.

The Shamir stone had been used by King Solomon in the building of his temple " without the sound of hammers "; now Aaron used the same magical Shamir stone to cut the stones for the breastplate of the high priest!

The twelve precious stones in the breastplate symbolized the Ten Commandments plus the Lost Two, or a total of Twelve Commandments! This breastplate also contained the *Urim* and *Thummim*. Historians do not know what these two articles were! Aaron said, " From the Urim and Thummim we ascertain the will of God!" But how was this done? Urim means: lights;

radiating principles; revelations. Thummim means: complete; sound; truth. These two can be called "lights and truth." Through their use the high priest obtained divine guidance for the people in difficult situations. They were not unlike the crystal balls of the secret chambers in Egypt. They were two small oracular images which uttered oracles by a *voice*.

The Urim and Thummim enabled Aaron to keep in constant communication with the great ship: a "Ship of Light" similar to the craft he had operated when he was "Merk" of Hesperus (Venus)! It was a two-way communications device. When difficult situations arose, advice could be obtained by communicating with the mentors from space in their craft, usually hovering many miles above the earth!

Korah, son of Izhar, had been Horemheb, the cheese-maker's son! He was jealous of Moses and sought to usurp his leadership. Horemheb was always a usurper of "thrones." After he (Korah) rebelled against Moses and Aaron he was destroyed with his followers by the earth opening beneath him and swallowing him up.

"And the earth opened her mouth, and swallowed them up, and their houses, and all the men that appertained unto Korah . . . went down alive into the pit, and the earth closed upon them . . ." (Numbers xvi: 32–33).

"And there came out a fire from the Lord, and consumed the two hundred and fifty men that offered incense" (Numbers xvi: 35).

A "fire" from the great craft could not be stood by Korah and his men because of its peculiar vibration which destroys negative force wherever it encounters it. The "men who offered incense" were the followers of Amun still in the ranks of the Children of Israel!

Now Moses was commanded to take Aaron his brother and then to "speak unto a rock" so that it might give forth water. But Moses "lifted up his hand, and with his rod he smote the rock twice: and the water came out abundantly . . ." (Numbers xx: 11).

"And the Lord spake unto Moses and Aaron, Because ye believed me not . . . therefore ye shall not bring this congregation into the land which I have given them. This is the water of Meribah; because the children of Israel strove with the Lord, and he was sanctified in them" (Numbers xx: 12–13).

Moses and Aaron were not to see the "Promised Land." The

lifetime dream of their hearts was not to be realized, for they had used the vril-rod power as they chose, instead of by orders from their mentors.

For forty years Israel had been guided by a " supernatural cloud " that wasn't a cloud at all, but visitors and helpers from another world of highly enlightened men. Moses could not possibly have delivered his people or the secret records out of Egypt and sustained them in the wilderness for forty years without the direct and miraculous help of the other-worldly (space) brethren. Miriam, Aaron, and Moses, their work done in this lifetime, all died in the same year. Miriam died when she was one hundred and thirty and was buried at Kadesh. Kadesh, which means clean, pure, sanctified, was the final resting-place of she who had once been Tantahpe, priestess of Isis. This time she had served Aton (One God) well; her work was finished for this time.

Aaron, who had been King Hadad of Edom, now perished atop Mount Hor at the age of one hundred and twenty-three. This mountain of the wilderness was on the very border of Edom! The entity had returned to the area of a former lifetime and vibration!

One of the Old Testament's most specific predictions of Jesus, the Christ, is found in Deuteronomy, Chapter xviii. A Prophet like unto Moses was to come in the future. This was what Moses was preparing for in his *Revelations*.

Psalm 81 is called " A Psalm of Asaph." However, this Psalm is also called " A Psalm for Asaph." And it is indeed a Psalm *for* Asaph and not *of* or *by* Asaph! Asaph had been appointed by David and Solomon to oversee the song services in the Temple worship. David wrote several Psalms for this official; dedicated them to him.

" This he ordained in Joseph for a testimony, when he went out through the land of Egypt: where I heard a language that I understood not " (Psalm lxxxi: 5).

Notice here that David changes to the first person, and says: " *I* heard a language that *I* understood not." He is speaking of Joseph, and then says " I " as if he meant he had been the entity Joseph!

This, of course, is true; an absolute proof is found in Psalm lxxxi that Joseph was later David!

" Thou callest in trouble, and I delivered thee; I answered thee in the secret place of thunder: I proved thee at the waters of Meribah. Selah " (Psalm lxxxi: 7).

In this verse God Himself is speaking, and says: "... I proved thee [David] at the waters of Meribah. ..." *Moses* was the man who was " proved " at the waters of Meribah! Why then does this verse say that David was the one who was " proved "?

Of course, the entity David later incarnated as the man Moses. Historians believe that David lived *after* Moses, where we have shown that actually David lived several centuries *before* Moses was born! Now if this verse were written by David, as we have said, you will ask: " But how could he write about himself as Moses being ' proved ' at the waters of Meribah if Moses hadn't lived yet? " More " ages in chaos " again!

Actually, the correct reading of Verse 7 would be:

" Thou shalt call in trouble, and I will deliver thee; I will answer thee in the secret place of thunder: I will prove thee at the waters of Meribah. Selah."

Ages later, after the chronology had become hopelessly confused, scribes couldn't understand why this verse should be written in *future* tense! You see, by this time they believed, quite erroneously, that David lived *after* Moses instead of *before*! They were certain that the verse should be in the *past* tense! So they changed it to " correct " it! This has happened often in history: the so-called " corrections " have only added to the impossible " chaos " of inaccurate chronological arrangement.

Verse 7, as originally written, was a prophecy given to David by God; a *promise* that God would be with David (Moses) in generations to come! "... I will answer thee in the secret place of thunder ... " means that David as Moses would be surrounded by a magnetic force field from the hovering space ship when he heard the *voice* and received his instructions; " the secret place of thunder " signifies a resonating magnetic field of force!

Moses, who had written Genesis from ancient existing documents, now completed his own manuscripts and books and handed them over to the priests. He commissioned Joshua to lead the people into the " Promised Land." After Moses had finished writing his records and book, he composed a song for the people to sing. David too had poured out his soul to God in song; and Hammurabi had also put laws on stone. Moses was now only doing what he had done before in other lifetimes!

" At one hundred and twenty, his eye not dimmed, nor his

natural force abated," the aged Moses climbed Mount Pisgah and, as he viewed the " Promised Land," into which he longed to go, God gently lifted him into another dimension—in a moment his soul had passed within the veil. He had reached the age where, worn with the rigours of the wilderness, he was no longer qualified for the task that was ahead of the Israelites. He would incarnate again in the years ahead to continue the *Work*—but this phase was over. He had brought his people into Egypt as Joseph and now he successfully brought them out.

Mount Nebo—the loftiest peak of Mount Pisgah, eight miles east of the mouth of the Jordan—the end of Moses' journey to prepare the way for the Christ who was to come—not to Egypt, but Israel! Nebo means: planet Mercury; quick messenger; celestial scribe; prophet.

Standing upon this peak, Moses saw the entire land of Palestine in panorama: the hills of Judea and Galilee, Mount Carmel, the snow-capped summit of Mount Herman, where Jesus was later transfigured! Moses knew, even now, that the " thunders of Mount Sinai [Horeb] " would give way to the " still small voice " of Jesus, the Christ! Through *Revelation* Moses had set the stage for the coming of the Greater Prophet.

" So Moses the servant of the Lord died there in the land of Moab, according to the word of the Lord " (Deuteronomy xxxiv: 5).

" No man knoweth of his sepulchre unto this day . . . " for, like Joseph, Moses was gently lifted into another world of time and space. His tomb will never be found, for it never existed! Moses found his reward; he had performed " all the signs and wonders which the Lord sent him to do in the land of Egypt."

After Moses had departed from the earth, there were many centuries of long, difficult service on the part of the " Goodly Company." They continued to serve in humble positions in many lands and places. However, until the Master Christ arrived, they continually prepared for that event.

To complete *Revelation* we will briefly mention certain incarnations of the Workers in the Light during this long period before the birth of Jesus, the Christ.

Cato, the artist of the Eighteenth Dynasty in Egypt, became Pharaoh Amenemopet, the " New King " from the Nile Delta, in

1020 B.C. Cato's son, Rahotep, had made the mask for Tutank-hamun; now Cato, as Amenemopet, wears a portrait mask of solid gold when he dies!

Isaiah, the Prophet of Redemption, was born *ca.* 765 B.C. He had been Prince Seti, ninth son of Ramses II who perished when the royal palace crumbled on the Last Night of the Greater and Final Exodus. During Isaiah's lifetime a meteor shower returned, being fragments of the shattered Lucifer, the planet in its destructive action which caused the earthquake that killed Prince Seti. Now, as Isaiah, Seti warns the people against destruction caused once again by Lucifer, which was responsible for his death in the falling palace in another lifetime.

Isaiah was the first of the Major Prophets and prophesied during the reign of Uzziah, King of Judah, and Ahaz, the grandson of Uzziah. He was contemporary with Hosea, Amos, Micah; also the Assyrian monarchs Tiglath-pileser III, Shalmaneser IV, Sargon, and Sennacherib.

Isaiah's chief contribution is the prophecy of the birth of Christ and that of His Kingdom there shall be no end. The Lord himself shall give a sign; a son whose name shall be called Immanuel. The fifty-third chapter describes in a poetic way the beauty of Christ and His sufferings and how He is " brought as a lamb to the slaughter " (Isaiah liii: 7), " who had done no violence, neither was any deceit in his mouth " (Isaiah liii: 9).

He foretells the spoiling of Syria, the fall of Assyria and Babylon, the overthrow of Tyre and general destruction of the land: " The earth shall reel to and fro like a drunkard " (Isaiah xxiv: 20).

He says that a remnant shall be saved, that the remnant of Jacob shall return unto God—that the Lord shall recover the remnant of his people which shall be left, from Assyria, Egypt, Pathros, Cush, Elam, Shinar, Hamath, and from the islands of the sea, and peace shall reign among them. He speaks with hope saying:

" He will swallow up death in victory; and the Lord God will wipe away tears from off all faces " (Isaiah xxv: 8).

The children of Israel shall be gathered one by one (Isaiah xxvii: 12); the great trumpet shall be blown and " they shall come which were ready to perish in the land of Assyria, and the outcasts in the land of Egypt " (Isaiah xxvii: 13).

Destruction is foretold:

" Woe to Ariel, the city where David dwelt! " (Isaiah xxix: 1).
Then he goes on to say:

" Thou shalt be visited of the LORD of hosts with thunder and
with earthquake, and great noise, with storm and tempest, and the
flame of devouring fire " (Isaiah xxix: 6).

After the destruction has taken place, he says:

" Then the eyes of the blind shall be opened, and the ears of the
deaf shall be unstopped.

" Then shall the lame *man* leap as an hart, and the tongue of the
dumb sing: for in the wilderness shall waters break out, and streams
in the desert " (Isaiah xxxv: 5-6).

The general contour of the earth is described after the destruction:

" Every valley shall be exalted, and every mountain and hill shall
be made low: and the crooked shall be made straight, and the rough
places plain " (Isaiah xl: 4).

Forgiveness is promised to Israel; her transgressions will be blotted
out. After the surface changes have taken place, the SECRET PLACES
OF THE LION shall be uncovered:

" I will go before thee, and make the crooked places straight;
I will break in pieces the gates of brass, and cut in sunder the bars of
iron:

" And I will give thee the treasures of darkness, and hidden riches
of secret places, that thou mayest know that I, the LORD, which call
thee by thy name, *am* the God of Israel " (Isaiah xlv: 2-3).
The kindness of the LORD shall continue:

" For the mountains shall depart, and the hills be removed; but
my kindness shall not depart from thee, neither shall the covenant
of my peace be removed, saith the LORD that hath mercy on thee "
(Isaiah liv: 10).

Great peace is promised:

" And all thy children shall be taught of the LORD; and great *shall*
be the peace of thy children " (Isaiah liv: 13).

In these incomparable words Isaiah reminds his readers of the
mercies of the LORD:

" Hast thou not known? hast thou not heard, *that* the everlasting
God, the LORD, the Creator of the ends of the earth, fainteth not,
neither is weary? *there is* no searching of his understanding.

" He giveth power to the faint; and to *them that have* no might he
increaseth strength.

" Even the youths shall faint and be weary, and the young men shall utterly fall:

" But they that wait upon the LORD shall renew *their* strength; they shall mount up with wings as eagles; they shall run, and not be weary; *and* they shall walk, and not faint " (Isaiah xl: 28–31).

In 1928 ancient library records were found at Ras Shamra, in northern Syria. There are striking similarities between the Ras Shamra texts and the Old Testament. The style especially resembles the Book of Isaiah. The reason why the Ras Shamra tablets and the literature of the Old Testament should be so similar lies in the fact that certain individuals incarnated later and continued to write in the same style and with the same purpose!

Later (*ca.* 384–322 B.C.), Isaiah incarnated as Aristotle, the Greek philosopher, pupil of Plato and tutor of Alexander the Great.

Jeremiah is called the Weeping Prophet. He prophesied during the reign of Josiah, Jehoiakim, and Zedekiah about 612–550 B.C. Jeremiah was contemporary with Zephaniah, Habakkuk, Ezekiel, Daniel. He had been Sinuhe, court physician for Pharaoh Akhnaton.

Jeremiah reproves Israel and Judah for their sins and pleads with them to return to the LORD (Aton—One God).

" Neither said they, Where is the Lord that brought up us out of the land of Egypt, that led us through the wilderness, through a land of deserts and of pits, through a land of drought, and of the shadow of death . . . " (Jeremiah ii: 6).

Remember, the great space ship had left the Children of Israel and followed them no more after they entered the " Promised Land." Therefore the statement: " . . . Where is the Lord [*voice* of the space ship] that brought us up out of the land of Egypt . . . "

" And I brought you into a plentiful country, to eat the fruit thereof and the goodness thereof; but when ye entered, ye defiled my land, and made mine heritage an abomination " (Jeremiah ii: 7).

This proves that the Israelites deserted Aton (One God) after their arrival in the " Promised Land." If they had not built a Golden Calf, but instead had received the original two sapphire tablets, they would not have reverted to pagan worship. We have already pointed out that because of their lack of understanding they were allowed to worship Aton (One God) from the lowest spiritual level. The period after Moses until the appearance of the Christ on earth was one of constant struggle between Amunism (Golden Calf or Apis worship) and Atonism (One God worship).

From Jeremiah ii: 6 we see that the people were not asking for this great power (Lord) that had "brought them up out of Egypt." Through Moses, Aaron, and Hur great manifestations of spiritual force and power came about, but the people had forgotten and were no longer serving Aton (One God).

" The young lions roared upon him, and yelled [gave out their voice], and they made his land waste: his cities are burned without inhabitant " (Jeremiah ii: 15).

Because the people were not serving Aton (One God) and not preparing for He who was to come (Christ), the " lions " of the secret places " roared " upon them (Israel). The " lions " made the " land waste " because without Israel's true purpose being served for the *Fulfilment* to come the land and the people were barren (" wasted ") of spiritual fruit or accomplishments.

In the Book of Exodus we find that is is claimed that Moses and Aaron ordered pagan blood sacrifice (Exodus xii: 43 to xiii: 16).

However, such pagan ritualism had been allowed; otherwise man would not even have worshipped the One God (Aton). Later, it was the task of inspired prophets like Isaiah, Jeremiah, and Amos to free the people from the bondage of " burnt offerings and sacrifices."

" For I spake not unto your fathers, nor commanded them in the day that I brought them out of the land of Egypt, concerning burnt offerings or sacrifices " (Jeremiah vii: 22).

God says here that he did *not* command the people to offer up such hideous sacrifice. This type of thinking still prevails as mankind believes God sent His precious Son to earth to be slaughtered like the lamb, and from the literal " blood " man is supposed to be washed pure as the " driven snow " and gain a quick and easy access to Paradise! Christ did not come to fail in His mission and go down in defeat on a bloody Cross! He came to teach, for only through understanding can man ever hope to reach his Infinite Father!

" But this thing command I them, saying, Obey my voice, and I will be your God, and ye shall be my people: and walk ye in all the ways that I have commanded you, that it may be well unto you. But they hearkened not, nor inclined their ear, but walked in the counsels and in the imagination of their evil heart, and went backward, and not forward " (Jeremiah vii: 23-24).

Here we find a direct reference to the fact that the people went "backward." But the "imagination of their evil heart" caused them to revert to the crude symbolism of blood sacrifice and animal slaughter.

"Since the day that your fathers came forth out of the land of Egypt unto this day I have even sent unto you all my servants the prophets, daily rising up early and sending them " (Jeremiah vii: 25).

Here we see that "all the servants " of God were back in life with the mission of "prophets." But God says: "Yet they hearkened not unto me, nor inclined their ear ... they did worse than their fathers " (Jeremiah vii: 26).

The people were not listening to the prophets; they continued in evil ways.

Jeremiah predicts evil to come from the north and a great destruction:

" ... the destroyer ... is on his way; he is gone forth from his place to make thy land desolate; *and* thy cities shall be laid waste, without an inhabitant.

" Behold, he shall come up as clouds, and his chariots shall be as a whirlwind: his horses are swifter than eagles " (Jeremiah iv: 7, 13).

They will call " peace, peace, when there is no peace " (Jeremiah vi: 14). This is comparable to the present time.

" The spoiler shall suddenly come " (Jeremiah vi: 26); and " the land shall be desolate " (Jeremiah vii: 34).

He tells of the utter ruin of the Jews and the prophecy of the captivity by Babylon.

He tells of false prophets that " prophesy lies in my name " (Jeremiah xxiii: 25), and warns the people not to heed their words.

He prophesies that Nebuchadrezzar, King of Babylon, will destroy the inhabitants and the nations round about (Jeremiah xxv: 9). And after seventy years the King of Babylon will be punished and that nation for her iniquity, including the land of the Chaldeans, and " will make it perpetual desolations " (Jeremiah xxv: 12).

The LORD promises that after seventy years he will cause the captives to return—that they will call upon the LORD and the Lord " will hearken unto you " (Jeremiah xxix: 12).

He gives great comfort to all seekers after truth:

" And ye shall seek me, and find *me*, when ye shall search for me with all your heart " (Jeremiah xxix: 13).

Baruch wrote down for Jeremiah his prophecies concerning Jerusalem and Jehoiakim, who burned them. Baruch wrote them down again, and other pronouncements were added. If the King would retire to Babylon before Jerusalem was taken, she would not be burned and the inhabitants spared; if he refused to do so, the destruction would take place. He chose to remain, and Jerusalem suffered the consequences.

Jeremiah was imprisoned for his prophecies, but was released by the captain of the guard of the Babylonians when Jerusalem was taken (Jeremiah xl: 5).

Jeremiah prophesies the destruction of Egypt by King Nebuchadnezzar:

" O thou daughter dwelling in Egypt, furnish thyself to go into captivity: for Noph shall be waste and desolate without an inhabitant " (Jeremiah xlvi: 19).

To this day Noph (Memphis) remains a desolate area in Egypt.

Jeremiah foretells judgment against Moab for her pride and contempt of God and his people. Also, in the latter days she will suffer captivity:

" Yet will I bring again the captivity of Moab in the latter days, saith the LORD " (Jeremiah xlviii: 47).

Edom shall also be a desolation (Jeremiah xlix: 17); Elam shall suffer, and "it shall come to pass in the latter days, that I will bring again the captivity of Elam, saith the LORD " (Jeremiah xlix: 39).

Babylon shall not be spared because she has striven against the Lord:

" Call together the archers against Babylon: all ye that bend the bow, camp against it round about; let none thereof escape: recompense her according to her work; according to all that she hath done, do unto her: for she hath been proud against the LORD, against the Holy One of Israel. . . .

" Behold, I am against thee, O thou most proud, saith the Lord GOD of hosts: for thy day is come, the time that I will visit thee " (Jeremiah l: 29, 31).

In the end Israel will be redeemed:

" And I will bring Israel again to his habitation, and he shall feed on Carmel and Bashan, and his soul shall be satisfied upon mount Ephraim and Gilead.

" In those days, and in that time, saith the LORD, the iniquity of Israel shall be sought for, and *there shall be* none; and the sins of Judah, and they shall not be found: for I will pardon them whom I reserve " (Jeremiah l: 19–20).

Ezekiel lived in the period of Jehoiachin at the time of Nebuchadnezzar, between 606–538 B.C. He was contemporary with Jeremiah and Daniel. Ezekiel prophesied twenty-two years. He was taken to Babylon in the First Captivity (606 B.C.). He had been Aaron, the older brother of Moses, during the time of the Greater Exodus. His prophecies fall into two sections: (1) Prior to the Fall of Jerusalem, and (2) after the Fall of Jerusalem.

The first chapter of Ezekiel opens with Ezekiel seeing the " whirlwind " and the " four living creatures," which describes perfectly the so-called " flying saucers " of today:

" And I looked, and, behold a whirlwind came out of the north, a great cloud, and a fire infolding itself, and a brightness *was* about it, and out of the midst thereof as the colour of amber, out of the midst of the fire.

" Also out of the midst thereof *came* the likeness of four living creatures. And this *was* their appearance; they had the likeness of a man " (Ezekiel i: 4–5).

Ezekiel portrays the Eagle, Lion, Bull, and Man, the mystery symbols:

" As for the likeness of their faces, they four had the face of a man, and the face of a lion, on the right side: and they four had the face of an ox on the left side; they four also had the face of an eagle " (Ezekiel i: 10).

He continues to describe the *living creatures*:

" And the living creatures ran and returned as the appearance of a flash of lightning . . .

" . . . and their appearance and their work *was* as it were a wheel in the middle of a wheel.

" When they went, they went upon their four sides: *and* they turned not when they went.

" As for their rings, they were so high that they were dreadful; and their rings *were* full of eyes round about them four.

" And when the living creatures went, the wheels went by them: and when the living creatures were lifted up from the earth, the wheels were lifted up.

" Whithersoever the spirit was to go, they went, thither *was their* spirit to go; and the wheels were lifted up over against them, for the spirit of the living creature *was* in the wheels " (Ezekiel i: 14, 16–20).

Ezekiel was commissioned by the visitors from space who came in the " whirlwind " (force field) of their craft to warn the House of Israel who rebelled against the Lord, " for they are a rebellious house " (Ezekiel iii: 27), to give them warning from the Lord to turn from their wickedness (Ezekiel iii: 19).

" Thus saith the Lord GOD; This *is* Jerusalem: I have set it in the midst of the nations and countries *that are* round about her.

" And she hath changed my judgments into wickedness more than the nations, and my statutes more than the countries that *are* round about her: for they have refused my judgments and my statutes, they have not walked in them " (Ezekiel v: 5–6).

Then follows the judgment of Israel; the remnant which will be scattered "into all the winds " (Ezekiel v: 10). " And they that escape of you shall remember me among the nations whither they shall be carried captives " (Ezekiel vi: 9). This is the Remnant that has been carrying the Light among the nations.

" . . . and they shall pollute my secret *place*: for the robbers shall enter into it, and defile it " (Ezekiel vii: 22). And has not this been done in Israel and in Egypt and other places where the Remnant have brought the Light?

Ezekiel reproves false prophets:

" And mine hand shall be upon the prophets that see vanity, and that divine lies: they shall not be in the assembly of my people, neither shall they be written in the writing of the house of Israel, neither shall they enter into the land of Israel; and ye shall know that I *am* the Lord GOD.

" Because, even because they have seduced my people, saying, Peace; and *there was* no peace . . . " (Ezekiel xiii: 9–10).

It is the false prophets of *Amun* today who are calling out peace, peace, when there is no peace!

God pleads for repentance for Israel:

" Cast away from you all your transgressions, whereby ye have transgressed; and make you a new heart and a new spirit: for why will ye die, O house of Israel?

" For I have no pleasure in the death of him that dieth, saith the

Lord GOD: wherefore turn *yourselves*, and live ye" (Ezekiel xviii: 31–32).

Ezekiel prophesies judgment against the Pharaoh of Egypt (Ezekiel xxix: 3) and against Egypt herself:

" And I will make the land of Egypt desolate in the midst of the countries *that* are desolate, and her cities among the cities *that are* laid waste shall be desolate forty years: and I will scatter the Egyptians among the nations, and will disperse them through the countries.

" Yet thus saith the Lord GOD; at the end of forty years will I gather the Egyptians from the people whither they are scattered:

" And I will bring again the captivity of Egypt . . . and they shall be there a base kingdom.

" It shall be the basest of the kingdoms; neither shall it exalt itself any more above the nations: for I will diminish them, that they shall no more rule over the nations. . . .

" Therefore thus saith the Lord GOD; Behold, I will give the land of Egypt unto Nebuchadnezzar king of Babylon; and he shall take her multitude, and take her spoil, and take her prey; and it shall be the wages for his army. . . .

" Thus saith the Lord GOD; I will also destroy the idols, and I will cause *their* images to cease out of Noph; and there shall be no more a prince of the land of Egypt: and I will put a fear in the land of Egypt " (Ezekiel xxix: 12–15, 19; xxx: 13).

The latter prophecy holds to this day. There is fear on every hand in the land of Egypt.

As the shepherd seeks out his flock, so will the Lord GOD seek out his sheep that are scattered (Ezekiel xxxiv: 12).

" Therefore will I save my flock and they shall no more be a prey. . . .

" And I will set up one shepherd over them, and he shall feed them, *even* my servant David; he shall feed them and he shall be their shepherd.

" And I the LORD will be their God, and my servant David, a prince among them. I the LORD have spoken *it* " (Ezekiel xxxiv: 22–24). The children of Israel shall be gathered together:

" And they shall no more be a prey to the heathen, neither shall the beast of the land devour them; but they shall dwell safely, and none shall make *them* afraid " (Ezekiel xxiv: 28).

No more shall the Wanderers be thrown to the lions for the sport of Roman emperors, or burned at the stake, or shot through with Egyptian spears because the " kingdom is at hand."

The resurrection of dry bones possibly relates to the reincarnation of souls who have gone on before who shall come back to enjoy the peace that will folllow in the New Age (Ezekiel xxxvii).

Gog and Magog which are symbolical of the heathen nations and the forces of evil in all nations, shall suffer in the latter days (in which we now live):

" And thou shalt come up against my people of Israel, as a cloud to cover the land; it shall be in the latter days. . . .

" And it shall come to pass at the same time when Gog shall come against the land of Israel, saith the Lord GOD, *that* my fury shall come up in my face. . . .

" . . . Surely in that day there shall be a great shaking in the land of Israel;

" . . . and the mountains shall be thrown down, and the steep places shall fall, and every wall shall fall to the ground. . . .

" . . . and I will rain upon him, and upon his bands, and upon the many people that *are* with him, an overflowing rain, and great hailstones, fire, and brimstone. . . .

" . . . and they shall know that I *am* the LORD." (Ezekiel xxxviii: 16, 18, 19, 20, 22–23).

A " holy war " is building up in the Middle East and is of great significance in connection with prophecy.

Daniel prophesied approximately between the dates of 606–538 B.C. He is a Prophet of the Captivity, and called the " Prophet of the Times of the Gentiles." He had been none other than the Law-giver, Moses, in a former lifetime!

In the third year of the reign of Jehoiakim, King of Judah, Nebuchadnezzar besieged Jerusalem and carried away many people to Babylon, including Daniel and his three friends, Hananiah, Mishael, and Azariah, whose names were subsequently changed to Belteshazzar, Shadrach, Meshach, and Abednego.

The King had the master of the eunuchs to bring certain of the Children of Israel, and of the King's seed, " in whom was no blemish " and " skilful in all wisdom, and cunning in knowledge, and understanding science," to whom they might teach the learning and the tongue of the Chaldeans (Daniel i: 4). The King appointed them a daily provision of the King's meat and wine so that at the end of three years they might stand before the King.

Now Daniel didn't want to defile himself with the King's meat and wine and asked the prince of the eunuchs for pulse instead (vegetables in general; particularly lentils, peas, and beans). At the end of ten days Daniel and his companions appeared fairer and fatter in flesh than those who ate the King's fare.

Nebuchadnezzar had a dream and he called in the magicians, astrologers, sorcerers, and the Chaldeans to interpret his dream. They could not, so the King ordered them to be slain. Then Daniel interceded for them and he and his friends asked Divine guidance:

"Then was the secret revealed unto Daniel in a night vision. Then Daniel blessed the God of heaven" (Daniel ii: 19). Daniel interpreted the dream to the King, telling of the different types of kingdoms, the latter of which is of great significance:

"And in the days of these kings shall the God of heaven set up a kingdom, which shall never be destroyed: and the kingdom shall not be left to other people, *but* it shall break in pieces and consume all these kingdoms, and it shall stand for ever.

"Forasmuch as thou sawest that the stone was cut out of the mountain without hands, and that it brake in pieces the iron, the brass, the clay, the silver, and the gold; the great God hath made known to the king what shall come to pass hereafter: and the dream is certain and the interpretation thereof sure" (Daniel ii: 44–45).

Now who could cut stone out of the mountain without hands? None other than those who built the Great Pyramid which was built with light energy! These are the Workers in the Light, the Visitors from Space, the Wanderers from other worlds. And the kingdom shall be that of Christ who shall rule and stand for ever.

For the interpretation of this dream Daniel was made overseer of the wise men of Babylon; and "Daniel requested of the king, and he set Shadrach, Meshach, and Abednego over the affairs of the province of Babylon" (Daniel ii: 49).

Nebuchadnezzar made an image of gold and required all the people to worship it. Shedrach, Meshach, and Abednego refused to do so and were cast into a fiery furnace, which was so hot that the men who took up the three to cast them into the furnace were burned (Daniel iii: 22).

Instead of three men in the furnace bound together, Nebuchad-nezzar saw four men loose, " walking in the midst of the fire," and he was much astonished. The form of the fourth " is like the Son of God," said Nebuchadnezzar.

Then Nebuchadnezzar spoke to Shadrach, Meshach, and Abednego and said: " . . . ye servants of the most high God, come forth, and come *hither*." Then the three came out of the furnace.

" And the princes, governors, and captains, and the king's counsellors, being gathered together, saw these men, upon whose bodies the fire had no power, nor was an hair of their head singed, neither were their coats changed, nor the smell of the fire had passed on them " (Daniel iii: 27).

The King then made a decree that no one should speak anything amiss against the God of Shadrach, Meshach, and Abednego. And these three were promoted in the province of Babylon.

Nebuchadnezzar had another dream of a great tree, which Daniel interprets. According to the interpretation the King would be driven into the field to eat grass as oxen and live with the beasts for a time, after which he would acknowledge the God of heaven.

At the end of twelve months, as the King was walking in the palace, he said: " Is not this house of the kingdom by the might of my power, and for the honour of my majesty? " (Daniel iv: 30).

" While the word *was* in the king's mouth there fell a voice from heaven, *saying* O king Nebuchadnezzar, to thee it is spoken; The kingdom is departed from thee.

" And they shall drive thee from men, and thy dwelling *shall be* with the beasts of the field: they shall make thee to eat grass as oxen, and seven times shall pass over thee, until thou know that the most High ruleth in the kingdom of men, and giveth it to whomsoever he will " (Daniel iv: 31-32).

" The same hour was the thing fulfilled upon Nebuchadnezzar " (Daniel iv: 33), and at the end of the appointed time Nebuchadnezzar acknowledged the most High and said:

" I Nebuchadnezzar lifted up mine eyes unto heaven, and mine understanding returned unto me, and I blessed the most High, and I praised and honoured him that liveth for ever, whose dominion *is* an everlasting dominion and his kingdom *is* from generation to generation " (Daniel iv: 34).

Belshazzar, son of Nebuchadnezzar, the last King of Babylon,

makes a feast and " They drank wine, and praised the gods of
gold, and silver, of brass, or iron, or wood, and of stone " (Daniel
v: 4).

During the revelry handwriting appeared on the wall. This
troubled the King so that " his knees smote one against another "
(Daniel v: 6).

The wise men of the kingdom were unable to interpret the handwriting, but the Queen told the King about Daniel " in whom *is* the
spirit of the holy gods " whom Nebuchadnezzar had made master of
the magicians, astrologers, Chaldeans, and soothsayers. So Daniel
was called and interpreted the writing which said:

" God hath numbered thy kingdom, and finished it.

" . . . Thou art weighed in the balances, and art found wanting. . .

" Thy kingdom is divided, and given to the Medes and Persians "
(Daniel v: 26-28).

" In that night was Belshazzar the king of the Chaldeans slain,
and Darius the Median took the kingdom, *being* about threescore
and two years old " (Daniel v: 30-31).

In the Medo-Persian State Daniel was placed above the presidents
of the provinces and set over the whole realm " because an excellent
spirit *was* in him."

The presidents and princes sought to find fault with Daniel, but
could find none. So they got the King to sign a decree which stated
that whosoever shall ask a petition of any God or man for thirty days
save of the King, he shall be cast into the den of lions, knowing
that Daniel would not cease praying to his God.

When Daniel heard of this he prayed and gave thanks before God
as he had done before three times a day.

Darius could not change the decree since " the law of the Medes
and Persians altereth not." So Daniel was cast into the den of lions
and " the king went to his palace and passed the night fasting . . . "
(Daniel vi: 18). Very early in the morning the King went hastily to
the den of lions and said to Daniel:

" O Daniel, servant of the living God, is thy God, whom thou
servest continually, able to deliver thee from the lions? " (Daniel
vi: 20).

Then Daniel answered:

" O king, live for ever.

" My God hath sent his angel, and hath shut the lions' mouths, that they have not hurt me: forasmuch as before him innocency was found in me; and also before thee, O king, have I done no hurt " (Daniel vi: 21–22).

So Daniel was taken out of the den of lions and " they brought those men which had accused Daniel, and they cast *them* into the den of lions, them, their children, and their wives " (Daniel vi: 24).

An *angel* had " shut the lions' mouths "—is it not obvious what *force* the heavenly messenger used to accomplish this purpose?

Darius then wrote a decree to all the people, nations, and languages, saying, " I make a decree, That in every dominion of my kingdom men tremble and fear before the God of Daniel: for he is the living God, and steadfast for ever, and his kingdom *that* which shall not be destroyed, and his dominion shall be *even* unto the end " (Daniel vi: 26).

Daniel's vision of four beasts (Daniel vii), his vision of the ram and goat (Daniel viii), his vision of the man clothed in linen (Daniel x), his account of the kings of the north and south (Daniel xi), refer to the latter days, and fuller understanding of these will be forthcoming as the time draws near. This is said to relate to the Times of the Gentiles.

The individual Joseph eventually became Moses, and then incarnated as Daniel, then as the prophet Nehemiah (445 B.C.). All four of these men served Aton (One God) at foreign courts! Between incarnations as Daniel and Nehemiah, the entity was in life as Ahmose II—Twenty-sixth Dynasty—Pharaoh of Egypt (569–525 B.C.). Formerly he had been Ahmose I, founder of the Eighteenth Dynasty. Is it not strange that over one thousand years separated Ahmose I from Ahmose II? Why did it take such a long period of time to produce the second Ahmose? The reason is obvious: it took the same vibration to produce the name again, and *Ahmose* is not unlike *Moses*!

Amos was a herdsman of Tekoa, a few miles south of Bethlehem. He prophesied during the days of Uzziah, King of Judah, and in the days of Jeroboam II in Israel. Isaiah was prophesying at this same time in about the year 745 B.C. to a later date. He had been the scribe Ahmose at the court of Akhnaton (notice similarity of *Amos* and *Ahmose*), and then incarnated as Hur of the Greater Exodus. Amos was a man of the common people, without training in the schools of the prophets.

He pronounces judgments upon six heathen nations: Syria, Tyre or Tyrus, Ammon, Philistia, Edom, Moab. Also he pronounces judgments upon Judah and Israel for oppression of the poor. He pleads for Israel:

" For thus saith the LORD unto the house of Israel, Seek ye me, and ye shall live " (Amos v: 4).

" For I know your manifold transgressions and your mighty sins: they afflict the just, they take a bribe, and they turn aside the poor in the gate *from their right*. . . .

" Seek good, and not evil, that ye may live: and so the LORD, the God of hosts, shall be with you, as ye have spoken.

" Hate the evil, and love the good, and establish judgment in the gate: it may be that the LORD God of hosts will be gracious unto the remnant of Joseph " (Amos v: 12, 14–15).

Amos condemns feast days, burnt offerings, solemn assemblies, peace offerings, etc. " Though ye offer me burnt offerings and your meat offerings, I will not accept them: neither will I regard the peace [thank] offerings of your fat beasts " (Amos v: 22).

His theme song is:

" But let judgment run down as waters, and righteousness as a mighty stream " (Amos v: 24).

" Have ye offered unto me sacrifices and offerings in the wilderness forty years, O house of Israel? " (Amos v: 25.) This verse shows us that it was definitely *not* the command of God that pagan sacrifice take place!

Amos was a prophet of the common people and championed their cause:

" Hear this, O ye that swallow up the needy, even to make the poor of the land to fail. . . .

" The LORD hath sworn by the excellency of Jacob, Surely I will never forget any of their works.

" Shall not the land tremble for this, and every one mourn that dwelleth therein? . . .

" And it shall come to pass in that day, saith the Lord GOD, that I will cause the sun to go down at noon, and I will darken the earth in the clear day " (Amos viii: 4, 7–9).

The foregoing verses predict physical destruction. Amos also predicts a famine of the world:

" Behold, the days come, saith the Lord GOD, that I will send a famine in the land, not a famine of bread, nor a thirst for water, but of hearing the words of the LORD.

" And they shall wander from sea to sea, and from the north even to the east, they shall run to and fro to seek the word of the LORD, and shall not find it " (Amos viii: 11-12).

Further desolation is also foretold:

" And the Lord GOD of hosts is he that toucheth the land, and it shall melt, and all that dwell therein shall mourn: and it shall rise up wholly like a flood; and shall be drowned as by the flood of Egypt " (Amos ix: 5).

All the Israelites shall be gathered:

" . . . and I will sift the house of Israel among all nations, like as corn is sifted in a sieve, yet shall not the least grain fall upon the earth. . . .

" In that day will I raise up the tabernacle of David that is fallen, and close up the breaches thereof; and I will raise up his ruins, and I will build it as in the days of old. . . .

" And I will plant them upon their land, and they shall no more be pulled up out of their land which I have given them, saith the LORD thy God " (Amos ix: 9, 11, 15).

According to the Divine Tetrad, the following Four Creatures are symbolic of the Four Major Prophets and later of the Four Evangelists.

Man (Angel)	Ezekiel	Matthew
Lion	Daniel	Mark
Bull	Jeremiah	Luke
Eagle	Isaiah	John

However, this ancient symbolic system does not accurately indicate incarnations of entities. It is correct in two instances, however.

Isaiah (Eagle) was later John; Jeremiah (Bull) was later Luke. But Daniel did not become Mark; and Ezekiel did not become Matthew. In the time of the Master Jesus, Daniel was in life as the father of Jesus—Joseph. Ezekiel was in life at this time as the young Mark! The correct symbology, then, as far as incarnations are concerned, would be:

Man (Angel)	Amos	Matthew
Lion	Ezekiel	Mark
Bull	Jeremiah	Luke
Eagle	Isaiah	John

In Egyptian symbology we find a direct comparison to the above. The four Egyptian Gods of the Dead stand before the Judge and have four different natures.

Man

Dog (Jackal)

Ape

Eagle

These Sacred Four Creatures as seen in ancient funeral tablets appear at the trial of the dead man and mediate to Osiris on his behalf.

Later, the original Dog or Jackal becomes a Lion, and the Ape becomes a Bull. The Man and Eagle remain the same. But the Four Creatures always act as mediators between man and the gods. They tell Isaiah to warn the people of the coming catastrophe and appear to Ezekiel in " wheels " and tell him to warn the people also. The Four Creatures pertain to space visitors, and this matter was fully dealt with and explained in the book, *Other Tongues—Other Flesh.* Space ships (" saucers ") were symbolized and incorporated into many world religions. For example, Ashur, the supreme national god of Assyria, was depicted standing on a *winged disc*!

One of the very strange references in the Bible is to the " hornets." (The Hebrew word for " hornet " means a machine which flies.)

" And I will send *hornets* before thee, which shall drive out the Hivite, the Canaanite, and the Hittite, from before thee " (Exodus xxiii: 28).

" Moreover the LORD thy GOD will send the *hornet* among them, until they that are left, and hide themselves from thee, be destroyed. Thou shalt not be affrighted at them: for the LORD thy God is among you, a mighty God and terrible " (Deuteronomy vii: 20–21).

" And I sent the *hornet* before you, which drave them out from before you, even the two kings of the Amorites; but not with thy sword, nor with thy bow " (Joshua xxiv: 12).

The " hornet " references refer to the time when the Children of Israel were ready to enter the " Promised Land " and were afraid of the native inhabitants they would meet there. But God tells the people:

" Thou shalt not be afraid of them: but shalt well remember what the LORD thy God did unto Pharaoh [Amunism], and unto all Egypt " (Deuteronomy vii: 18).

He goes on to say that the Lord thy God brought thee out of Egypt by " . . . signs, wonders, and the mighty hand, and the stretched out arm . . . " (Deuteronomy vii: 19).

Of course, we know that the people were guided out of Egypt and protected by the hovering space craft. Now as the people are ready to finally enter their " Promised Land " God says:

" . . . the LORD thy God " shall do the same " unto all the people of whom thou art afraid " (Deuteronomy vii: 19).

A promise is given to the people that the *hornets* (space ships) will be " sent before thee." In other words, just before the gigantic craft abandoned the Children of Israel, after guiding them as a " cloud " for forty years, it (and smaller craft or " hornets " inside of it) made a demonstration of power and force to the native inhabitants that the Israelites would have to deal with. This made it much easier on the people who had wandered for four decades— they would be respected by those who had been shown such power. But God tells the people not to be afraid of the *hornets* for He is with them (Deuteronomy vii: 21).

Joel (*ca.* 720 B.C.) spoke of the coming day of God and coming judgment. He predicted the Gospel Age and, like John, in Revelation, he forecast the Earth's Harvest. Later he incarnated as John the Baptist. Elijah also became the Baptist! How could *two* men become *one* man? We will explain this apparent " contradiction " in *Fulfilment*!

Elijah, Prophet of God, *ca.* 875–800 B.C., was a native of Gilead, the Land of Jephthah. He was a child of the wild loneliness of mountain ravines; he wore a cloak of sheepskin or coarse camel hair, with his own thick long hair hanging down his back.

His mission was to drive the worship of the false god Baal (Amun) out of Israel. The way had to be prepared for the Christ!

Elijah went to Mount Horeb (Sinai), where Moses had been given the Law, and he was conscious that the time of his departure from earth had come. He headed straight for the land where Moses had departed centuries before him. He went to Mount Nebo, the loftiest peak of Mount Pisgah.

Elijah had been a prophet of " fire." He then called down " fire " from " heaven " on Mount Carmel; and he had called down " fire " to destroy the officers of Ahaziah. Elijah, like Moses before him, divided waters. He used his mantle instead of a rod, and divided the waters of the Jordan (II Kings ii: 8).

Elijah heard the same *voice* that Moses heard, and he was translated from the earth in the same manner as the great Law-giver.

" And it came to pass, as they [Elijah and Elisha] still went on, and talked, that, behold, there appeared a chariot of fire . . . and parted them both asunder; and Elijah went up by a whirlwind into heaven " (II Kings ii: 11).

The prophet who had called down " fire " now left in a chariot of that same " fire." A " whirlwind " or force field (vortex) carried him off so that it wasn't necessary for him to pass through the experience of so-called death!

" And Elisha saw it, and he cried, My father, my father, the chariot of Israel, and the horsemen thereof . . . " (II Kings ii: 12).

The " chariot of Israel," indeed! For it was the same space craft that had guided the people of the Exodus; it was the same craft that lifted Moses into another dimension of time and space; and it was the same great mother-ship that had released its scout ships (" hornets ") on those who opposed the entry of the Israelites into the " Promised Land." Now it took away Elijah after his mission was accomplished. The prophet's mantle had fallen from him, and Elisha picked it up so that he might succeed Elijah as Prophet of God (II Kings ii: 13).

Although the entity Elijah was not Moses, he nevertheless was very close to the work and vibration of the latter. Elijah was the guardian and administrator of the Divine Law: Moses had been the giver of this same law!

Elijah knew that he would be removed from earth in the same manner as Moses, so he went to where the " angels " (space visitors) had taken the Law-giver, and Elijah was borne away also. The translation of these two men was a forecast of the eventual " Rapture of the Church "—that glad day when " angel chariots shall sweep in and swing low to gather us up to welcome the returning Christ."

The " Rapture " of the Church will be effected in the same manner as the translation of Moses and Elijah; that is why space visitors in so-called " saucers " are here today! The " handwriting is on the wall " !

Later, Elijah returned as the Angel Sandalphon. This was one of the " angels " (messengers from another world) who approached Ezekiel several hundred years later from the " wheels." But as Sandalphon, Elijah was *not* in a new body! He had not reincarnated on another world—remember, he was taken there bodily by the " chariot of fire "!

" Angel " in ancient languages means: " birds of God," " messenger," and " a man whose soul is winged." The present space visitors are certainly " messengers " or " birds of God." So Elijah was Sandalphon, a " man whose soul was winged." And he certainly was " winged " ever since he had been translated by the chariot air space ship!

Not only do we find Elijah leaving the earth in a space ship, but we find him returning (in the same body) later in a space craft to speak with Ezekiel!

Many strange legends have been preserved concerning the birth of Pythagoras (590–500 B.C.). He had been Thutmose III, who brought the treasures from Solomon's Temple to Egypt. Ancients claimed he was no mortal man, but one of the gods who had taken a human body to enable him to come into the world and instruct the human race. This, of course, is true, since Pythagoras was one of the " Goodly Company."

Pythagoras established a university at Crotona, a Dorian colony in Southern Italy. He gathered around him a select group of students whom he instructed in the secret wisdom which had been revealed to him, and also in the fundamentals of occult mathematics, music, and astronomy, which he considered to be the triangular foundation of all the arts and sciences.

Gautama (Sakyamuni, Siddhartha) Buddha was the founder of Buddhism. He was born near Kapilavastu (the modern Kohana), India, 568 B.C. He died near Kushinagara, Oudh, 488 B.C. This entity had been in life before as the great Priest of Salem, Melchizedek (Psalms cx: 4; Hebrews v: 6), and later incarnated as the greatest Master of all time—Jesus, the Christ! Siddhartha, which means, " he who gains his end," was certainly appropriate, for during the *Fulfilment* the Christ gained the end for which he was sent by the Infinite Father!

The artist Cato, of Akhnaton's court, became the Master Kong (Kong-fu-tse, Kung-fu-tse), who is known to the world by the

Latinized form of his name, Confucius. This Chinese sage lived 551–478 B.C. He had also lived as Pharaoh Amenemopet of the golden mask.

The famous Iemhotep became Amenophis at the time of Akhnaton. He incarnated as Baruch, *ca.* 586 B.C. The name Baruch, which means, " one upon whom blessings are poured," certainly fits this entity. He had been deified twice in earlier lifetimes by the Egyptian people after his death! In *ca.* 300 B.C. he again entered life as Euclid of Alexandria, the mathematician, and " father of geometry." He was born in Egypt, the land where he had twice before been deified and lived great lives!

The good Akhnaton came into life again in 469 B.C. as the Athenian philosopher Socrates. When he was accused of impiety and innovation and condemned to death in 399 B.C., Simmias and Cebes were present at his death. It will be remembered that young Tutankhamun was one of those present when Akhnaton drank the poison and died in doomed Akhetaton. This time when Socrates drank the fatal hemlock in prison, Simmias, who had been Tutankhamun, was present. So we find the former relationship of murdered individual-witness (Akhnaton-Tutankhamun) repeating itself in Socrates-Simmias!

In conversation with Cebes, a pupil of Socrates asks this question: " Do you now tell me likewise in regard to life and death. Do you not say that death is the contrary of life? "

" I say so."

" And that they are produced from each other? "

" Yes."

" What, then, is that which is produced from life? "

" Death," said Cebes.

" And that which is produced from death? "

" I must allow," said Cebes, " to be life."

" Then, Cebes, from the dead are living things and living men produced? "

" It seems so," he replied.

" Therefore," said he, " our souls exist in Orcus, after death."

" I think so."

" Of their stages of generation, then, is not one, at least, obviously distinct? For dying is surely an intelligible idea—is it not? "

" Certainly it is," said he.

" How then," he continued, " shall we do? Shall we not oppose in turn to this the contrary process of generation, but shall Nature fail in this? Or must we allow some process of generation contrary to dying? "

" By all means."

" What is it, then? "

" Reviving."

" Therefore," said he, " if reviving is granted, this should be the process of generation from the dead to the living, viz. reviving? "

" Certainly."

" We allow then in this way that the living are produced from the dead, no less than the dead from the living; but, such being the case, it appeared to me to furnish adequate proof that the souls of the deceased exist somewhere, from whence they return again into life."

" Such, Socrates, appears to me to be the necessary result from what has been admitted."

" Observe, now, Cebes, that we have not, in my judgment, made these admissions without reason; for if those things which are produced were not continually to alternate with each other as if revolving in a circle, but the generation were direct from the one (contrary merely to its opposite, nor should take a circuit and come around again to the first), are you aware that all things at last should assume the same figure, submit to the same affection, and cease to be produced at all? "

" How say you this? "

" There is no difficulty in comprehending what I say; but if, for instance, falling asleep be granted, and that awaking, which is produced from sleeping, were not to alternate with it, be assured that all things coming to an end would render the fable of Endymion a mere jest, and he no longer would be considered of importance, because all things else would be influenced by an affection such as he was, by sleep; further, if all things were confounded together, and never divided asunder, the theory of Anaxagoras would soon be realized—ALL WOULD BE CHAOS.

" Thus, my dear Cebes, if all things which had partaken of life should die, and when dead should remain in the same state of death and not revive again, would there not be an unavoidable necessity that everything should persist at last, and nothing revive?

" For if living things were produced from anything else than what had died, and those living things should die, what remedy would there be against all things being finally destroyed by death? "

" None whatever, Socrates, in my mind," answered Cebes; " but to me you seem to speak the clearest truth."

" Such," said he, " Cebes, the case unquestionably seems to me, and that we do not acknowledge these things under the influence of delusion; but there is in reality a reviving and producing of the living from the dead, a surviving of the souls of the deceased, and happiness for the good, but misery for the evil amongst them."

Socrates' extraordinary mind and genius excited the envy and malice of some, while it elicited the warmest admiration of many. This can also be said of Akhnaton! In the groves of Academus, the Lyceum, and on the banks of Ilissus he was followed by those who listened with delight as he discoursed of immortal things. Did not Akhnaton discourse of immortal things at Akhetaton, followed by those who sought the *Greater Light*?

Cebes had been Genubath, son of Hadad; and he had been the young son of Tutankhamun who was buried with the boy-king in his tomb. So we find the former relationship of father-son (Hadad-Genubath; Tutankhamun-young son) now changed to that of companions and students together, Simmias-Cebes.

The great teacher Philolaus (Philos, Phylos), *ca.* 480 B.C., took refuge first in Lucania and then at Thebes, Egypt, where he had Simmias and Cebes as pupils. So we find young Simmias returning to the Egypt in which he had been a Pharaoh and lived many lifetimes.

While at Thebes with Philolaus, Simmias attempted to discover the secret, hidden chambers of the SECRET PLACES OF THE LION at the Great Pyramid and Sphinx. However, he did not succeed. He knew he had been " Ratut " and he desired to find the tablets he himself had written centuries before. But this was not to come until he incarnated during the time of Jesus, the Christ!

Amunhotep III, the " Magnificent," who had also lived as Ramses II, the " Great," came back into life in 427 B.C. as the Greek philosopher Plato. Plato was a student of Socrates, so we find the former relationship of father-son (Amunhotep III - Akhnaton) now changed to student-teacher (Plato-Socrates).

The entity that had been Sitamun, second wife of Amunhotep III, and later Istno-fret, wife of Ramses II, returned to life as a male entity in the second century B.C. She became the Greek mathematician and Pythagorean, Nicomachus.

The entity who had been the Prophet Joel incarnated as John, son of Zacharias the priest and his wife Elisabeth. He was the forerunner of Jesus Christ. John the Baptist signifies a high intellectual perception of Truth, but one not yet quickened of Spirit!

The stage was now set for the appearance of Him who would lead the entire world out of darkness and into the Light of a greater Understanding.

The *WORD* had been *Prepared* in many lands; it had *Dawned* in Egypt as the Aton (One God); it was *Revealed* during the Greater Exodus in the "burning" bush and through the Two Tablets; now it was to be *Fulfilled*!

Chapter Four

FULFILMENT

THE *WORD* was fulfilled. . . .
   " . . . there shall come a Star out of Jacob, and a Sceptre shall rise out of Israel . . . " (Numbers xxiv: 17).

The promise of an Eternal King, to arise out of David's Family, was repeated over and over again: to David, to Solomon, and again and again in the Psalms, and by the prophets Amos, Isaiah, Micah, Jeremiah, and Zechariah over a period of several hundred years.

By and by, in the fullness of time, the angel Gabriel was sent to Nazareth, to Mary, who was of the family of David. Gabriel said:
   " . . . Fear not, Mary: for thou hast found favour with God. And, behold, thou shalt conceive in thy womb, and bring forth a son, and shalt call his name JESUS, He shall be great, and shall be called the Son of the Highest: and the Lord God shall give unto him the throne of his father David: And he shall reign over the house of Jacob for ever; and of this kingdom there shall be no end " (Luke i: 30–33).

In the child Jesus, the Davidic promises found their Fulfilment!

The angel told Mary, " . . . the Lord God shall give unto him [Jesus] the throne of his *father David*. . . . " This is very interesting, since Joseph, father of Jesus, had been Moses, and in an earlier life-time the other Joseph, son of Jacob. He was also David, so when the angel called David the *father* of Jesus, he was quite accurate, for Joseph had been David!

It will be remembered that Menelik was the son of Solomon and Sheba (Hatshepsut); therefore his (Menelik's) descendants who ruled as kings of Abyssinia would be directly related to David and Solomon. So we find Menelik and Jesus, both come from the " seed of David "! This is proof that the same pattern and vibration existed in ancient Israel and Egypt. The scene of the Plan shifted back and forth between these two countries until the correct area and time came about! The Christ was either to incarnate as the Pharaoh Sananda, a descendant of Menelik, or as Jesus, son of Joseph. In either case the Christ would be directly descended from David! Yet he was finally born in Bethlehem, city of David!

The unfortunate theory of Mary's "perpetual virginity" has absolutely no basis in fact! Is virginity to be regarded as any holier than motherhood? Mary had other children besides Jesus, and this is substantiated by the statement in Luke ii: 7 that Mary "brought forth her first-born son." Why "first-born" if there were no others?

The four "brethren" of Jesus mentioned in Matthew xiii: 55 were the sons of Joseph by his first wife, Martha, and were therefore his half-brothers. They were: James ("James the Less"; Galatians i: 19); Joses; Simon (Simeon); and Judas (Jude, Thaddaeus). The "Judas" mentioned here had to be the Apostle Jude, for it is mentioned in the Bible that "Judas was the brother of James" (Luke vi: 16). It does not mean he was the brother of *James* and John, sons of Zebedee; therefore he had to be the brother of "James the Less." And this James had been Huya during the reign of Akhnaton.

Now Jesus had a full younger brother and two full sisters. These were the children born of the union between Joseph and Mary. The brother was Lazarus and the sisters were Mary and Martha! (Matthew xiii: 56.) This Martha had been Tantahpe and then Miriam in former lifetimes! So we find the former relationship of father-daughter (Maya-Tantahpe); then brother-sister (Moses-Miriam), now a relationship of father-daughter again (Joseph-Martha).

The true Hebrew derivation of the name Lazarus is disputed. However, the name is a form of Eliezer. Remember that Moses had a son by the name of Eliezer (Exodus xviii: 4). So we now find Joseph (who had been Moses) giving one of his sons the same name: Lazarus, or *Eliezer*!

The former Queen Meritaton, who later became the Egyptian princess who took Moses from the water, was now in life as the wife of Lazarus. So the former relationship of son - foster-mother (Moses-daughter of Seti I) was now one of father-in-law - daughter-in-law (Joseph-wife of Lazarus).

" Now when Jesus was born in Bethlehem of Judaea in the days of

Herod the king, behold, there came wise men from the east to Jerusalem, Saying, Where is he that is born King of the Jews? for we have seen his Star in the East, and are come to worship him " (Matthew ii: 1-2).

The followers of Zoroaster had been told earlier that Zoroaster would incarnate again on earth, and the sign would be " a great brilliant star in the east." So He who had been Shem and Melchizedek, Zoroaster, and Gautama Buddha now came into life for His supreme accomplishment as Jesus, the Christ!

King Herod called in the Wise Men and asked them what time the star appeared in the heavens (Matthew ii: 7). This means it was not an ordinary star, for it had not been seen before in the sky!

" When they had heard the king, they departed; and, lo, the star, which they saw in the east, went before them, till it came and stood over where the young child was. When they saw the star, they rejoiced with exceeding great joy " (Matthew ii: 9-10).

It has been calculated that there was a conjunction of Jupiter and Saturn in 6 B.C. However, this can scarcely explain how "the star went before them till it came and stood over where the child was." Some astronomers think that possibly the " Star of Bethlehem " was a star that had exploded and burned brightly for a while. Many stars a year explode in the Milky Way Galaxy, but that would not fit the case either! Neither was the star the Wise Men saw the " supernatural light " that the theologians think it was! It was a space craft, the same one that had led the Children of Israel out of Egypt and provided " manna " for forty years, and sent out scout ships (" hornets ") to pave the way for the Israelites to enter the " Promised Land." This craft had departed from earth after the action of the " hornets " near the River Jordan. (The waters of the Jordan were parted and the walls of Jericho collapsed.) Now the ship returned again to herald the birth of the Christ who is supreme in our Solar System—the Son of God!

Now when the Wise Men came Jesus was not in the " manger," as is generally believed, but in a " house " (Matthew ii: 11). The Three Wise Men were in actuality representatives of the space craft—they came from the " east " where the " star " had appeared! One of these Wise Men was Mer (who brought myrrh), and he had formerly lived as Ahmose, scribe of Akhnaton, and then as Hur, husband of Miram.

Jesus Christ is called a " star " from the Light of His divine wisdom and from the Light with which He comes into the world. " Stars " of the heavens signify spiritual men because of the knowledge of good and truth such men possess.

" Star out of Jacob " means knowledge concerning the Lord (Jesus) and His human form; and " Sceptre out of Israel " means Divine Truth as to government. In other words, a Master (" Star ") would come to the world as a descendant of Jacob and would appear as a man (human). He would eventually cause all nations and world governments to be ruled and governed by Divine Truth!

Immediately after the birth of Christ shepherds in fields near by saw " the angel of the Lord," and the " glory of the Lord shone round about them " (Luke ii: 9).

" And suddenly there was with the angel a multitude of the heavenly host praising God . . ." (Luke ii: 13).

" And it came to pass, as the angels were gone away from them into heaven . . . " (Luke ii: 15).

The " angel " who appeared was Gabriel (" man of God ") the same one who had appeared to Mary, and the " glory or light of the Lord shone about them." This was light from the great ship. Evidently, several beings appeared with Gabriel and, after delivering their message, they departed back to " heaven."

The shepherds saw the Christ Child in the " manger " some time before the Three Wise Men came, for Christ was no longer in the " manger " but in a " house " when the latter arrived.

After the Wise Men departed (Matthew ii: 12–13), the " angel " Gabriel appeared to Joseph in a " dream." The " angel " told Joseph to " arise " and take Jesus and his mother Mary into Egypt. Actually, Gabriel was in charge of the space craft and he contacted Joseph telepathically (in a " dream ") through the magnetic force field of the ship (which is used for communications).

Joseph, when he was in life as Moses, had taken his wife Zipporah and child, put them on an ass, and went from Midian into Egypt. Did he do the same thing now with Mary and the child Jesus? He did not, contrary to modern-day conceptions of the flight into Egypt.

" . . . he took the young child and his mother by night, and departed into Egypt " (Matthew ii: 14).

Gabriel had warned Joseph that King Herod would seek Jesus and kill Him if they didn't leave Bethlehem at once. So Joseph put Mary on an ass with the child and led them out of the City of David; out into the open fields. Then they were all picked up by the space craft, and therefore guided by Gabriel into Egypt. This same Gabriel had given Daniel the seventy weeks' prophecy (Daniel ix : 21). Now Gabriel aids Joseph, who had been Daniel! Daniel said: " Yea, while I was speaking in prayer, even the man Gabriel, whom I had seen in the vision at the beginning, being caused to *fly swiftly*, touched me about the time of the evening oblation."

Because they began their journey on an ass, and because early historians couldn't understand how else they could have travelled to Egypt, the idea prevails to this day that they made the entire long journey on such a creature! But when we speak of the " flight " into Egypt we are speaking literal truth! It was a *flight* in the truest sense of the word!

The stay in Egypt was short—only two years. Herod died, and it was safe to return. Joseph and Mary resided in the city of On (Heliopolis) while in Egypt. This was the same city where Joseph, father of Jesus, had lived as another Joseph—son of Jacob! The entity returns to the former vibration of another lifetime.

" But when Herod was dead, behold, an angel [Gabriel] of the Lord appeareth in a dream to Joseph in Egypt, Saying, Arise, and take the young child and his mother, and go into the land of Israel ... And he 'arose, and took the young child and his mother, and came into the land of Israel " (Matthew ii: 19-21).

" Arise " and " arose " do not mean that Joseph was " dreaming " and had a vision, and then had to get up out of bed. It means that by a " dream " he received a message telepathically from Gabriel and " arose " to the space craft. When the original Scripture verses are translated correctly in some future day, it will be obvious what was meant! And originals exist for nearly all the Books of the Bible —their secret hiding-places will be revealed.

Jesus had " risen " in a space ship and was taken into Egypt, and two years later returned the same way.

The " Goodly Company " had told of the coming of a great and wonderful King in the family line of David who would rule and bless the entire world. This King had been named long before he appeared: " The Messiah " (Hebrew), or " The Christ " (Greek).

Both words mean the same thing: the "One Anointed" of God to perform the world *Work* of which the prophets had spoken. "Jesus" was his personal name. "The Messiah" or "The Christ" were the names of the office he came to assume.

John the Baptist was the son of Zacharias, the priest, and his wife, Elisabeth. Gabriel also appeared to Zacharias and told him that his wife Elisabeth would have a child. This priest, Zacharias, had been Aaron and then Ezekiel in other lifetimes. Elisabeth had been Elisheba, wife of Aaron. So we find the former husband-wife team (Aaron-Elisheba) returning in the same relationship (Zacharias-Elisabeth). Actually, Elisabeth is the same name as Elisheba!

Now the entity who had been the Prophet Joel incarnated first as John the Baptist, and he withdrew from ordinary life to become a hermit of the desert (Luke i: 80). Many years passed before the boyhood friends, Jesus and John, met (nearly thirty years).

While John was in the desert he became ill, and the entity that had been Joel departed from the flesh, and he who had been Elijah (Elias) took over the physical form of the Baptist!

Gabriel had told Zacharias, "And he [John] shall go before him in the spirit and power of Elias [Elijah] . . ." (Luke i: 17). Later, Jesus Himself said that Elijah returned to life as John the Baptist (Matthew xi: 14).

Joel could not carry out this mission, and Elijah took over to fulfil the purpose of the Baptist. Joel then incarnated at once as Thomas the Doubter! This Joel had been the Hittite ambassador to Egypt, who gave the iron knife to young Tutankhamun. So we find the former relationship of prince-foreign ambassador (Tutankhamun-Hittite official) returning as father-son (Zacharias-John).

The mission of the Baptist was finally completed when he baptized Jesus and a *voice* from heaven said: ". . . This is my beloved Son, in whom I am well pleased" (Matthew iii: 17).

The place chosen for the introduction of Jesus, the Messiah to the world, was the lower Jordan, at the very spot where the waters divided for Joshua to cross on Israel's entrance into the "Promised Land." Directly to the east, at the edge of the Jordan valley, were the towering heights of Mount Nebo, where Moses was given a glimpse of the "Promised Land," and then translated from the earth. There, in the same area, the "fire chariot of Israel" had carried Elijah away. Five miles to the west, at the edge of the valley, was Jericho, whose walls really fell because of the last act of the great, hovering space craft and its "hornets." The waters of the Jordan had been separated by the craft's force field, even as the Red Sea had been parted (Joshua iii: 16–17).

The "captain of the host of the Lord" appeared to Joshua when Joshua "lifted up his eyes and looked" (Joshua v: 13–14). Then this "captain" told Joshua to take off his shoes—"for the place whereon thou standest is holy" (Joshua v: 15). This is what the *voice* commanded Moses to do; a direct contact had to be made with the ground!

Seven priests bearing seven trumpets were to encompass Jericho for seven days. On the seventh day, after circling the city seven times, with the host of the Lord hovering above waiting for the appointed time, and amidst the shouts of the people and the blasts of trumpets, the walls of Jericho crumbled from the action of the great ship's magnetic field.

This same area of the Jordan provided the *vibration* for the Baptism of the Christ! "Miracles" had taken place here many times before. Even Bethel was near, where Abraham had erected an altar to the One God (Aton), and where Jacob saw the "heavenly ladder" with angels ascending and descending. Jacob, of course, saw space visitors! Nearby, southward, on the same mountain ridge as Bethel lay Jerusalem, the Holy City—city of the priest Melchizedek. And now Melchizedek was Jesus, the Christ!

The so-called "missing years" in the life of Jesus, before His Baptism, found Him journeying to Britain, Egypt, and Tibet. While in Britain He resided in an area that was later to be the location of the famous Glastonbury Abbey. While in Egypt he penetrated the SECRET PLACES OF THE LION at the Great Pyramid, under the Sphinx, and elsewhere!

On the first day of the feast of unleavened bread, the Twelve Disciples came to Jesus and asked Him, "Where wilt thou that we prepare for thee to eat the passover?" (Matthew xxvi: 17.)

Jesus said: "I will keep the passover at the house of Mary, mother of John (Mark), for my time is at hand." The Twelve Disciples made ready the Passover in the Upper Room in the house of Mary of Jerusalem, mother of the young John, later named Mark (Acts xii: 12). This Upper Room or Chamber represents the high state of mind that we assume in thinking about spiritual things.

And this may be attained through prayer, by going into the silence with true words, or in deep spiritual meditation.

" Now when the even was come, he [Jesus] sat down with the twelve " (Matthew xxvi: 20). These Twelve were (Matthew x: 1-4): Simon, who was called Peter (he had been Akhnaton, and later Socrates); Andrew (Peter's brother, who had been an Aton priest during Akhnaton's reign); James (brother of John, a son of Zebedee); John the Beloved (he had been Prince Seti, then later Isaiah, and Aristotle); Philip (he had been Amunhotep III, and later Ramses II; then Plato); Bartholomew or Nathanael (he had been Mahu, chief of police under Akhnaton); Thomas (he had been Joel, and incarnated as the first entity to live as John the Baptist; Elijah took over the body of the Baptist, and the former occupant took over the body of Thomas—more wholesale " body swapping " similar to the happenings of the David-Ahmose I period); Matthew the publican (he had been Ahmose the scribe at Akhetaton, then became Hur, and later Amos); James the Lesser (he had lived as Huya, major-domo for Queen Tiyi, mother of Akhnaton); Lebbaeus, whose surname was Thaddaeus (Judas); Simon the Canaanite; and Judas Iscariot who betrayed Jesus (this entity had assassinated Pharaoh Akhnaton and later Tutankhamun).

These Twelve looked to Simon Peter, not because of his age, since he was a young man the same age as Jesus, but because he had once been the good Akhnaton—he who heralded the Dawn of Aton (One God) to an unbelieving world. Jesus picked these men of varied backgrounds because he could tell by his *inner vision* who they had been in the past and what particular mission they were in life to serve while he was on earth!

The home of Mary of Jerusalem was a meeting-place for the early followers of the Master Jesus. She was a wealthy widow who supported the work of the Christ in His wanderings. Barnabas, being Mark's uncle, made this home his headquarters while in Jerusalem.

It has been claimed that Mark never knew Jesus, and received the information that he placed in his Gospel second hand from Peter. However, this is not true. Mark was twelve years old when the Last Supper took place in his home. At the age of twelve a Hebrew boy was considered a man, and was therefore no child in the eyes of his contemporaries!

Mark served the Disciples and the Christ in that Upper Room on that night; he watched the entire proceedings as he waited at the top of a stairway not too far from the large and long rough-hewn table. It was he who filled the *Cup* for Jesus when the Master wished to drink (Matthew xxvi: 27).

Mark had been reared in a home that was full of spiritual atmosphere and power! Although only twelve years old, he had been educated in the finest schools of the day. He spoke and wrote several languages. Mark was impressed deeply by the devout men who gathered at his mother's home night after night to hear Jesus speak. Mark had heard the Master's words to His select Inner Group! Only the Twelve heard the most important sayings of Jesus outside of Mary and her son Mark. It is little wonder that John Mark yielded himself at an early age to the Infinite Father's leadership!

Before the Last Supper of bread and wine was instituted, Jesus told His Twelve that one of them would betray him. Judas Iscariot, deeply feeling his guilt, said, " Master, is it I? " Jesus said, " Thou hast said it! " Judas then left the Upper Room, and the bread and wine were taken. Afterwards Jesus and the Eleven sang together in fellowship (Matthew xxvi: 30); they they went out into the Mount of Olives. This was a ridge of hills near Jerusalem to the east of the city. The ascension of Jesus took place there later; David had gone up the Mount of Olives when he was fleeing from Absalom; Ezekiel had seen great space ships on top of this mount—and now he who had formerly been Ezekiel was in life as the young Mark!

" Then did the cherubim lift up their wings, and the wheels beside them; and the glory of the God of Israel was over them above. And the glory of the Lord went up from the midst of the city, and stood upon the mountain which is on the east side of the city [Mount of Olives]. Afterwards, the spirit took me up, and brought me in a vision by the Spirit of God into Chaldea, to them of the captivity. So the vision that I had seen went up from me " (Ezekiel xi: 22–24). So, in the exact place from where Ezekiel had seen the space visitors, Mark now made his home!

" Then cometh Jesus with them unto a place called Gethsemane . . . " (Matthew xxvi: 36). This garden was adjacent to the home of Mary of Jerusalem, and was where she had a press for extracting unguents and ointments. In fact, the word Gethsemane means "oil-press." It was her garden, and Jesus and the Eleven had taken a stroll there after the Last Supper had been consummated in the house. The garden and the home were at the foot of the Mount of Olives.

While Jesus and the others walked and talked, Mark cleared the room for his mother. When he went to take the Cup he stood back in amazement. It was only an old, rough clay cup from his mother's own kitchen—but it was now shining with a faint luminescence! In the dim light of the massive room, it glowed ever so faintly— almost imperceptibly—but quite visible to the discerning eyes of youth! Mark picked it up, wrapped it in his cloak, and went directly to his own room.

He quickly removed his garments and lay down, but he couldn't sleep—his thoughts were on Jesus outside in the garden. Who was this man who seemed so familiar to him? He knew his entire future in the world was to be connected with the life and work of Jesus.

The Jesus that Mark knew was not the dark, effeminate creature that is pictured by modern artists. Jesus was a powerfully built man who commanded respect not only because of His fantastic mental and spiritual qualities, but because of His athletic prowess as well!

Would the most perfect man of all time be enclosed in an emaciated body that is today portrayed as hanging on the Cross? No, a thousand times no! Jesus was *Perfect*—spiritually, mentally, and PHYSICALLY! His body was firm and strong, displaying no unmanly softness or delicacy. He looked as if He were moulded from the finest marble; there was not a blemish or mark upon Him! He was light and fair, and lithe as the finest athlete.

He was six feet tall and weighed approximately one hundred and eighty pounds. His hair was golden red, and was worn short in the Roman style. He had only a suggestion of a golden beard, but allowed it to grow longer during the last year before the Last Supper. His face was not soft and feminine; it was finely chiselled and possessed strong, masculine lines; the jaw was well set and square; the forehead high, with a slight bulging which was per-ceptible more at one time than another.

Jesus, in appearance, looked like a mixture of two types. He was almost typically Roman and almost typically Greek, yet conformed to neither perfectly. He was calm, handsome of face, and forceful as any perfect man must be!

As young Mark pondered on the Christ, the meaning of the Last Supper, and the walk in his mother's garden, he heard confusion and loud shouting. He quickly got out of his bed and, looking out of the window, saw Roman soldiers coming into the vast olive groves. He did not take time to dress, but quickly wrapped a sheet around him, and dashed out into the darkness; ran through the groves towards the torches held high by the Roman soldiers he saw approaching Jesus!

These soldiers slowly walked towards the Master with drawn swords. One of them slashed out with his weapon and cut off the ear of Malchus, servant of the high priest. Simon Peter did not cut off this man's right ear, as is generally believed (John xviii: 10).

Another soldier came close to Jesus and raised his sword to smite the Master. Mark saw this and rushed in to ward off the blow. The sword missed the Christ, but cut off Mark's thumb—thus *marking* him for life. He was ever afterwards called the " marked " because of his love for Jesus, and the missing thumb attested to this devotion. Since he heartily disliked the name John, he added the Roman name Marcus (Mark) and became John Mark.

Jesus rebuked the soldier: " Put up again thy sword . . . for all they that take the sword shall perish with the sword " (Matthew xxvi: 52).

" Thinkest thou that I cannot now pray to my Father, and he shall presently give me more than twelve legions of angels? " (Matthew xxvi: 53).

This refers to the fact that " angels " or messengers from space (" heaven ") would have instantly come to the aid of Jesus if He had desired it. But that was not the Plan.

The eleven Disciples fled from the garden, leaving Jesus and Mark with the shouting Roman soldiers (Mark xiv: 50).

" And there followed him [Jesus] a certain young man, having a linen cloth cast about his naked body; and the young men [Roman soldiers] laid hold on him: And he left the linen cloth, and fled from them naked " (Mark xiv: 51–52).

The description of the " naked young man " is only mentioned in the Gospel of Mark. Here Mark is telling of his own experience in the garden with the Christ. For a short distance he walked side by side with Jesus and took His hand. The two looked at each other for a long moment, and then Mark forgot the physical features of this Son of Man. Those features, outstanding as they were, faded into insignificance when one looked deep into the eyes—the EYES!

There was tremendous power there; power of such magnitude that Mark gasped. All thoughts fled from him as he seemed to wing his way through the star-filled night; out . . . out, into galaxies of unheard-of spiritual light. There was gentleness there too; unbelievable gentleness—compassionate, loving, brotherly; all-knowing! Mark couldn't take his gaze from the Master's eyes. He felt as though he had left the denseness of earth and was looking into the very heart of God!

Then the soldiers took hold of Mark and asked him who he was and what he had to do with this man Jesus. He tore away from them, leaving the sheet in their hands.

" And they led Jesus away to the high priest . . . " (Mark xiv: 53).

Jesus made a great impression on the Roman governor, the illustrious Pilate. This great man of Rome did not want to crucify Jesus, but the priests of Amun once again prevailed! Pilate's wife, Procula, became a Christian after the Crucifixion when she went to the home of Mary, mother of John Mark, to attend the meetings which continued even though the Master was no longer visibly with the workers.

Procula had dreamed of Jesus and never forgot him (Matthew xxvii: 19). Pilate himself ever afterwards asked only one question: " What is Truth? "

Mark was at Golgotha when Jesus was crucified. Golgotha was a hill just outside Jerusalem. It is also called Calvary. Golgotha, in the Aramaic-Jewish language, means " place of the skull." The skull is the place where intellect is crossed out, that Spirit may win an eternal ascendancy. Jesus (the intellectual) was crucified at the *place of the skull*, that Christ (Truth) might become all in all. Jesus was nailed to the Cross through His *wrists* and feet, and not through the *hands*, as usually believed and portrayed today.

A storm broke out in all its fury; lightning split the heavens and darkness came upon the land (Matthew xxvii: 45).

" And about the ninth hour Jesus cried with a loud voice, saying, Eli, Eli, lama sabachthani? . . . " (Matthew xxvii: 46.) However, Christ was not saying: " My God, my God, why hast thou forsaken me?" Throughout the ministry of Jesus, His teachings and acts reveal that faith in the One God was the dominating and fundamental element in His character. Therefore it is not reasonable to conclude that in the final and supreme test of His life He lost that faith! How could He have surrendered to absolute doubt and despair by saying, " ... why hast thou forsaken me? ... "

Robert B. Stacy-Judd was absolutely correct when he interpreted Christ's last words as: " My wounds will be kept open by those who defame me!" His translation is based on the Maya language, and that language in turn is based on the original Mother or Solar Tongue—the Universal language of the " angels." The only alteration made by Stacy-Judd is the deleting of the first " h " in " sabach-thani," and changing the " s " to a " z." " S " and " Z " are synonymous in the Maya and other ancient languages. The first " h " in the last word was either used as a conjunction or is a complete mistake. Thus, " sabachthani " becomes: zabac (h) thani.

Ancient records at Lake Titicaca confirm Stacy-Judd's research. The words of Christ were not uttered in the colloquial idiom of the times, but were spoken in the classic speech of very ancient lineage, as preserved by the secret societies and mystery schools of the masters.

When Christ uttered those words, He gave a two-way message to the world. First of all, those who would defame Him and betray His cause would perpetuate that Cause throughout history. Secondly, those who followed Him and were unwavering in their faith would become a healing balm to His wounds.

" Eli, Eli, lama zabacthani! " cried Jesus.

" Some of them that stood there, when they heard that, said, This man calleth for Elias [Elijah] " (Matthew xxvii: 47).

" The rest said, Let be, let us see whether Elias [Elijah] will come to save him " (Matthew xxvii: 49).

The people knew that Elijah (Elias) had been translated into " heaven " by a " chariot of fire "; they thought that perhaps this same Elijah might come to save Jesus and take Him away into " heaven." But such was not the Plan! No space visitors, no Gabriels, no " hornets " or mother-ships came to intervene!

" Father, into thy hands I commend my spirit. . . . It is finished! " And Jesus, the Christ, died on the Cross, Friday, April 7, A.D. 30 (see Appendix).

Indeed, it was " finished "—the *Fulfilment* had come to man; Christ's mission was a success. He " gave up the ghost " at the very hour in which Paschal lambs were being sacrificed in the Temple. Therefore the theory developed that He came into the world only to fail in his mission and therefore had to be crucified so that all men might be saved through the shedding of His literal blood. Once again this is pure paganism and based on the idea that salvation can be secured through blood-smeared altars!

Let it be remembered that Jesus came into the word to *LIVE*, not to *DIE*! It is in His *life* that man finds salvation! His words that fulfilled the ancient prophecies—his way of life—these are man's eternal salvation. His death is not to be considered as the Will of the Father. The Fundamentalists today who glory in the " blood " are the pagans of yesterday who lusted after the smell of bloody altars, for they felt that here was true salvation from sin! Yet there is great significance attached to the " blood " of the Christ!

Jesus' blood had to be shed; therefore, the Fundamentalists are correct in a sense, but they do not understand the deeper spiritual meaning. The literal blood of the Christ had to be shed through the piercing of His side.

" But one of the soldiers with a spear pierced his side, and forthwith came there out blood and water " (John xix: 34).

" . . . They shall look on him whom they pierced " (John xix: 37).

It had been prophesied that Jesus would be pierced:

" And I will pour upon the house of David, and upon the inhabitants of Jerusalem, the spirit of grace and of supplications: and they shall look upon me whom they have pierced . . . " (Zechariah xii: 10).

" For dogs have compassed me: the assembly of the wicked have inclosed me: they pierced my hands and my feet " (Psalms xxii: 16).

The shedding of the blood liberated certain elements so that they might enter the earth through the Christ Spirit; that is why it had been spoken of earlier, and these elements could not have been released in any other way.

Blood—the blood of anyone, carries that certain individual's frequency. And there is no other frequency exactly like it anywhere in Creation! Therefore transfusions are not desirable!

The crystalline formation of the blood carries light energy throughout the body. That *is* the LIFE! The blood itself is *not* Life; but it is the medium through which Life enters the body and is carried to all its parts. No one or no thing is alive because of the action of a heart, liver, or brain, or quantity of blood. The LIFE is without and we live as we assimilate it. Therefore the blood is the " life stream." When Jesus' blood fell upon the ground of earth on Golgotha, it assured the world that the Christ would return again!

He could not return unless His particular frequency and vibration was *in* and *on* the earth! There is, therefore, a definite tie or bond between him and the Planet Earth. He *must* return!

Now when the side was pierced, some of the witnesses to the Crucifixion standing by tried to get some of the blood on them. They rushed to Jesus' side where the blood spurted and ran down in many small rivulets to the ground. What did this action mean? It certainly is not pleasant for anyone to have warm, human blood spilled upon him! Remember that the Children of Israel during the Exodus period in Egypt were told:

" And they shall take of the blood, and strike it on the two side posts and on the upper door post of the houses . . . " (Exodus xii: 7).

" And the blood shall be to you for a token upon the houses where ye are: and when I see the blood, I will pass over you, and the plague shall not be upon you to destroy you, when I smite the land of Egypt " (Exodus xii: 13).

Because of the blood of the Lamb, and its particular vibrational frequency, the Israelites were ensured safety in Egypt. The milling crowds around the Cross of Jesus knew this! Remember they had said, while Jesus was before Pilate: " . . . His blood be on us, and on our children " (Matthew xxvii: 25). Did this mean that they would be responsible for Christ's death, or did it mean the *safety* angle again? Think it over!

Those on whom the blood spilled, even if it was of microscopic quantities, were assured of being a part of the Remnant that would remain! John the Beloved was one of those who received the blood, and he never died a natural or even a violent death on earth!

The frequency of the Christ's blood assured those on whom it fell that He would return to them and several were immediately awakened to Cosmic Consciousness at that instant! Mary, mother of

Jesus, Mary Magdalene, Peter, John, Philip, Mark, and Manilus the Centurion were among those who received the blood gift.

When the blood ran on to the soil of earth, an unbreakable and eternal ray was established between the Christ and His world. This contact makes it possible for Him to return—and SOON!

Blood signifies Divine Truth. It also signifies things celestial, and in a supreme sense the human essence of the Lord; consequently essential love or His mercy towards mankind. Blood was therefore called the blood of the covenant, and was sprinkled upon people in the Jewish Church. Jesus' blood represented the Divine Truth proceeding from the Divine Good of His Divine Love.

The blood and water which issued from the side of Jesus signifies the *conjunction of the Christ with the human race* by Divine Truth, spiritual and natural, proceeding from the Divine Good of His love.

For centuries after the Crucifixion (and even today) it was accepted as theological fact that the literal blood of Jesus granted complete and everlasting salvation to those accepting Him. Do they not still sing about being " washed in the blood of the Lamb " and " fountains of blood "? But they do *not* receive the actual blood by going to an altar and saying, " I accept the Lord "! But there is no need to receive the literal blood now, for the whole purpose of the Crucifixion was to release the vibration (blood). We are not saved because of Christ's blood that we accept, but we shall be saved because that blood was deposited on the earth, thereby sealing the promise of His return! The blood, however, is a symbolic yet physical manifestation of that promise.

Christ's body was symbolic of the Great Pyramid. The latter contains secret chambers that will eventually be revealed to mankind. Like the Pyramid, Christ's body contained " secrets " of the sacred *vibration*; when his side was pierced, this was released, a symbolic representation that the SECRET PLACES OF THE LION will be opened in the New Age of Truth!

Theologians throughout history have misinterpreted the Crucifixion scene and its deeper spiritual meaning! They still believe today that the literal blood will give them eternal salvation and a quick, free passage to Paradise! It will not do any such thing! But since it was shed, man had the promise of Christ's return and eventual salvation on a dark planet! Because those standing near by attempted to get the blood on them, man has ever afterwards believed in the power of the literal blood. This is correct, but interpreted on the lowest level of understanding in the churches of today. They still serve the Bread and Wine symbolizing Christ's broken body and blood; this is a ritual memorializing the permanent contact that was made between Jesus (Heaven) and earth on that Friday in A.D. 30.

Let us be fully aware that our Infinite Father is not filled with delight at the sight of " fountains of blood " or " blood-smeared worshippers." Individuals do not need to receive the literal blood themselves. Since Christ lived many centuries ago, there isn't any of the blood left anyway. Going to an altar or praying over a Communion cup won't bring back any of the original blood either! This part of present belief and ritualism developed out of the fact that witnesses near by rushed forward to receive the blood. The *salvation* part of the side-piercing lies in the fact that " a tie was established between Jesus and the earth." By living the Words and Life of the Christ, we can expect salvation at the time of the Second Coming. Going to an altar of any kind won't ensure you anything unless you LIVE CHRIST! Then, and then only, will His blood of the covenant guarantee you Divine safety at the " time of chaos."

The blood shed that day was symbolic of a great Plan to purify and redeem the race of mankind on earth by pouring into its life currents a new and purer stream through Christ. There is a living potency in His blood; yet the red blood of flesh by itself does not carry the power to " cleanse your conscience from dead works to serve the living God." It is the " blood of Christ . . . through the Eternal Spirit," that cleanses. Christ was the Fulfilled Word of God, and the life of that Word was a form of energy far transcending any ordinary life current inherent in blood as we think of it. Yet it was the peculiar frequency of Christ's blood brought about by the high energy of the Word that introduced into man's mind a spiritual principle; a principle that manifests in mind and body in concrete form when rightly appropriated.

Remember, the blood represents life; it is the vehicle that carries life through the avenues of the body, but it is not life itself. The blood shed for our " sins " symbolizes a complete conjunction between Jesus and the earth; or, the Father and mankind.

" Behold, he cometh with clouds; and every eye shall see him, and they also which pierced him . . . " (Revelation i: 7).

Let us state here the prevalent belief of Fundamental religionists:
1. God sent His only begotten Son to earth to die for our sins.
2. The literal blood, once we accept it, assures out eternal salvation.
Now let us state the true inner meaning of the above:
1. God did *not* send His Son to earth to die—he came to LIVE so that man might learn from the Life and Words (teaching) of Jesus.
2. The literal blood does *not* assure individual salvation, but it does assure the world that Jesus will return.

The confusion that has arisen from so-called " blood atonement " is obvious from the above and from the happenings at the Cross. " Blood *atone*ment " means: At-one-ment, or complete communion and conjunction with the Father—harmonious at-one-ment with Divine Truth (Blood). A new race on earth will shortly demonstrate eternal life; the lifting up of the whole man—spirit, soul, and body —into the Christ-consciousness of oneness (at-one-ment) with the Father. By means of this reconciliation (at-one-ment) that Christ established by the shedding of His blood and the imparting of its frequency to earth, mankind will regain the original estate as true " Sons of God." " Be ye therefore perfect, even as your Father which is in heaven is perfect " (Matthew v: 48).

" And, behold, the veil of the temple was rent in twain from the top to the bottom; and the earth did quake, and the rocks rent; And the graves were opened; and many bodies of the saints which slept arose " (Matthew xxvii: 51-52).

Remember, there were earthquakes before when the Plan was being fulfilled!—Earthquakes in Egypt on the night of the Final Exodus; quakes at Mount Sinai (Horeb) when Moses received the Tablets! Bodies had been thrown out of their ruined tombs and graves in Egypt as they were during the final hour on Golgotha! The " veil was rent in twain " in the Temple! By the graves being opened and the veil removed, it symbolized that mankind had received another look into the SECRET PLACES OF THE LION! In Egypt when such happenings took place, man was in the period of *Revelation*; now the same occurrences symbolized the apex of the *Fulfilment* period!

Man would now see beyond the veil of the " Mystery of Mysteries "; the new vibration which issued from the Christ assured this! When the veil was rent the Father proclaimed that the barrier between God and man had disappeared.

The centurion Manilus looked up into the blackness of heaven; as once again the Sun of Aton was blackened even as it was during the Exodus; and with a voice full of knowing, he shouted to the grief-stricken multitudes: " People of Jerusalem, I am Manilus the centurion, an officer of Imperial Rome. I have never believed in gods, yet this day I have seen the power of the Living God who is *One* [Aton]. I have awakened to a new understanding and shall ever more serve the Cause of He whom you have slain this day. Truly this man was the Son of God! "

As the crowds left Golgotha for Jerusalem, the storm became furious. Looking back at the Cross, they saw the body of Christ glowing in a brilliant violet-white light! The world was in total darkness, but Christ was now literally the " Light of the World." This was symbolic of the fact that the Divine Truth which He brought with Him on His mission to Earth became the" Light of the World " to a planet which was spiritually starved!

During the Final Exodus manna fell from " heaven " and Moses brought forth water from the rock. This was a forerunner of the Christ who symbolized the Bread and the Water of Life. If a man eat and drink of this he shall live for ever!

Moses had performed " miracles " with ancient instruments such as the vril rod, etc. Jesus performed " miracles " but He needed no instruments or paraphernalia! He used the power of MIND alone— mental power which all men possess and could use if they but followed the *Great Path* Jesus opened to mankind through the Fulfilment!

" And when Joseph had taken the body, he wrapped it in a clean linen cloth, And laid it in his own new tomb, which he had hewn out in the rock: and he rolled a great stone to the door of the sepulchre, and departed " (St. Matthew xxvii: 59–60).

The Holy Shroud or Mantle of Turin, the property of the House of Savoy (Italy's ex-sovereigns), is kept in the Cathedral of Turin, Italy. This is the actual " clean linen cloth " that Joseph used to wrap the body of Jesus! It is a piece of cloth about 3.7 feet in width and 14.4 feet in length. On its surface is visible what appears to be a large photographic negative of a man. When this design is photographed it is discovered that the negative is a positive of the design on the cloth. In other words, the new negative now has become a positive of the negative on the Shroud.

The chemical reactions of the spiced mixture on Christ's body and bodily excretion caused the impression of his body to be indelibly placed on the cloth. Joseph and Nicodemus, both members of the Sanhedrin, had anointed the body with a mixture of myrrh and aloes and folded it in a white linen cloth, according to the prevailing burial custom of the Hebrews.

This cloth or mantle belonged to Joseph, just as the tomb did. But the mantle was far older. It was a sacred possession which had belonged to Elijah, and was the mantle which he used when he smote the waters of the Jordan just before he was translated (II Kings ii: 8).

This mantle of *power* shows the true blood and portrait of Jesus, the Christ. The marks of His brow, scourge marks, pierced side, and His wrist and feet wounds are all plainly visible!

Later, Simon Peter and John entered the tomb of Jesus, and saw the cloth lying there. Peter picked up the mantle to preserve it as a sacred relic.

" . . . he [John] stooping down, and looking in, saw the linen clothes lying; yet went he not in. Then cometh Simon Peter following him [John], and went into the sepulchre, and seeth the linen clothes lie . . . " (John xx: 5–6).

Over and over again Jesus had plainly said He would be raised from the dead three days after the Crucifixion. Early in the morning Peter, who had been staying at the home of Mary of Jerusalem, took young Mark and went to the tomb of Joseph of Arimathea. The early morning had been windy, but suddenly it was calm—as still as death! The two came to the entrance of the tomb, where a gigantic stone blocked the entryway and two Roman soldiers stood guard.

Peter sensed something; he wasn't certain just what it was, but he felt that he was in the presence of tremendous power! Suddenly a tiny shaft of brilliant white light streamed down from above and penetrated the small window of the tomb just to the right of the blocked doorway.

" And, behold, there was [or had been] a great earthquake: for the angel of the Lord descended from heaven, and came and rolled back the stone from the door, and sat upon it. His countenance was like lightning, and his raiment white as snow . . . " (Matthew xxviii: 2–3). There had also been an earthquake as Jesus expired on the Cross, at the giving of the Two Tablets on Mount Sinai (Horeb), and during the Final Exodus from Egypt. An earthquake seems to be the Creator's way of calling attention to momentous events! The guards were startled and fell back in fear, for the ground shook. It was still quite dark and they did not see the tiny shaft of light which was plainly visible to Peter and Mark. But the soldiers felt something and saw the "star" above them. Their blood was chilled and they trembled because of the force which they could neither fully see nor understand.

The guards ran from the tomb, and later told the story that the stone was rolled away—but the stone was NEVER ROLLED AWAY! The guards and their superiors told such stories to protect themselves from ridicule and cruel punishment for having left their post of duty and for inventing such fantastic tales.

As Peter held Mark by the hand, both heard a high-pitched hum, and looked up to the sky to the area from which came the shaft of light; they saw a brilliant white twelve-pointed "star" slowly circling the tomb! But this was no ordinary star! The "star" that had heralded the birth of Jesus now returned to raise him from the *death* which is not eternal—raise Him to another dimension of existence!

The humming sound became louder and louder, then suddenly stopped. The great stone began to glow, faintly at first, but gradually it became bright until both witnesses could see through it as though it were finely polished crystal. The light inside of the sepulchre was a violet brilliance and appeared to pulsate slowly. The stone itself had been transformed into a gigantic *amethyst* of unbelievable beauty!

The "angel of the Lord descended from heaven" as the beam of pure white light (Matthew xxviii: 3), then the violet light "rolled back the stone" by changing its atomic structure and making it possible for Christ to walk through it! However, it was not actually rolled aside. Why would such a physical act be necessary to allow the Christ to pass out of the tomb? After all, He later demonstrated His ability to come and go at will. He could appear and disappear as He chose!

Then the violet light concentrated on the reclining figure wrapped in the linen shroud. After a few moments, this form rose from those coverings without even unwrapping them! The rising light took bodily form and Peter and Mark recognized their Master, Jesus, the

Christ. What a beautiful and blessed time was this Resurrection morning! As the two watched, Jesus walked through the now transparent, but solid, stone as easily as though it were composed of nothing but the misty morning air!

The Master Jesus put His arm around Peter and kissed the forehead of young Mark. At that moment, memory returned to the two and Peter remembered that he had once been the good Akhnaton; Mark recalled his short life and reign as Tutankhamun. The former relationship of half-brothers (Akhnaton-Tutankhamun) was now one of friendship (Peter-Mark). Mark looked to Peter as his father since his own father was not in life. Indeed, Peter often called the young Evangelist " Mark, my son."

Peter knew that his denials uttered during a time of fear were now forgiven him, and the two witnesses to this first Easter Morn knew that the Plan they had served and laboured for so long ago in Egypt was now *fulfilled* in the happening of this day! Akhnaton and Tutankhamun had prepared the way for a Pharaoh Sananda who never appeared because it was not yet time. Now Sananda had lived his life as the humble Jesus, and had risen from the dead to prove to all men everywhere that LIFE IS ETERNAL!

Jesus left a " sign " on the forehead of the youthful Mark, and told him that since he was now marked for life because of his thumb severed by a Roman sword in the garden of his mother, he would also bear the print of the Golden Sun Disc (Aton) on his forehead for eternity. Jesus told Mark that some day he should tell this to a man who did not yet know Him, but who would come to serve the Cause after he was struck by a blinding light (Saul of Tarsus).

The dark of early morning was now vanishing quickly, and Jesus stepped back from Peter and Mark; the violet light appeared around Him once again, and a great golden crown seemed to encompass His magnificent head, the beam of white light dropped down from above, and the Master Jesus began to rise into the air on the brilliant beam until He had vanished from sight. The last words heard by the man and youth were: " Take ye the Message to all the world; I am the Resurrection and the Life! "

Peter went directly to the home of the " Sons of Thunder "—the sons of Zebedee, James and John. There he relayed what he had witnessed. In the meantime, Mark hid near the tomb.

Shortly after Peter left the sepulchre, Pilate himself and other Roman officials visited the tomb. They did not believe the story told by the soldiers. What did the guards mean by their feeling of fright and the sense of fantastic power? The stone was not rolled away. How could this dead Jesus have left the tomb? In order to make sure all was in order, Pilate ordered the stone rolled away, and discovered an *empty* chamber—the SECRET PLACE OF THE LION had given up its most treasured secret of Truth!

How could the body be gone with the tomb still sealed? Pilate asked his now famous question: " What is Truth? " He told the soldiers to forget the entire matter, and the other officials claimed, when questioned later, that fanatical followers of the Nazarene came in the night and overpowered the guards, then rolled away the stone in order to steal the body of their Christ! (Matthew xxviii: 13.) Pilate knew better, but reported the same false tale to the Emperor Tiberius Caesar in Rome.

The soldiers rolled the stone away; Pilate said: " Now let us be gone before we are found here by this empty chamber of death that has suddenly become a strange symbol of life . . . for where is he who was dead! "

Now, after Peter had left the tomb to go to the home of James and John, young Mark hid himself near by and watched the actions of Pilate and the officials. Then Mary Magdalene came and found the tomb empty. After she left he entered the tomb. The women now approached the tomb: " And they said among themselves, who shall roll us away the stone from the door of the sepulchre? And when they looked, they saw that the stone was rolled away: for it was very great. And entering into the sepulchre, they saw a young man sitting on the right side, clothed in a long white garment; and they were affrighted " (Mark xvi: 3–5).

In some places in the Bible it mentions the one young man sitting on the right side, and in other places it mentions two angels in white sitting, one at the head, and one at the feet, where the body of Jesus had lain (John xx: 12).

When the women entered the dimly lit sepulchre, their eyes being unaccustomed to the change in light, they mistook Mark for an " angel." They did not recognize him. Besides, the Bible says: " . . . they saw a young man sitting on the *right* side. . . . " This was the area of the tomb window, and light was now pouring in this window. Mark was sitting directly in its path, which made him appear to be an " Angel of Light." Therefore, because of the change of light and the sudden appearance of the young man in white, they were startled. Mark's white garments reflected the light and, besides, a certain vibration was still perceptible in the tomb, and this made the entire scene appear somewhat hazy to the women. They felt *power* and fled from the tomb to tell the other Disciples! They did not flee as the guards had who were dazed and frightened, but they were wild with excitement, full of anxiety and wonder—they were bewildered, yet happy.

The order of events of the Resurrection Morning are:

1. Peter and Mark approach the tomb.

2. A white light from the " star " above enters the window on the right side of the tomb.

3. The two guards flee from the tomb in fright.

4. Jesus is raised from the dead and speaks to Peter and Mark.

5. Jesus ascends to the hovering craft.

6. Peter goes to the home of James and John.

7. Mark hides near by the now empty tomb.

8. Pilate, Roman officials, and the two soldiers come to the tomb and roll away the stone to check the remains of Jesus.

9. Pilate knows others are approaching the tomb, so he commands all to leave the area.

10. Mary Magdalene was ahead of the group of women, and when she saw the tomb empty ran to the house of James and John, where she also found Peter (John xx: 2). She saw no " angels " at the tomb, because Mark hadn't entered it yet.

11. Mark leaves hiding-place and goes in tomb.

12. The other women draw near and hear the " angel," who was really young Mark: " Be not affrighted: Ye seek Jesus of Nazareth, which was crucified: he is risen; he is not here: behold the place where they laid him " (Mark xvi: 6).

13. The women leave to tell the other Disciples. Then Mark leaves the tomb and goes to his mother's home.

14. John arrives at the tomb first (John xx: 4) because he had not yet seen the evidence of Jesus' Resurrection. Peter followed him, not running, because he had been there earlier in the morning with young Mark.

15. John saw the linen shroud in the tomb but did not enter, and

Peter, coming behind him, entered the tomb and also saw the shroud (John xx: 5–6).

16. John followed Peter into the tomb: " Then went in also that other disciple [John], which came first to the sepulchre, and he saw, and believed " (John xx: 8).

17. Mary Magdalene, following hard after Peter and John, returned to the tomb, and remained after they left. She was alone and weeping.

18. Mary Magdalene looked into the tomb and saw two "angels"; then Jesus himself appeared to her. The two " messengers " in the tomb were Gabriel and another occupant of the " Star Ship " who had returned to the tomb with Jesus from the ship that had hovered over the area earlier in the morning when Jesus was raised from the dead.

19. Jesus told Mary Magdalene: " . . . Touch me not; for I am not yet ascended to my Father . . . " (John xx: 17). Jesus did not want Mary to touch Him, for if she had she would have changed His frequency. Since His Resurrection had been accomplished by a beam from the craft completely changing His atomic structure (and that of the great stone), a change in vibrational frequency would have resulted in disintegration of His form. He had touched Peter and Mark earlier when He first emerged from the tomb. However, a female-negative polarity at that moment, since He was out of the violet beam, could not have been stood. Later other women touched Him (Matthew xxviii: 9), and no harm was done.

20. Mary Magdalene leaves the tomb to speak with the other Disciples (John xx: 18).

" An angel," sitting upon the stone (Matthew); " A young man," sitting in the tomb (Mark); " Two men " stood by them (Luke); " Two angels," sitting in the tomb (John); these different and apparently contradictory expressions simply mean that part of the time two " angels " were visible, and part of the time only one was visible. At least, that is what modern theologians tell us. But why were two visible, and then only one?

When *one* is mentioned, it refers to Mark in the tomb. Indeed, Mark himself speaks of the " young man " sitting in the tomb; he should have known since he was the one who did the sitting!

When *two* " men " or " angels " are mentioned it refers to Gabriel, who had been present when Jesus was ushered into the world, and now escorted Him out of the same world; and to another " messenger " of the " Star Ship."

Fundamentalists believe that " myriads of angels hovered over the tomb that morning." This is true, in a sense—" angels " did hover over the tomb. But what *was* and *is* the nature of so-called " angels "? Remember, it is the same " angels " who will have charge of the general Resurrection (Matthew xxiv: 31).

After the Resurrection and Ascension the Disciples gathered together and were taught by Mary, mother of Jesus, concerning the deeper meanings of what the Christ had meant when He said: " Ye must be born again! " She explained to them how the Resurrection of Jesus was symbolic of the Greatest Truth! This Truth is that *all* men live time and time again so that spirit will come to know itself and that all might teach perfection as they continue up the worlds in ever-expanding grandeur!

Yes, the Resurrection symbolized the Greatest Truth ever revealed to man—the entire purpose of *Fulfilment*. One of the words translated *resurrection* in the Bible is the same as that of the name of the Rose of Jericho. This strange plant, when it dries up, either because of drought or for some other reason, pulls up its roots, rolls down its stem, rolls away as a ball, and then puts it roots down again in some other new place, to again lift itself upright to new life! The other Scriptural word translated resurrection means: " always rising again."

Mary told the Disciples that all men were like the Rose of Jericho. When they die (dry up) for any reason, they leave the earth (pull up their roots) and eventually return (put their roots down again) to life again on the earth (lift themselves upright to new life). This, of course, means nothing more than REINCARNATION!

Jesus taught the Doctrine of Reincarnation, but it was removed later by a theological group that wanted to keep man in ignorance of this great Truth! This will be dealt with in detail in the sequel to this book, entitled, *Another Mountain*.

Man *always rises again*! No matter what his failures, no matter what the efforts of the past or the desires and goals not yet attained, he will attain his godhood once again as he *rises* with the Christ above the limitations of Time and Space! Man shall live and die unto eternity until he becomes ONE awith ALL PERFECTION! Great Truth exists in the SECRET PLACES OF THE LION—yet the Truth of

Eternal Life is the greatest; Christ proved it by demonstrating it to the world. Resurrection is the continuation of life as we progress ever upward and forward. Man's mind shall be raised from sense to spiritual consciousness. The Resurrection of Jesus was a forerunner of the Resurrection that will come to all men. Jesus abolished so-called " death " by bringing life and immortality to light.

" For since by man came death, by man came also the resurrection of the dead " (I Corinthians xv: 21).

The Resurrection is the lifting up of the whole man into the Christ-consciousness. And the whole man is: spirit; soul; body. All the faculties of mind are lifted up until they conform to the absolute ideas of Divine Mind. A Resurrection shall take place here and now in all who conform their lives to the Spiritual Law under which it works.

Jesus had said: " And I, if I be lifted up from the earth, will draw all men unto me. This he said, signifying what death he should die " (John xii: 32–33).

He was indeed *lifted up* by the force field which translated him, even as Moses and Elijah had been translated to other dimensions of Time and Space. Yet Jesus could still lower that vibration and be visible to his Disciples. " . . . All power is given unto me in heaven and in earth " (Matthew xxviii: 18).

" . . . lo, I am with you alway, even unto the end of the world . . . " (Matthew xxviii: 20). During the forty days between the Resurrection and Ascension of Jesus, He appeared to the Disciples, singly or in groups, ten or eleven recorded times. This was to banish from their minds any doubt as to his continued existence as a *living man*! (Acts i:3.)

" But ye shall receive power, after that the Holy Ghost is come upon you: and ye shall be witnesses unto me both in Jerusalem, and in all Judea, and in Samaria, and unto the uttermost part of the earth. And when he had spoken these things, while they beheld, he was taken up; and a cloud received him out of their sight. And while they looked steadfastly toward heaven as he went up, behold, two men stood by them in white apparel " (Acts i: 8–10).

Jesus told the Disciples that they would teach the *Fulfilled Word* all over the earth. Then he was taken up on the white beam and was received into the " Star Ship " which hid itself in a " cloud " of its own manufacture. This is very similar to so-called " saucers " of today which have been observed producing artificial clouds to make themselves inconspicuous.

They saw the two " angels " again from the ship who were Gabriel and his assistant. These two had also been seen by the women at the empty tomb. They spoke to the assembled group of Disciples:

"... Ye men of Galilee, why stand ye gazing up into heaven? this same Jesus, which is taken up from you into heaven, shall so come in like manner as ye have seen him go into heaven " (Acts i: 11).

Jesus shall " *come in like manner* "!

The Disciples then returned to Jerusalem from the Mount of Olives (Olivet). The mount was east of Jerusalem and was where Ezekiel had seen " the cherubim lift up their wings, and the wheels beside them."

" And the glory of the Lord went up from the midst of the city, and stood upon the mountain (Olivet) which is on the east side of the city [Jerusalem] " (Ezekiel xi: 23).

Space craft appeared again on the Mount of Olives to remove Jesus from the world; but they were to bring Him back again in like manner. The Ascension of the Christ symbolized the eventual elevation of all men on earth to Divine Truth and Good.

When the Disciples arrived back in Jerusalem, they went to the Upper Room in the home of Mary, mother of Mark (Acts i: 12–13). This was the same room where the Last Supper had taken place, and they continued in prayer in this room until the day of Pentecost, A.D. 30 (fifty days after the Crucifixion). During this time St. Matthias and Joseph (Barsabas) were appointed as possible successors to the twelfth Apostleship left vacant by Judas Iscariot. Both men had been Aton priests at Akhetaton. Matthias secured the twelfth position finally through election (Acts i: 23–26).

It was during the ten days after the Ascension of Jesus that his mother, Mary, taught the Disciples concerning the meaning of *resurrection*, or living again and again (reincarnation) (Acts i: 14). She told them that man never returns to life as a plant or animal (transmigration, metempsychosis), but always remains a man or a woman.

The Resurrection of Jesus became the one unceasing and unvarying focal point of the teaching of the Apostles and Disciples.

Paul (Saul) was a Jew born in Tarsus, a city in Cilicia. On the road to Damascus " suddenly there shone from heaven a great light round about " him (Acts xxii: 6). The light was seen by those with him but they did not hear the voice of Jesus which spoke to Paul (Acts xxii: 9). The light actually temporarily blinded Paul (Acts xxii: 11), who had lived before as Pharaoh Meneptah, son of Ramses II. It will be remembered that Meneptah was blinded and burned by a brilliant light on the road also!

The Apostle named Joseph was a Jewish man of Cyprus, of the tribe of Levi, and they called him Barnabas, which means " son of exhortation." This Barnabas had been Moses, then lived as Joseph, father of Jesus, the Christ. When Jesus was twelve years of age, his father Joseph took him up to Jerusalem. He (Joseph) lived a short time after this, and when he passed away he immediately reincarnated as another *Joseph*, later called Barnabas!

Barnabas persuaded the Jerusalem Disciples to receive Paul. He was sent to receive the Gentile Church at Antioch. He went to Tarsus to get Paul and set him to work. He accompanied Paul on his First Missionary Journey. Barnabas was a good companion for Paul, who represents the Word of the Spirit of Truth. He believed in Paul and convinced the Apostles at Jerusalem that Paul's change of heart was sincere.

The Church at Jerusalem heard that the Greeks were turning to the teachings of Jesus and it sent Barnabas to Antioch to investigate. Antioch was the Third City of the Roman Empire, surpassed only by Rome and Alexandria. It contained over half a million people and was the doorway from the Mediterranean to the great Eastern highways. It was known as Antioch " The Beautiful," and " Queen of the East." Multitudes in this city accepted the teachings of Jesus, and the city became the birthplace of the name " Christian " (Acts xi: 26). It was the centre of an organized effort to Christianize the entire world!

It had been revealed to Paul in Damascus at the time of his conversion that he was to carry the Gospel to the Gentiles. Every step in his experience from that time on was in preparation for his missionary work. These experiences reached a climax in Antioch, which city became a " springboard " for the Word to the outer reaches of the world.

Paul and Barnabas had intense missionary zeal and made great plans for the spreading of the *Word*. They went to Jerusalem and, while there, Peter was imprisoned; James, brother of John was murdered; and Herod died (A.D. 44).

While visiting in Jerusalem, Paul and Barnabas stayed at the home of Mary, mother of John Mark. Barnabas was an uncle of John Mark. Mark was " son to sister of Barnabas "—Barnabas' nephew. The former relationship of Tutankhamun in the House of Maya was now reversed to Barnabas (Maya) in the House of Mark (Tutankhamun)! What Maya had done for the young Pharaoh, the young Evangelist was now doing for his uncle!

Paul, who had been Pharaoh Meneptah, now worked with Barnabas, who had been Moses, and Mark, who had been Aaron; and Philip, who had been Ramses II, father of Meneptah, was numbered among the Twelve.

Paul and Barnabas returned to Antioch and took John Mark, who was now twenty-six, with them (Acts xii: 25).

It is believed by some theologians that Peter took the *Cup* of the *Last Supper* with him when he fled to Antioch in A.D. 36. However, he did not take it, but did take the Holy Shroud or Mantle that he had picked up in the empty tomb after the Resurrection of Jesus!

John Mark had the Cup in his possession since it belonged in his mother's home and had been picked up by him after the Last Supper in the Upper Room. He now took it with him as he journeyed to Antioch with Paul and Barnabas! It was left in Antioch for several years as a treasured possession of the workers there.

As Barnabas, Paul, and Mark went forth from Antioch, they were as definitely under the guidance of " angels " and " messengers " as were the Children of Israel when they followed the " cloud." They went first to Cyprus, an island of the Mediterranean Sea seventy miles off the coast of Syria. It was not their main objective, but it was important as the first lap of their missionary journey. Cyprus was the home of Barnabas, and Jewish Christians from there had been the first to preach the Word in Antioch. Therefore it is not strange that the three, led by Barnabas, decided to enter Asia Minor by way of Cyprus.

During the first months of their missionary experiences, the three travelled and laboured together in ideal fellowship. They were all sincere workers for the Plan and were full of faith in the ultimate triumph of the Christ throughout the earth.

"Now when Paul and his company loosed from Paphos, they came to Perga in Pamphylia: and John [Mark] departing from them returned to Jerusalem" (Acts xiii: 13).

Paphos was on the western shore of Cyprus. From there to Perga on the southern shore of Asia Minor it was a hundred water miles by direct line. Mark had not forced himself upon the missionary party but was welcomed as a fellow worker in the Lord. Paul did not want to give up Mark, for the young man had served the two older men. He looked after the supplying of their daily needs while they preached and taught the people. He was also the recorder of the journey and wrote the account of all that happened. Like Paul, he wanted to serve the Gentiles and carry the message to the entire world.

John Mark had two natures: one a polite and brilliant exterior; the other a deep spiritual nature, which was called out and developed by the confidence that his uncle Barnabas placed in him.

John means: grace and mercy of the Lord, and God's gift.

Mark means: brilliant, shining, polite.

The Bible never states *why* John Mark left Barnabas and Paul at Perga. Some religionists say that Mark was nothing but a deserter who was timid, full of fear, and possibly was not yet sold on Gentile evangelization.

It was not a timid Mark who warded off the blow of the sword in the garden, thereby losing a thumb. It was not a fearful Mark who stayed with Jesus in the garden after all the others had fled. And he was so sold on Gentile conversion that he never used the name John again. He preferred his Roman name of Marcus, the "Marked One." Jesus Himself had called him "The Marked," and he never used his original name again.

Why did Mark make such a decision at Perga in Pamphylia? In the night Mark had heard a *voice* speak to him, and he knew it was the Master Jesus. He was told that a greater work awaited him in Jerusalem and Rome. "Mark, my evangelist, go to thy mother Mary and prepare thyself for the work with Simon Peter who needs thee."

Peter favoured the Jews, and at first did not want to allow Gentiles into the Church, Mark would be needed by Peter to help him. Mark was well educated and as Peter's personal recorder and secretary could assist the great Apostle in his ministry. Mark translated Peter's writings into Greek and Latin so that the Gentiles might receive the Word.

Mark had felt that on this First Missionary Journey to be organized for giving the Word to the Gentiles, he was serving the best purpose, for he knew his duty was amongst the non-Jewish world. Yet, the *voice* told him that the greater work would be done by him through Peter. Mark went to Paul and said:

" The Damascus road was a place of decision for you, Saul of Tarsus. It meant a complete change in your life, and led you to your present ministry to the Gentiles. Now, Perga in Pamphylia is a place of decision for me. I cannot go on with you; I must return at once to Jerusalem."

These words wounded Paul deeply, for he did not understand. This wound had not healed when the time came later for the Second Missionary Journey. Mark later wanted to go with Paul, but Paul would not allow it. Therefore Barnabas separated from Paul on account of Mark. The separation was not in anger—but was sharp. However, later they worked together again.

Barnabas then took Mark and went to Cyprus, and Paul took Silas and went to Syria. This Silas had lived as Nathan, the prophet, under David, and later as an Aton priest under Akhnaton.

Mark had been an observer on the journey with Barnabas and Paul, and, after leaving Paphos, with several days on the ship for quiet meditation, Mark was pondering his *real duty* when the *voice* of Jesus spoke to him. By the time the ship anchored in the harbour at Perga his mind was made up.

He was young, mentally alert, and spiritually discerning. Yet the youth of Mark's day were taught to respect their elders, and Mark hesitated to express his convictions to the older men of recognized wisdom and spiritual power. Modesty was one of Mark's outstanding characteristics, and his spiritual struggles were his very own. Mark knew that the fellowship with Barnabas and Paul had been important, yet he felt that there was something lacking in their ministry, for he knew that he had a contribution to make to the *Work* amongst the Gentiles of which Barnabas and Paul were not deeply conscious, and which they were not prepared to make. Mark felt that the need could be met by his return to Jerusalem. Besides, the *voice* of his beloved Teacher had told him this was so!

Mark did not realize the full import of what the Master Jesus had in store for him. Details of his work would be given to him as he proceeded. However, since Mark gave practically no explanation of why he was leaving the group, Paul was shocked by the sudden decision. Mark said to him:

" Beloved brother Paul, I have been led of the Spirit to return to my home in Jerusalem. The same Lord who guides thee guides me also, and I must do that which he asks. Years ago Peter and I witnessed His resurrection. Since you saw Him in the blinding light you know of what I speak. That blessed morning He told me, since I was marked for life by the Roman sword that sought His life, I would also bear the mark of the Golden Sun Disc [Aton] on my forehead for eternity. He told me to tell this some day to a man who knew Him not then, but would come to serve the Cause after he was struck by a blinding light. And that man is you, Paul. I feel that this is the time I must tell you this. This sign I carry must carry me into another service and to other lands. You, my dear companion Paul, have a great mission to the Father's children, yet that mission is not my mission. We shall work together again, but my mission is of another nature. Jesus needs us all, and we must follow where He leads."

The three separated; Mark returned to Jerusalem and Paul and Barnabas went on into Asia Minor.

In A.D. 1910 there was found, in the ruins of an ancient cathedral on the site of Antioch, a chalice containing an inner cup that was thought by some scholars to be the actual cup that Jesus used on the night of the Last Supper! The Chalice of Antioch had been connected with the Cup that Jesus used, but the inner cup discovered with it was not the original!

Remember that Mark had picked up the Cup from where Jesus sat at the long table in the Upper Room. It was Mark's home and the Cup belonged to his mother, Mary. When the Thirteen were served that night, all the Twelve were served liquid in silver cups. However, Jesus had asked young Mark to bring him a plain, clay cup! The clay cup brought by Mark was identical in size and shape to the silver ones, but was used about the home as second-best table equipment. Mary, the mother of Mark, was a wealthy widow, and would naturally have silver vessels for her guests to eat and drink out of!

Jesus wanted a cup which was made of the clay of earth! The symbolism of his desire is obvious! The Cup (made of earth) symbolized the Body of the Christ, and the wine symbolized Jesus' blood that would be shed on the Cross. The Cup also represented the earth that would receive the blood of Christ. The wine inside the Cup again symbolized the blood. The *Cup* represents spiritual truth or truth of faith.

Mark had seen the Cup glow in the dimly lit Upper Room. He took it with him to his own room and put it away for safe keeping. For fourteen years after the Crucifixion he kept it, although it was shown periodically to many of the Disciples as they gathered in the Upper Room of Mark's home.

Mark had taken the Cup with him when he went to Antioch with Barnabas and Paul. There he left it with members of the Church of Antioch (founded A.D. 42).

As leader of the Twelve, Peter visited all the leading church centres of the Roman world. In A.D. 50 he had been in Antioch to visit the Church there. Earlier in A.D. 36 he had taken the Holy Shroud or Mantle there and left it with the brethren. Peter now wished to return the Cup to Jerusalem, for the brethren were anxious to have it in their possession once again. The *Cup*, and not the *Cross* was the greatest symbol of Christendom!

Peter had with him in A.D. 50, in Antioch, the silver cup he had used himself at the Last Supper! This he gave to Linus, the Greek artist who fashioned the magnificent chalice that held the humble clay cup! Linus had just completed the chalice and it rested in a secret chamber of the Antioch church. Linus took Peter to the chamber and they replaced the original Cup of Jesus with Peter's silver cup which was the same size and shape. Of course, it fitted perfectly!

Peter then returned with the clay cup to Jerusalem, where later in the same year of A.D. 50 the Council of Jerusalem was held. Although God had expressly revealed to Peter that Gentiles should be received into the Church without circumcision, and the Apostles and elders were convinced, yet a powerful sect of Pharisee disciples persisted in teaching that it was necessary.

The Antioch brethren had begun an aggressive campaign to Christianize Gentiles without requiring circumcision. The Church was rent with discord over the question. However, the Apostles at this council gave unanimous and formal expression to the judgment that the old ritual was not necessary for Gentiles.

Peter had felt that the brethren in Jerusalem were becoming uneasy over the situation at Antioch, and knew that they wanted the Cup back in Jerusalem and not in the hands of the Gentile converts. Therefore he switched the cups, and the original once again found its way to Jerusalem.

Twenty years after the Crucifixion of Jesus, the Greek artist who was Linus made the silver chalice for the Cup of the Last Supper. This Linus had been Solomon of the lions and the lion-throne; also he had lived as Rahotep of the lion-throne and the Golden Mask. Linus means " lionlike."

The relationship of Pharaoh-young artist (Akhnaton-Rahotep) was now one of Apostle-great artist (Peter-Linus). Only the scene had changed from Thebes to Antioch.

This same Linus later is a friend of Paul in Rome and sent a salutation to Timothy (II Timothy iv: 21). Timothy himself had lived as Pharaoh Smenkhkare during the eighteenth Dynasty of Egypt! And Meriten, sister of Tutankhamun and Smenkhkare, returned as Lois, grandmother of Timothy! (II Timothy i: 5.)

Linus became a Christian after being commissioned by the Church to make a receptacle that would hold the clay cup. The chalice was to be of pure silver, and Linus was to place designs of grape vines, bunches of grapes and birds on its surface along with the figures of Jesus and His Apostles. Jesus' right hand was to touch a plate with five loaves and two fishes. Just beyond the plate, a dove; by his side a lamb, and vines—all Christian symbolism. However, only ten of the Apostles were finally placed on the chalice. This was because Linus did not get to personally see all of them so that he might copy their features. But what of Jesus? Linus had never seen the Master! It was while he concentrated on what Christ must have looked like that he had a *vision* where Jesus appeared to him. Linus, greatly impressed, became a Christian, and finished the chalice shortly before Peter arrived in Antioch in A.D. 50.

The cup of Peter which was placed in the chalice after the clay cup was removed was a much-used object, and was poorly made and crudely executed. The silver shell or chalice made by Linus, however, was magnificent. Silver artisans today claim that it is the work of a great silversmith of the first-century Grecian School!

Linus succeeded in capturing the face of the Christ to show the gentleness, power, and magnificence of Him in such a way that it has never been equalled in Christian art. The heads of the Apostles were equally well done. The character, the very souls of the great men were portrayed in the metal.

Paul was shown as a man with a lean, thin face. His head was bald and he wore a long Van Dyck beard. His eyes were large and somewhat hypnotic.

Peter was portrayed as a young man with a full round face. His hair was very heavy and curly and he wore a close-clipped beard.

Jesus was shown on the chalice as a handsome man with His hair worn short in Roman style! The face shows no beard! The eyes are kind and gentle beyond belief!

On the shores of the Sea of Galilee a few years ago scientists discovered a life-sized statue of marble. The inscription on its base reads: " I, Mary Magdalene, had this statue made of Jesus, the Christ, who did so much for me, in order that the world might know how he looked." This statue conforms in every way to the Jesus represented on the Chalice of Antioch!

Of course, Jesus wore His hair long and had a beard at the time of the Crucifixion, but most of His life He was clean shaven!

The Cup remained in Jerusalem until A.D. 63. During this year Joseph of Arimathea, although a member of the Sanhedrin, was marked for assassination because he was too prominent a follower of the Christ. He was a wealthy shipowner and traded with Britain in tin. To save his life so that he might carry on the work, he sailed for Britain in one of his own vessels. Twelve companions went with him. At that time he took with him the clay cup— but *not* the Chalice of Antioch. The latter still remained in the city where Linus had made it and still contained Peter's silver cup!

Joseph had gained his great wealth in the tin trade. Almost the only deposits of tin and lead known to the ancient world came from the Mendip Hills just north of Glastonbury, and many ancient writers show that this trade was widespread. A song is still current among Cornish miners that says: " Joseph was a tinman."

Jesus had gone to Britain in his youth with Joseph, and Joseph returned to the spot where the Christ had lived while there! He also took with him the Spear which had pierced Jesus' side at the

Crucifixion! Philip had had the Spear in his possession but told Joseph to take it with the Cup to Glastonbury! Joseph kept both sacred objects in a secret chamber and it was later hidden in a crypt beneath the Abbey.

Recently an object was found that has been called the " Glastonbury Chalice." This is the chalice that was made for the clay cup in Britain, just as Linus had made one to hold it at Antioch!

Joseph died at Glastonbury and was buried there. His tomb has been found, but the knowledge of such a great discovery has been suppressed!

The Cup later disappeared from the Abbey as it was translated into another dimension of Time and Space. It shall make its appearance on earth again in the years ahead!

Therefore the Chalice of Antioch is authentic in that it once held the Cup of Jesus, but it no longer holds that Cup any more than the Glastonbury Chalice holds it!

The events that took place later in Rome are too numerous and cannot be added to this manuscript, but will appear in the forthcoming book, *Mantle of Gold.*

However, Mark did finally go to Rome to work with Peter as Peter's recorder and secretary. The ancient Pharaohs and others who comprised the " Goodly Company " were now in life as humble men. First they had incarnated as rulers and leaders, but at the time of Jesus the situation was reversed! They had been persecuted as Pharaohs, and they were still persecuted.

What difference if a man wears a crown or a ragged cloak if he is destroyed for teaching the Word of the Infinite Father? Indeed, he may serve the Infinite One in a greater way as a pauper than as a prince! The Workers in the Plan did not reincarnate as Roman emperors. The rulers at that time were earth souls who were allowed to rule the people, since the Plan had not succeeded at Akhetaton, and the world was given over to the negative forces for a time so that they might eventually seek the Greater Light again!

While Mark was in Rome, he wrote his Gospel at the request of Roman Christians who desired a written memorial of the Word. His Gospel was the first of the four to be written!

In his *Hypotyposes*, Clement of Alexandria (A.D. 190) says: " After Peter had announced the Word of God in Rome and preached the

Gospel in the Spirit of God, the multitude of hearers requested Mark, who had long accompanied Peter on all his journeys, to write down what the Apostles had preached to them."

Peter, while working with Mark in Rome, wrote his First Epistle.

" The Church that is at Babylon [Rome], elected together with you, saluteth you; and so doth Marcus, my son " (I Peter v: 13).

" Babylon " here has to be the Roman capital, since Babylon on the Euphrates was in ruins; New Babylon (Seleucia) on the Tigris cannot be meant; and the Egyptian Babylon near Memphis, or Jerusalem, do not fit the designation. Besides Rome is called " Babylon " in very ancient Christian literature and documents. In Revelation, Chapter xvii, Rome is called " Babylon." In those times the Workers had to be careful how they spoke of the ruling power and had a name for it that they, among themselves, but not an outsider, would understand.

Mark founded the Church of Alexandria (Coptic). Some theologians believe this took place A.D. 41-44, during the reign of Claudius. This is according to the Chronicle of Eusebius. However, this could not be true since Mark was with Barnabas and Paul in A.D. 44 as they journeyed to Antioch.

The New Testament is silent in regard to Mark's activity during A.D. 50 to 60. This was the period that he was in Egypt and also in Rome.

Mark had been appointed Bishop of Alexandria by Peter, and, while there, went to the Great Pyramid area and the Sphinx many times. Here was Tutankhamun of another lifetime searching for the records he himself had helped write. Here also was Simmias of another lifetime looking for the documents he had not succeeded in locating while in the school of Philolaus (Phylos) at Thebes.

Mark penetrated the SECRET PLACES OF THE LION under the Sphinx in the Temple there and obtained access to the secret inner chambers of the Great Pyramid. Certain tablets and records were removed by him at that time and taken to the Church of Alexandria. Why did he take these records? Because the knowledge they contained was to be revealed to the brethren at Alexandria—those who were *in* the Light and serving that Light! The time had come for this information to be made known.

Amunism was still waging a " holy war " against all those serving

Aton (One God). The evil priests knew Mark had somehow discovered some of the ancient tablets. In no way could they get him to tell the secret. Therefore, while meditating one day, he was dragged from the church and through the streets of Alexandria. That night he was thrown in prison, where the Christ appeared to him and comforted him. The next day the procedure of the preceding day was continued, and the Evangelist passed on to be with his Master.

Anianus was his successor and knew the secrets of the records, but he did not know where they had come from! These tablets were buried with Mark in a hidden crypt near the church.

Mark did not die in A.D. 62–63, as St. Jerome claims. He could not have died then if he was alive when II Timothy iv: 11 was written. He was with Paul when that Apostle was martyred in A.D. 67. Therefore he couldn't possibly have died in A.D. 62 or 63. Mark was dragged through the streets of Alexandria, Egypt, by the Amun priests on the pagan feast of the idol Serapis. This was on April 24, A.D. 70. He died the next day on April 25.

Peter and Paul were martyred on the same day during the Neroian persecution, on June 29, A.D. 67. Paul was beheaded outside the walls of Rome on the Ostian Way. Paul actually had been in Spain (Romans xv: 24, 28). But he did not remain there long, and returned to Rome to work with the brethren there. The old differences between Mark and Paul were now gone, for Paul understood why the young Evangelist had to leave him at Perga. The two loved each other as brothers as they now served the Lord Jesus together.

Paul had been initiated into the ancient mysteries, for in I Corinthians iii: 10 he calls himself a " master builder " or adept.

Paul wrote his Second Epistle to Timothy from Rome:
" For I am now ready to be offered, and the time of my departure is at hand. I have fought a good fight, I have finished my course, I have kept the faith " (II Timothy iv: 6–7).

Paul begged Timothy to rejoin him as quickly as possible. He was alone with Luke since Peter was concerned at that time with the Emperor Nero, and Mark was off on an evangelistic mission which took him temporarily from Rome.

" Only Luke is with me. Take Mark, and bring him with thee: for he is profitable to me for the ministry " (II Timothy iv: 11). The beloved physician Luke had been the physician Sinuhe at Akhetaton. Later he was Jeremiah the Prophet.

Timothy located Mark, and informed him of Paul's message from Rome. He knew that it looked very bad for both Peter and Paul, since Nero was now conducting daily blood-baths for his amusement. Two men as outspoken as Peter and Paul could not hope to live long under such circumstances.

Timothy and Mark arrived in Rome several days before the death of Peter and Paul.

We have already spoken of the four Egyptian Gods of the Dead: Dog (Jackal), Ape, Man, and Eagle. These correspond to the symbols of the Four Evangelists: Matthew, Mark, Luke, and John.

> Matthew................Man (Angel)
> Mark...................Lion
> Luke...................Bull (Calf, Ox)
> John...................Eagle

These four figures are common to almost all periods of art. They are found in Egypt and Assyria and Israel. Ezekiel spoke of them and so did John while on Patmos. These four creatures, through the Four Evangelists, represent Jesus under four aspects.

Matthew is represented as a Winged Man or Angel because he commences his Gospel with the human generation of the Christ, and because in his writings the human nature of Jesus is stressed more than the divine nature.

Mark is symbolized by a Lion, as he dwells on the Resurrection or rising again of Jesus and because in his Gospel he sets forth the royal dignity of Jesus and His power manifested in His Resurrection from the dead. He opens his Gospel with the mission of John the Baptist. "The voice of one crying in the wilderness" is appropriately figured by the Lion, whose roaring voice is heard in wilds and deserts.

Luke is represented as the Bull (Calf, Ox) because in his Gospel he particularly dwells on the Priesthood of Jesus, and His sacrifice.

John is known as the Eagle because, as the eagle soars on its powerful wings high towards heaven, John soared in the "spirit" upwards to the heaven of heavens to contemplate the divine nature of the Christ and to bring back to earth revelations of sublime mysteries.

The Four further represent these aspects of Jesus:

Matthew . . . . INCARNATION
Mark . . . . RESURRECTION
Luke . . . . PASSION (CRUCIFIXION)
John . . . . ASCENSION

Peter knew that he had served his purpose for another lifetime and was taken before Nero since he was the leader of the Apostles. He was crucified head downwards in the Neroian Gardens on the Vatican. When he was condemned to crucifixion by Nero, he said: " I am not fit to die as my Lord died! Grant me this last desire, Nero . . . place me head downwards on the cross "!

While he suffered his last moments on that cross, Mark and Linus approached the great Apostle. He whispered to them: " Marcus, my son . . . return to Alexandria; the brethren have need of thee! . . .

" Linus, beloved disciple, you shall take my place in Rome . . . draw the Lord's people together in the Faith! . . .

" Saul of Tarsus shall be with me this night when we join our blessed Jesus! "

A centurion had lit the faggots under the cross on which Peter hung; the flames leaped up furiously, and Mark and Linus fell back. Then they both perceived a glowing body of light next to the burning body of Peter. This was the spiritual body of Paul who had left the scene of his own martyrdom to be with Peter!

Here was Mark watching the final moments of Simon Peter. This same relationship had existed before for these two entities. First, at Akhetaton, then in a prison, and now in Nero's garden! Mark, as Tutankhamun, watched Akhnaton, who was now Peter, die. Then Simmias, who had been Tutankhamun, watched Socrates, who had been Akhnaton, die. Now Mark (Tutankhamun, Simmias) watched the martyrdom of Peter (Akhnaton, Socrates)!

The hearts of the brethren in Rome were greatly saddened by the simultaneous death of Peter and Paul. How would the Work survive without their great leadership? They thought that all was lost for the Cause. This was similar to the feelings of the Workers when Akhnaton died in Egypt; they thought then, as now, that all was lost!

Paul had died by being beheaded near Rome at a place called

Aquae Salviae (now Tre Fontane), somewhat east on the Ostian Way. He joined his fellow-worker Peter in death during the end of the reign of Nero in A.D. 67.

The following year, on July 9, A.D. 68, the cruel and childish Nero fled Rome and committed suicide.

A record was written down of the end of Peter and Paul by Mark and Linus. This record, along with others, was placed in an ancient sepulchre outside Rome. The writings were placed beneath a great stone in a cave that was used as a tomb. A hastily made sign was placed near the entrance. Some day in the future an earthquake will reveal this tomb, and the writings of Mark and Linus will be found!

For some time the remains of Peter and Paul were kept in a vault on the Appian Way.

Linus, who had made the silver chalice, was now in Rome! (II Timothy iv: 21.) He had been a student of both Peter and Paul.

The Cloak or Robe worn by Jesus on the day of His Crucifixion had been secured by a Roman soldier on Golgotha through the casting of lots (Matthew xxvii: 35).

This Roman soldier soon after the Ascension of Jesus became a Christian, and later the Robe was given to Paul to be kept in his charge. Paul speaks of this in his Second Epistle to Timothy:

" The cloak that I left at Troas with Carpus, when thou comest, bring with thee, and the books, but especially the parchments " (II Timothy iv: 13).

Paul could have secured cloaks in Rome; then why did he want Timothy to bring such a garment with him on a long journey? The answer is obvious: This was no ordinary " cloak "!

The Robe or Cloak of Jesus had been left with Carpus, and Paul wanted Timothy to bring it with him when he picked up Mark and came to Rome. He asks for books, but he is especially concerned with " the parchments "! The books would have contained widely known information, but " parchments " implies secret records and knowledge of the workings of the brethren which had just been put into writing!

After Timothy brought the Robe to Rome, it was given to Linus, who treasured it throughout his life! The " parchments " were part of the writings that Linus placed in the cave-tomb along with the report on the death of Peter and Paul!

Peter had desired that Linus succeed him in Rome. Therefore

the Robe was passed to each successor for generations! The Robe now rests in a vault deep under St. Peter's in Rome!

Some records (*Apost. Const.*, VII, 46) claim that Linus was a " son of Claudia." However, this is not true. Other records say he was from Tuscany; this is equally untrue. He was born in Antioch, and after his death he was buried beside Simon Peter.

Who was Claudia? She was the *wife of Mark*! She was very prominent in Rome, and was related to the Caesars. Claudia had met Mark when he and Peter were in the Imperial Palace on numerous occasions. It was easy for Claudia to become a Christian. She had always been one at heart, even before she heard of the Christ.

She was a shy child, and no one ever knew what she was really thinking. When she entered the Temple of Jupiter, and of the other gods, she had the outward appearance of great piety—everyone thought that she was a great adorer of the gods. But she was literally an iconoclast! She would paint beards on the female deities, and breasts on the male gods! The priests always ended up by blaming some poor Christian for the ghastly acts! No one would have believed that demure, sweet Claudia, the adored of the gods, would have done such a thing!

She is mentioned as a Christian woman of Rome (II Timothy iv: 21) in the Bible. She was, however, a Briton by birth. She was the daughter of the Roman who governed Britain. Her mother was a native of that land. However, the Roman official had brought his own wife with him from Rome. Claudia's mother was a native woman that the Roman had been indiscreet with; yet he loved this child, since his own wife was unable to bear children. Her father named her Claudia after the Emperor Claudius I, a relative of her Roman father, and naturally of herself. Claudia is the feminine form of Claudius.

Although Claudia was a very fair child, and later a beautiful woman, she was lame in one foot. That is also why she was named as she was, for Claudia means: broken; lame.

Claudia was taken to Rome by the legal wife of her father. This woman loved Claudia, even though she was not her own child, and made a great noble lady of the child.

Claudia had known that a great teacher (Jesus) had been in Britain at Glastonbury, but she did not know His name. Yet she loved the spot where He had lived during those so-called " missing " years.

When Mark told her that the Master of Glastonbury was the same as the Master Jesus, she embraced Christianity at once!

Claudia came into life in the strange way she did in order to obtain the vibrations of the sacred areas of Britain! She had been a former Queen of Egypt! The former relationship of husband-wife (Tutankhamun-Ankhsenamun) was now repeated in Mark-Claudia.

Some ancient traditions also claim that Claudia was the wife of Pudens; or that she was the daughter of King Cogidubnus of Britain. However, neither one of these assumptions is accurate! She was the wife of Mark, and was martyred with him later in Alexandria!

Peter's wife was Concordia (Perpetua) and she died on a cross in Nero's garden the same night that her husband was martyred. She had lived before as the beautiful Queen Nefretiti. So we find the former relationship of husband-wife (Akhnaton-Nefretiti) repeating itself in Peter-Concordia.

For several centuries after the Ascension of Jesus, the "Goodly Company" incarnated over and over again. Sometimes they were mentioned in history, and many more times they were forgotten. But the service to the Cause of Aton (One God) will never be forgotten Cosmically!

Simon Peter returned as Epictetus, the Greek Stoic philosopher in A.D. 68. He came into life almost immediately after his crucifixion during the Neroian persecution. He was born a slave in Phrygia, and was later banished from Rome. He taught the Stoic philosophy at Rome and Nicopolis in Epirus. He recognized conscience as the supreme principle, and insisted upon self-renunciation and self-restraint.

You might ask: "But why would Peter return as a Stoic? Wouldn't he continue to be a Christian?"

This incarnation was one in which this entity overcame certain weaknesses that were evident when he denied the Christ after He was taken from Gethsemane. Self-renunciation and restraint were the order of the day for Epictetus. Besides, the Stoics drew their philosophy mainly from their predecessors, Socrates and Aristotle. And Epictetus had been Socrates! The best Stoics came nearer to the truly Christian rule of life than any other of the ancient schools of philosophy. It is obvious why Simon Peter lived as Epictetus!

Uriah, the Hittite, who had lived as Tutu at Akhetaton, returned as St. Clement I of Rome (ca. A.D. 91–100).

Amunhotep II incarnated as Justin the Martyr (*ca.* A.D. 100–165). Tantahpe, priestess of Isis who used the ancient sistrum in the temple, later lived as Miriam, sister of Moses. She then entered life later as St. Cecilia (died *ca.* A.D. 230). This Cecilia was a Roman martyr and became patron saint of music. The same pattern repeats again and again: Tantahpe-sistrum; Miriam-harp; Cecilia-music.

Linus returned (*ca.* A.D. 340–420) as St. Jerome, monk and scholar, and maker of the Latin version of the Bible known as Vulgate.

Jeroboam had become Horemheb, the cheese-maker's son, and usurper of thrones. Now he incarnated as the Emperor Diocletian who ruled A.D. 284–305.

He who had lived as Hiram of Tyre and as head Aton priest and brother of Maya, then Ramses I, became Justinian I, the Roman Emperor (A.D. 527–565). He was born in A.D. 483 and married the dancing-girl Theodora in A.D. 523. She had lived as Nefretiti and Concordia, and was now the wife of the greatest emperor of all the long line of Roman Caesars. Yet he was of the " Goodly Company " and the other emperors were not, as we have explained.

Mark incarnated as St. George, Roman tribune, and brother of Marcus of Rome, another tribune. This Marcus had been Genubath and later son of Tutankhamun. So we find the former relationship of father-son (Hadad-Genubath; Tutankhamun-young son) now becoming a brother relationship in George-Marcus. These two entities had also been Simmias and Cebes. St. George was not the cruel George of Cappadocia that some historians claim he was. He died in Lydda (Diospolis) in Palestine by the order of Diocletian because he had torn down the Emperor's edict of persecution against the Christians at Nicomedia.

The former relationship of Tutankhamun and the usurper of thrones, Horemheb, was now one of tribune (George) and emperor (Diocletian).

St. George was martyred April 23, A.D. 303. Mark had died on April 25. Now George dies on almost the same day! He was not George of Cappadocia, since the latter was killed in A.D. 361. George had visited Britain on an imperial expedition and visited the area of Glastonbury while there—he was searching for the *Cup* of the *Last Supper*! And since he had been Mark, who once possessed that *Cup*, it was logical for him to seek it again! His remains rest in a church at Lydda, which was built by the Emperor Justinian.

George went to Palestine with his mother after the death of his father. He returned to the area of a former work, for he had lived in the Holy Land with his mother Mary when he was Mark! He was strong and robust of body, and by his courage and conduct was advanced in the army by the Emperor. When Diocletian waged war against the Christians, George laid aside the marks of his dignity, and complained to the Emperor himself about the bloody edicts. He was cast in prison, and then tortured, led through the streets, and beheaded.

Fortunata was a Christian maiden who bravely endured torture and death at Caesarea in Palestine in A.D. 303 in the persecution under Diocletian. She had lived as Ankhsenamun, wife of Tutankhamun, and as Claudia, wife of Mark. She died in the same year as St. George—A.D. 303. The former relationship of husband-wife (Tutankhamun-Ankhsenamun; Mark-Claudia) was now one of Christian martyrs (George-Fortunata).

Mark and Marcellianus were Roman twin brothers who had secretly been Christians for many years before being discovered by the authorities. They were finally arrested, but the execution was delayed so that they might be persuaded to deny the Christ. They bravely underwent the most appalling tortures before being beheaded on June 18, A.D. 286. Their great heroism led to the conversion of many individuals. They had lived previously in Egypt as the identical twins who had brought from their country the secret power of the magnetic field which protected the tombs of the Pharaohs. At that time they died with other slaves in front of the tomb of Tutankhamun.

The Law brought by Moses had been a mere interlude until such time as mankind should be ripe for a complete revelation. The time was " ripe " when Jesus came to *fulfil* the *Word*!

" Even so we, when we were children, were in bondage under the elements of the world: But when the fulness of the time was come, God sent forth his Son, made of a woman, made under the law, To redeem them that were under the law, that we might receive the adoption of sons. And because ye are sons, God hath sent forth the Spirit of his Son into your hearts. . . . Wherefore thou art no more a servant, but a son; and if a son, then an heir of God through Christ " (Galatians iv: 3–7).

The " children " during the " bondage " of Egypt had seen for a short time the Greater Light under Akhnaton. Then came the Law that served its purpose but from which man had to be redeemed. Then came the " fulness of time " when man was to be accepted not as a " servant " but as a Son of God himself through the *Fulfilment* of the *Word*!

Through millennia it had been a trying period for the " Goodly Company " as they served again and again. Yet their power increased in proportion to that service.

" He giveth power to the faint; and to them that have no right he increaseth strength. Even the youths shall faint and be weary, and the young men shall utterly fall: But they that wait upon the Lord shall renew [change] their strength; they shall mount up with wings as eagles; they shall run, and not be weary; and they shall walk, and not faint " (Isaiah xl: 29–31).

Some of the Workers in the Light had literally " mounted up with wings as eagles," as they were translated to other Space-Time areas.

Isaiah, who was later John the Beloved, had spoken truly. Those who received the *Fulfilment* under Jesus the Christ shall never in all Eternity " be weary nor shall they faint."

The *Word* had been *Prepared*; it had *Dawned*; it was *Revealed* to mankind; then it was *Fulfilled*.

Now it remains to be *DISCOVERED*!

Chapter Five

DISCOVERY

THE *WORD* was discovered. . . .
Thousands of the world's most valuable documents, gathered from all ancient countries, and written upon papyrus, parchment, wax and vellum, tablets of stone, wood, and terra cotta, were placed in the special library buildings of Alexandria.

Julius Caesar ordered the fleet burned in the harbour in 51 B.C. This caused many buildings and valuable manuscripts to be lost, thus causing the Dark Ages on earth!

However, the most important information was saved and taken to the secret chambers of the Sphinx and Pyramid by the Teachers of the Mystery Schools! After Caesar had the fleet set on fire, several hours passed before the first buildings began to burn. The librarians, aided by hundreds of slaves attached to the repository, succeeded in saving the most sacred and important of the documents. These are now buried deep within the SECRET PLACES OF THE LION!

In A.D. 389 the edict of Theodosius caused the destruction of the remaining parts of the library left standing after the conflagration of 51 B.C.

The negative forces of Amun (False God) continually tried to erase the memory of Atonism (One God worship) from the face of the earth. When these forces were too powerful, the great secrets of Light were buried or secreted away for a while; never wholly lost, but hidden until man should have need of them again!

The followers of Amun had tried to erase all memory of Akhnaton and his great labour in Egypt. They tried even harder to see to it that future generations knew nothing at all of the Christ; in fact, they hoped that man would be completely unaware that Jesus ever lived at all! The " Goodly Company " returned in the Dark Ages as reformers, priests, and leaders of Truth. Great religious leaders were necessary to lift the earth up and out of the tight hold that Amunism still had upon it. In Egypt they had overthrown Aton, but now a different pattern emerged. Since they couldn't defeat the new Christian way of life, they decided to make it the State religion with themselves as its head, of course!

The priests of Amun became the priests of the Cross! They removed from the sacred teachings the Doctrine of Reincarnation taught by Jesus and the Apostles. They knew that if man was aware he had a chance in many lifetimes to overcome his weaknesses and inherit the "Kingdom" they would not have the necessary control over him they desired. They took the Living, Resurrected Christ and put him back on the blood-smeared Cross. They tore the memory of that Cross and what it stood for out of their hearts and hung it around their fat, sweaty necks! While Christ had said that man needed no one to intercede for him as he went to the Father, the priests of the "long, flowing robes of Amun" now raised themselves up as intermediaries between man and God! The hoary hand of Amunism pressed harder and firmer upon earth; harder and firmer until the planet almost suffocated in ignorance, superstition, lust for power, and falsity! But the Workers in the Greater Light prevailed!

Christ said: "Beware of the scribes, which desire to walk in long robes, and love greetings in the markets, and the highest seats in the synagogues, and the chief rooms at feasts; Which devour widows' houses, and for a shew make long prayers: the same shall receive greater damnation" (Luke xx: 46–47; also, Mark xxi: 38–40; Luke xi; Matthew xxiii: 5–7).

When Jesus spoke of the "Pharisees and scribes," he was referring to the followers of *Amun*—the hypocrites of *then* and *now*!

As we mentioned before, race leaders incarnated as great rulers in Egypt; then during the time of Rome's great power these leaders were humble men who taught the people. During the Dark Ages they once again incarnated as great reformers and teachers. Now, during the tribulations of the twentieth century, they are again in life as humble workers. The ancient Roman rulers sit on the thrones of the world again! The Plan has always followed the pattern of: first, the rule of Darkness, then the rule of Light for a period of time—to be followed by the Darkness of Falsity again!

Philip the Apostle returned as Arthur, the not so legendary king of ancient Britain, leader of the Knights of the Round Table (*ca.*

A.D. 500). At this time Barnabas came into life as Merlin the venerable magician and seer.

Tiyi, the wife of Amunhotep III, returned as Guinevere, wife of
King Arthur. So we find the former relationship of husband-wife
(Amunhotep III-Tiyi) repeating again in Arthur-Guinevere. At the
court of Amunhotep III, Merlin had been Maya, and was also Moses
and Barnabas!

Akhnaton returned as a Saxon king after the Arthur period.

The great artist of Egypt known as Cato had returned as Confucius and, during the *Discovery* period, incarnated as Lao Ming,
teacher of the Cambodian nation of the Middle Ages. He taught at
Angkor Wat, an ancient Khmer temple at the city of Angkor.
This city now lies in ruins in French Indo-China. One of his young
students there had been his son Rahotep during the time of the
Golden Mask in Egypt.

At one time during his evangelistic career, Mark had been sent
by Peter on a missionary journey around the eastern and northern
coasts of the Adriatic. Mark was accompanied by his friend and
companion Hermagoras. Hermagoras had lived as Cebes and then
later as Tribune Marcus of Rome. Mark had once been " Merk "
of the " Ships of Light " on Lemuria; so the name " Hermagoras,"
meaning " Son of Mercury," fit Mark's disciple very well. He had
been the actual *son* of Mark when they had lived as Hadad-Genubath;
Tutankhamun-young son; and of father-son in other lifetimes.

Mark and Hermagoras had reached Aquileia, then a flourishing
maritime city, and a favourite residence of the Roman emperors.
It was then called Roma Secunda. Peter consecrated Hermagoras
Bishop of Aquileia.

When Mark left the city his ship was caught in a storm, and driven
westward and southward amongst the islands of the lagoons, where
it ran aground on the one on which now stands the church of San
Francesco della Vigna (St. Francis of the Vineyard). There, as he lay
in his boat asleep, waiting for the rising tide to float it off, he received a vision of the Lord. The Christ said:

" Pax tibi Marce Evangelista Meus " [Peace to thee, O Mark, my
Evangelist]. A great city will arise here to thy honour."

Four centuries passed, and the prophecy of Jesus received partial
fulfilment when the Goths and Vandals, and finally the Huns under
Attila, burned Aquileia, Altinum, and other mainland towns, and

forced the inhabitants to flee to the lagoon islands. And there they founded the great city of Venice!

Another four centuries passed, and the prophecy received complete fulfilment in the dedication of the city of Venice to St. Mark!

During the period of *Discovery* the body of St. Mark was to return to the area of a former work and time—the city of Venice! After his martyrdom in Alexandria he had been buried very near the first Alexandrian church along with the secret record tablets he had rediscovered at the Great Pyramid and underground Sphinx temple.

In the year A.D. 829 two Venetian sea captains arrived in Alexandria. They were Tribunus of Malamocca and Rustious of Torcello. These men had been sent by the reigning Doge of Venice, Giustiniano Partecipazio, to obtain the body and records of St. Mark and bring them to Venice.

The Mohammedans, but especially the followers of Amun, were destroying the church where St. Mark was buried. Columns and marbles were being carried away to build temples, and the Doge remembered the prophecy that Mark would some day be connected with their city of Venice. He decided to send the sea captains to obtain the body and those sacred items buried with it.

The two seamen located the priest Theodorus, and the monk Stauracius, who was the custodian of the ancient church. Stauracius took the men to the secret crypt where the sarcophagus of Mark was located. The monk knew that the records must be removed from Alexandria, where Amunism searched in vain for the Tablets of Truth as they tore down the church stone by stone.

Stauracius and the two captains removed the records and the body, but the difficulty was getting the precious treasure to the Venetian boat in the harbour without being detected. Finally the monk thought of a plan. The prize they were to take to Venice was placed in a large basket, and on the top of this was placed the flesh of swine! The two seamen swung the basket from a pole across their shoulders. They shouted to the custom-house officers: " Kanzir! Kanzir! " (" Pork! Pork! ")

Turbaned officials asked to see the contents of the basket that was finally placed on the Venetian boat, but they turned away in disgust and contempt as they held their nostrils. How they hated the pork— the flesh of swine!

Finally, the body was wrapped in a big white sail and was hoisted to the masthead for greater safety. The ship, with her white sails, was conspicuous because of the large *red cross* on one sail! Remember, Mark lived later as St. George (*ca.* A.D. 303). The symbol of George is the *Red Cross*! On the boat in A.D. 829 that was commissioned by the Doge to bring the body of Mark to Venice a large red cross had been placed to designate it as the ship which was bringing the ancient records along with the body! The workers knew Mark was later George, so they used that symbol to mark the boat—a mark that would be immediately recognized by the mystery students everywhere.

Mark finally went to Venice, where Jesus had told him a great city would " arise to his honour." The body was at the masthead near the red cross of St. George!

Stauracius guarded the records while they were on board the ship, and when he arrived in Venice he was made *primicerio* of St. Mark's Church. The Doge himself had actually lived as St. Mark! He who had rediscovered the secret records in Egypt that he had written when Tutankhamun now lived as the reigning Doge! It was his duty to see to it that the records received a safe hiding-place— that was the purpose of that incarnation! How fitting it was for Mark (Doge) to receive his own body and records!

The body and records were deposited in the Ducal Palace when they first arrived in Venice. Three years later the hidden chambers of the new Church of St. Mark, built expressly to receive them, were ready. The Doge supervised the entire procedure, for he erected the new church. The prophecy made to the shipwrecked Evangelist Mark had now received complete fulfilment, for not only had a great city arisen, but it had arisen to his honour, as Jesus had said.

With Mark's body, the Doge found a ring—the ring that had been placed on the Evangelist's hand when Peter consecrated him Bishop of Alexandria. The Doge, knowing he had been Mark, and knowing it was now his duty to protect the tablets, took the ring and placed it on his own finger!

The church was begun in 830, and finished in 834 by Giovanni, the brother and successor of Giustiniano. The latter died the following year after the body arrived in Venice. His mission was completed, and his brother, who had lived as Hermagoras, completed the church. The former relationship of Bishop-Disciple (Mark-Hermagoras) was now one of brothers (Giustiniano-Giovanni).

Under the Church of St. Mark, facing the Piazza St. Mark, to this day are the records of ancient Eighteenth Dynasty Egypt, waiting to be rediscovered! And above the Piazza and Church stands the symbolic winged *Lion of St. Mark*—a fitting marker for more SECRET PLACES OF THE LION!

The great continent of North America, which had previously known highly developed Lemurian and Atlantean culture, then suffered a cultural hiatus for several thousand years, suddenly found itself the motherland for many groups of Indian peoples.

The legends of all Indian tribes abound with stories of how they finally came to the " surface " of the earth to find that the land was covered with silt and mud. They knew that a great ocean had covered this land previous to their emergence!

Anthropologists try to explain the legends away which say that the Indian people sprang from the bosom or womb of Mother Earth to enter life on the surface. They explain these so-called " myths " away by saying that the ignorant, superstitious, primitive aboriginals of North America watched the corn and other growing things emerge from the soil to life in the sunlight of earth. Therefore it is surmised that the Indians guessed that they too must have come from the Mother Earth in like manner. However, while this might be symbolically true, it is certainly not the whole story!

Anthropologists, historians, and other researchers will discover that the " myths " and " legends " of superstitious primitives are neither mythological nor products of ignorant savages! An actual happening was the beginning for all legendary accounts!

So, the Indian people of North America came *up* from the underground caverns to dwell as surface men once again. The catastrophes of Lemuria and Atlantis, plus the detrimental effects of intense cosmic ray bombardment, had caused the remnant of many races to go literally underground.

There are reasons why such a great continent was left practically undisturbed by civilization until the time of Christopher Columbus (A.D. 1492). It was to serve as the cradle for a new race of men!

However, there were SECRET PLACES OF THE LION in America too! The ancient telonium record tablets were still in the South-western area, and the " wild men of the forest," or the Indians, inherited a great legacy which they preserved for a time when future man would have need of the ancient Truth. The white man could have learned a great deal from the red man. In fact, he could still learn a great deal today, if he would only listen. But, of course, he will not listen because he is blinded by his own importance on the world scene. He hasn't time for ignorant savages! Which is more savage: killing your fellow man with a bow and arrow or vaporizing thousands upon thousands in a second with the super-weapons of a so-called "highly advanced culture"? The only thing modern man appears "highly advanced" in is the wholesale and total destruction of all his fellow men and every decent thing that ever found existence on the earth—"planet of sorrows"—known anciently on other worlds as the dark "Red Star."

The "Goodly Company" found life in North America *ca.* A.D. 1100–1300. The purpose of such lifetimes was again to *discover* the SECRET PLACES OF THE LION and *protect* them, *preserve* them if damage had occurred during the intervening centuries since they were last secreted away, and to *prepare* them for the man of the modern world who would shortly make his appearance after the coming industrial revolution!

In the American South-West there are *three* areas which were originally part of the Seven Sacred Cities of Cibola! These areas are: Mesa Verde, Montezuma Castle, and Casa Grande. These were supposed to be a group of native villages in the country north of Mexico. Some were visited by Spanish explorers of the sixteenth century. However, the cities themselves were made of mud bricks, not gold. The fabulous treasure that the explorers heard about was a reference to the records of antediluvian times now resting in hidden caverns near the site of the great Pueblo Indian structures.

These three Indian cultural centres enjoyed a great religious revival and were the "Meccas" for the Indian tribes of North America. The same entities who had lived in the south-western area when it was known as Telos now returned as the leaders of the religious ritualism of the red man. "Ships of Light" came from neighbouring planets, as they had thousands of years before, to bring about the exodus from doomed Lemuria!

About A.D. 1200–1250 they came for another reason. They did not remove anyone, because no exodus was necessary. They came to survey the area that had undergone great terrain changes several thousand years previously when the records had been placed *in* and *on* the earth. The telonium tablets had been placed in caverns, subterranean temples, and in buried space ships themselves! The Indian leaders and their people were visited by the brothers from outer space and, from that meeting, legends of the " fair-haired gods from the sky " rapidly took form. The true meaning was forgotten as the stories were passed from one generation to another by word of mouth.

The South-Western Indians today believe that the " sky gods " and " gods of the sun " will return soon and take them away with them!

The entity who had been Moses returned to the area where he had once been the " Ruling Prince of Lemuria." He was not a native Pueblo Indian, but came from the great cultural centres of Mexico. She who had been " Lady of the Sun " returned as a brother of the Indian from the south. The former relationship of Ruler-Historian (Prince-" Lady of the Sun ") was now one of brothers (Indians from the south). The two were teachers and historians. They brought a message and knowledge with them from the highly advanced civilization of Mexico. They arrived at Montezuma Castle and prophesied for many years by telling the tribes that a great craft of the " sun " would come in the future. Later, they went to Mesa Verde.

This land in America is known today by the Indian people as " Land of the Sun People." It is also " Land of the Lion." *Arizona* itself contains the meaning, for " ari " in Hebrew means " adult lion."

" Merk," who landed at Telos, had lived as Tutankhamun, Aaron, Mark, and St. George; he now returned in another " Ship of Light." " Lady of the Sun," now a male entity, greeted him when he landed at Mesa Verde, even as this individual had greeted him thousands of years before in Telos!

The great Sun Temple at Mesa Verde, which has long been an enigma to archaeologists, was built to commemorate the coming of the " sun " ship to the Indian people. Their legends today state that when some of their people learned to make " weapons of lightning " they constructed this unusual temple.

Inside the Sun Temple are two round structures which are spoken of in legends: " The gods with weapons of lightning assembled in one structure, while the mortals with ordinary weapons assembled in the other." The " gods of lightning " were, of course, the space visitors. They instructed some of the Indian leaders in the use of the Resonating Magnetic Force (Fourth Great Primary Force).

At one corner of the Sun Temple visitors to the ruins at Mesa Verde can still observe a strange symbol in the rock. It appears to be a natural formation, yet it looks like a rayed sun disc. This is the exact spot where the great " sun " ship landed in the thirteenth century A.D. The " disc " and its " rays " were created by the force field of the ship. It was done deliberately so that a marker might be established at this location. Holes drilled in the centre of the rock disc are still visible today, and were used along with wooden pegs to determine certain sun positions.

There is nothing in archaeological history to compare to the structure known as the Sun Temple! It never had a roof, therefore some scientists believe it was never completed. However, this is not true—it was never intended to have a roof! The passageways and chambers are unique and were developed out of ritualism stemming from the visitation from space at that very spot!

When it was discovered that most of the ancient records were still available and secure, the survey group returned to Hesperus (Venus).

The Indian leader from the south guarded the secret places as he had protected those in Egypt when he lived as Maya. Now, when he eventually left Mesa Verde, again the secret hiding-places were lost, for only he and the checkers knew the location!

Indian legends and symbolism are rich with evidence that outer space visitations were made periodically in various parts of the New World. When the Indians are asked today why the visitors of old don't put in an appearance as often as they once did, they say quietly: " After the coming of the white man, they didn't come to the Indian people very often."

The common " sun disc " symbol found in cave drawings, and made up of concentric circles, is not actually a sun symbol. It represents the " wheels within wheels " like those seen by Ezekiel— space ships at the River Chebar in the sixth century B.C., and near the Grand Canyon in the thirteenth century A.D.

The eastern Indians of America have legends of the " Star People " and the " People Above." The Mandan Indians of South Dakota believe that the universe is in three layers: above world; the land we live on (earth); and the lower land. They believe that there are people living on these three lands. In other words, there are underground races, surface races, and people living "above" in the heavens.

The Mandans believe that comets and constellations are people who once lived on the earth as holy people. The people of earth broke the divine rules and did not treat the holy people as they should, so the holy ones went back to the sky and are making their home there now.

This obviously refers to the time when space visitors were on the earth amongst the Indian people. Evidently the Indians finally treated them in a way that made them leave. The visitors then went " back to the sky " or home to their own world. The visitors are now making their " home " amongst the stars and constellations.

Sacred medicine bundles were common to many tribes, and some of these bundles were supposed to contain articles representing sacred beings who lived in the world *above* (space). Some of these bundles were called " Above Bundles," or " Star Bundles." Originally the bundles contained actual gifts and other articles from the space visitors which had been given to their Indian hosts. Imagine finding an ancient bundle today which contains a piece of unknown metal that belonged to a Venusian craft several hundred years ago! More SECRET PLACES OF THE LION!

This wouldn't be any stranger than articles that have already been discovered in North America. Articles of indisputable Egyptian origin have been found in graves of the temple mound builders in the Mid-Western United States. How did objects like scarabs, etc., come to be buried with Indians who perished in *ca* A.D. 1100–1300? How did such items get from Egypt to America?

Egyptian lamps and other objects have been found deep in the frozen wastes of Alaska and northward. Unfortunately these enigmas are pushed aside and brushed off by the scientists, who are afraid their pet theories will collapse in the light of such evidence.

The Navajo Indians have a legend of a fair, blond God who came to earth from out of the sky in a whirling lightning-cloud. He instructed them in good government. They marvelled at his great wisdom, and he told them he would return and help them again if they needed him.

Almost all primitive people have legends about the " little people " or " gods " who ride in " flying boats." Such tales persist through the centuries from India to America.

The people of the desert today—white men and red men alike—have seen many strange things that they refuse to discuss or report to the outside world. They have found that world a sceptical one and are content to be withdrawn from it as much as possible.

Both Navajo and Hopi Indians have sighted space ships or " saucers " on numerous occasions, but they are reluctant to talk about it, even to each other. Several years ago a very large spherical object, over thirty-five feet in diameter, was sighted by many Indians. As it travelled slowly through the sky it appeared to change in shape from oblong to pear-shaped—" all churning and twisting with the colours of the rainbow."

This craft began to descend to earth on the south-east side of Navajo Mountain. It hovered very close to the ground for some time. Many people rushed forward to greet it, but it rose silently up and away. A modern Hopi Indian who witnessed this near landing, said: " Yes, we know what they are—those are the people we are waiting for! "

Primitive people all over the world have tales about the " white, fair-haired gods " who will return to them to assist them and raise them to new life again.

The Chippewa Indians of the north country speak of the " little men who came in stone [or metal] canoes." These beings were supposed to be able to make their canoes go under water. An old Chippewa told me: " When our ancestors would approach these canoes on the lakes, they would suddenly go under the water. We thought they drowned, but then we would see the same great canoe come up in another place later! "

The legend of the " Magic Kettle " is also of Chippewa origin. Many years ago a great medicine man and several warriors were on a journey. One night they saw a brilliant " light " drop out of the sky and strike the side of a hill. The next morning they went to investigate. They found an enormous " kettle." It was round and had strange animals carved or portrayed on its surface.

The " Magic Kettle " of the Chippewas with its animal figures sounds very much like the " wheels " of Ezekiel with their figures of the Four Beasts!

For those who but take the time to look deeper into the hidden meanings of ancient mythology, there awaits an experience that would be quite difficult to explain!

Millennia ago pyramids were not only located in Egypt, but were to be found in a wide band that encircled the globe. When the Aztec Calendar Stone is finally deciphered (for it is not now understood in its true meaning) it will give the location of such pyramids that *existed* and *exist* in America!

These structures were cleverly concealed before the arrival of men like Cortes and Coronado. A famous diver some years ago even discovered a stone pyramid of immense size under one of the larger lakes of Wisconsin!

The knowledge contained in the Aztec Calendar Stone parallels that placed symbolically in the Great Pyramid! The Calendar Stone was the imperishable record for the New World; the Great Pyramid the same record for the Old World.

The gigantic tongue which protrudes from the face of the Sun God on the Aztec Calendar Stone symbolizes *Light*. The " Light " in the form of record tablets and writings was placed in the pyramids of America as well as in the secret chambers of Egypt and elsewhere. SECRET PLACES OF THE LION are to be found throughout the world!

Hernando Cortes (A.D. 1485–1547), the Spanish conqueror who destroyed the great knowledge of the Aztec civilization, had lived as the usurper Horemheb. He who had been the Indian from the south returned as the Emperor Montezuma. Montezuma had also been Maya. So we find the former relationship of assassin-victim (Horemheb-Maya) still the same in Cortez-Montezuma.

Men like Cortez, Coronado, and Pizarro were attempting to discover the SECRET PLACES OF THE LION in the New World just as they had worked for the same goal in other lifetimes in the Old World. However, they failed, for the hidden chambers of the *Most High* are well guarded and protected. Man never receives the knowledge contained there until it is time for him to do so.

The records had been rechecked in the thirteenth century A.D. Then in the sixteenth century the ancient hand of Amunism reached out to destroy once again knowledge of Truth. Cortes burned the Aztec codices and, under the sign of the " bloody cross," murdered, raped, and pillaged. But the Truth was not permanently ground into the dust any more than it was when Horemheb usurped a throne to accomplish the same purpose!

Montezuma, before his death, had the most important records secreted away. They will soon be discovered in chambers under the Aztec temple ruins in Mexico. They have gone through many periods of rest and reactivation. Their final discovery is near when they shall never be hidden again.

Coronado, in another lifetime, had been one of the scientists responsible for the destruction on Lemuria. He returned to look for the time capsules that had been buried thousands of years before. But he didn't find the Seven Cities of Cibola or their secrets!

On November 16, 1532, the Inca Atahualpa was captured by Pizarro, the Spanish conqueror of Peru. Atahualpa had lived as Tutankhamun, and Pizarro had been one of the assassins who murdered Pharaoh Smenkhkare during the Eighteenth Dynasty in Egypt.

Pizarro was really looking for the great "Sun Disc" of gold which had been brought earlier from the Motherland Lemuria. Other explorers in South America searched in vain for the fabulous "El Dorado"—they were never successful. This referred to the lost cities in the interior of the Brazilian Matto Grosso—the great cities belonging to one of the colonies of Mu.

The Golden Sun Disc of the Incas had been made from the "best gold"—transmuted gold! When Pizarro killed King Atahualpa, the messengers from all over the Land of the Inca were bringing objects of gold to Pizarro so that he would not destroy their Inca. When they heard Atahualpa was dead they did not continue to bring gold to Pizarro. The conqueror had been too impatient. If he had waited only a little while he would have possessed one of the world's greatest treasures! For the "Sun Disc" was more than just an image of veneration. When it was struck, it gave forth certain vibrations, the frequency of which made teleportation possible for the sun priests. This could be accomplished when certain objects were used to strike the disc. Striking it, one could also cause earthquakes!

The disc was hidden along with life-size solid gold statues of the former Inca rulers. The greatest objects had been held to the last so that Pizarro would receive only the less important gold objects. Why were the statues of life size? Because the *actual bodies* of the dead Inca emperors were *transmuted* to *solid gold*—this was their method of mummification!

The Sun Disc is now in the charge of the Brotherhood of the Seven Rays near Lake Titicaca, Peru.

The prophet Amos had become Matthew, and later was Francis of Assisi (A.D. 1181–1226), the Italian friar who founded the Franciscan Order.

Cato, later Confucius, lived during the Ming Dynasty which ruled China from A.D. 1368–1644. During this period art flourished (artist Cato vibration) and there were important revisions of Confucian philosophy (Confucius vibration)!

The entity that lived as Queen Tiyi and Queen Guinevere returned, A.D. 1412–1431, as the "Maid of Orleans," Jeanne d'Arc (Joan of Arc), who aroused the spirit of nationality in France against the English.

John the Beloved lived again as Leonardo da Vinci (A.D. 1452–1519), the great Italian painter, sculptor, architect, musician, engineer, mathematician, and scientist.

Joseph Barsabas returned as John Calvin (A.D. 1509–1564), the religious reformer and theologian.

One of Egypt's venerable seers returned as Nostradamus (A.D. 1503–1566). His magnificent deductions were based on the use of a crystal ball which originally had been brought from outer space during the building of the Great Pyramid. Nostradamus foretells the advent of atomic power and warns of the eventual destruction of civilization by means of the release of such energy. He holds out but one ray of hope: "the heavens shall show signs," meaning that we will be given one final chance to determine our destiny. This of course refers to the signs of the space visitors in the skies of Earth!

> "Leave, leave, go forth out
>   of Geneva, all
> Saturn of gold, shall be
>   changed into iron,
> The contrary of the positive ray
>   shall exterminate all,
> Before it happens, the
>   Heavens shall show signs."

He had a great deal to say about the happenings of our present age:

" The great swarm of *bees* shall rise, and it shall not be known whence they come. . . . "

The " hornets " of the Bible and the " bees " of Nostradamus are the " saucers " of today!

" The celestial bodies that are always visible to the eye, shall be darkened for these reasons, the body with the *forehead*, sense and head invisible, diminishing the sacred prayers."

The occult knowledge of " prophets " shall flourish during this period, keeping alive the hope of the world.

On June 27, 1558, Nostradamus wrote his epistle to Henry II of France, in which he said:

" . . . So many evils shall be committed by the means of the infernal prince, Satan, that almost the entire world shall be undone and desolate. Before these events many *unusual birds* shall fly through the air, crying, ' Huy huy! ' [' Now, now! ']. A little while after they shall vanish. After this shall have lasted a good while, there shall be renewed a reign of Saturn and a golden age. God the Creator shall say, hearing the affliction of His people, Satan shall be put and tied in the bottom of the deep, and there shall begin an age of universal peace between God and man. The ecclesiastical power shall return in force and Satan shall be bound for the space of a thousand years, and then shall be loosed again."

The " unusual birds " and the " swarm of bees " are already here as space visitors crying " Now, now! "

He who had been Mark and St. George returned to life as Father Ricardo, a priest who suffered during the Spanish Inquisition. Later he was Dr. Robert Browne (A.D. 1550–1633) of England, a leader among the early Separatist Puritans and father of Congregationalism.

Plato, who was later Philip, incarnated as Emanuel Swedenborg (A.D. 1688–1772), the Swedish scientist, philosopher, theologian, and mystic.

Baruch, who had lived as Iemhotep, Amenophis, and Euclid, returned as Sir William Herschel (A.D. 1738–1822), the German-born British astronomer.

Akhnaton, later Peter, incarnated as William Lloyd Garrison (A.D. 1805–1879), a great leader in the abolition movement in the United States! He who had fought for Truth in Egypt under Aton, now advocated the legal extinction of Negro slavery.

He who had been Thutmose III, and later Pythagoras, was studying at Oxford in A.D. 1850. He now resides at Shigatse in Tibet as Koot Hoomi Lal Singh (Master K. H.).

The cheese-maker's son, Horemheb, who later lived as the conqueror Cortes, returned to life to fulfil his mission as one of the discoverers of the tomb of Tutankhamun. He who had done everything in his power to destroy the Written Word of Aton (Truth) now had to return and reveal ancient Truth to the world. As a British archaeologist in Egypt (A.D. 1873-1939), he completed his karmic debt to his fellow man!

A controversial religious figure known as Joseph Smith entered life to repeat an unusual vibration (A.D. 1805-1844). He was a young man when the Angel Moroni visited him in his room in a brilliant light.

Moroni told young Smith that there was a book deposited, written upon gold plates, giving an account of the former inhabitants of this continent and the source from which they sprang. Also, Moroni told him that there were two stones in silver bows—and these stones, fastened to a breastplate, constituted what is called the Urim and Thummim—deposited with the plates; and the possession and use of these stones were what constituted " seers " in ancient times; and that God had prepared them for the purpose of translating the book.

Of Moroni, Smith says: " . . . I saw the light in the room begin to gather immediately around the person of him who had been speaking to me, and it continued to do so, until the room was again left dark, except just around him, when instantly I saw as it were a conduit [tube] open right up into heaven, and he ascended till he entirely disappeared, and the room was left as it had been before this heavenly light had made its appearance."

It appears that the messenger Moroni ascended by the magnetic beam of force, not unlike Jesus, the Christ, when the latter ascended into the " cloud."

During the work of Joseph Smith, " messengers from heaven descended in clouds of light "; not unlike the time of Moses, the Lawgiver, who had also received tablets or plates and heard the *voice* of the messenger!

He who had lived as Joseph, son of Jacob; Maya; Joseph, father of Jesus; and Joseph Barnabas, returned in the nineteenth century A.D. as *Joseph* Smith.

Hyrum, brother of Joseph Smith, had lived as Hiram, King of Tyre, and later was the Emperor Justinian!

Brigham Young (A.D. 1801–1877) succeeded to the leadership of the Church when Joseph and Hyrum were shot and killed in 1844 by an armed mob with painted faces. Young had lived as Solomon, later the artist Rahotep, and was in Rome as Linus, the Greek artist who fashioned the Silver Chalice of Antioch! It is very significant that Young's home in Salt Lake City, Utah, has two *lions* guarding the entrance! The symbol of the " lion " has always been associated with this entity.

When the Tabernacle in Utah was built, no nails were used in its construction! This is similar to the Temple of Solomon that was built without the " sound of hammers."

There are several points in the life of Joseph Smith which are clues to his past lives. He received previously unrecorded conversations between *Moses* and God. The fact that he had lived as Joseph of the " coat of many colours " is evidenced by the following, which Smith received:

" Behold thou art *Joseph* and thou wert chosen to do the work of the Lord, but because of transgression if thou art not aware, thou wilt fall . . . nevertheless my work shall go forth."

Smith repeatedly said: " No man knows my history." And no one did know his history. But he knew it, and knew it well. His past lives had been revealed to him during the visits of Moroni.

Smith planned an elaborate tomb which, he wrote in his journal, must be called " the tomb of Joseph, a descendant of Jacob." And indeed he was a true descendant of Jacob, for this Jacob had once been his father!

In the *Book of Mormon*, Nephi, son of Lehi, secured records on brass plates from Laban in Jerusalem. Joseph Smith secured plates of gold through the agency of Moroni. Moses also obtained sacred plates.

The Moses pattern is evident throughout the life and deeds of Joseph Smith. Also, the pattern of David and Solomon is evident; once again the many wives symbolize the many churches of the world united together in the Kingdom of the Christ! But this pattern should not have been repeated during the nineteenth century for man should have only one mate! Man learned through ancient forms of plural marriage, but the *Greater Light* showed man that he must become *one* with his single mate! The similarity in the lives of Moses and Smith can be seen by the following:

1. Brilliant lights; hearing a *voice*.
2. Receiving and interpreting tablets or plates.
3. Never going into the "Promised Land" where they had led their people. (Moses was translated; Smith was assassinated.)

The sun disc that was displayed at Nauvoo, Illinois, on the temple was a fitting symbol for the unfortunate yet rewarding life of Joseph Smith. Once again he had served the *Disc of the Sun*—Aton, the One God! At the time of Akhnaton he had seen the *Word* Dawn as Maya; during the Final Exodus from Egypt he had witnessed the *Word* Revealed by the giving and interpreting of the Two Tablets; during the Discovery of the *Word* he received and interpreted the Plates of Gold, which will be rediscovered in the future!

Moses lives again today; he walks the earth to aid in completing the Final Plan for earth in *Discovery*! He now works under the ancient symbol of the caduceus, the staff carried by Hermes or Mercury as messenger of the gods!

The "Goodly Company" walk the earth as men and women again, but the world knows them not! Is Joseph still an interpreter of dreams that are dreamed? Is Peter a man of valour and new horizons? Is Calvin a Presbyterian ministerial student? Is Nero serving humanity as a philosophical researcher? Does Mark still search for the "secret places"? Does Claudia still bear the mark of her name? Is Simon still the Zealot? Is Linus still the artist? Does "Lady of the Sun" still search for facts? Does Timothy now work with Luke? Has Sitamun realized her dream of channelling the Word? Is Matthew a man of the desert? Is Matthias an "Angel of Light" with bright visions? Does Jude find service at the sign of the Tree and Serpent? Did Paul found Unity? Is Miriam still interested in music? They are all in flesh, except Judas Iscariot! Yet the world knows them not—and will not know them except that they serve!

Moses went into Egypt during his present lifetime, but it was a different Egypt; the living ghost of a former magnificent world culture. The Egypt of old is gone, but the entity had to return to get into the old vibrations. He had to touch the monuments, the ruins; to walk in the hot sands; to awaken to old memories. The land found affinity with inherent vibrations of the past and the consciousness opened up to the duties of the present!

Great discoveries will be made in Egypt in the near future. Fantastic finds will be unearthed also in the United States and in South and Central America. Startling records will be discovered in the depths of the numerous caves that riddle Yucatan. History records numerous instances of valuable secrets being buried under threat of impending doom.

The Book of the Word of Truth opened in the world when race leaders incarnated as rulers; now that Book closes as the same workers return as unknowns. Yet the time is close when they shall reveal their true natures; not their identities of old, but their purpose on earth in the service of God and Man. They are of another separate creation and find life only in love of service.

Once man looked to Pharaohs and Kings—now he needs to look only to himself in his relationship to his Creator! There are still the unscrupulous priests of Amun who would rob man of his rightful inheritance, but they will not succeed; they will not be able to withstand the intense vibrations of a new Cosmic Order!

" The stone which the builders refused is become the head stone of the corner " (Psalms cxviii: 22).

" Unto you therefore which believe he is precious: but unto them which be disobedient, the stone which the builders disallowed, the same is made the head of the corner " (I Peter ii: 7).

The only type of building which adequately answers the description of that spiritual building of which Christ is spoken of as " chief cornerstone and headstone of the corner " is the Great Pyramid in Egypt! Only in the topstone of a pyramid can a cornerstone be at the same time a headstone, or a capstone, wherein all its four sides meet—a twofold condition which cannot be fulfilled in any other type of building.

Christ, the spiritual headstone, is absent from us now in the Body; so too is the Great Pyramid headstone, which represents the missing Christ. It was rejected by later pyramid builders even as the Christ was rejected of men (Isaiah liii: 3).

" . . . Behold, I lay in Zion for a foundation a stone, a tried stone, a precious corner stone, a sure foundation: he that believeth shall not make haste " (Isaiah xxviii: 16).

The " foundation stone " refers to the Christ at His First Coming. When the time arrives for His Second Coming He will become the " headstone of the corner."

" Now therefore ye are no more strangers and foreigners, but fellow citizens with the saints, and of the household of God; And are built upon the foundation of the apostles and prophets, Jesus Christ himself being the chief corner stone; In whom all the building fitly framed together groweth unto a holy temple in the Lord: In whom ye also are builded together for a habitation of God through the Spirit " (Ephesians ii: 19–22).

When Christ returns soon in the " clouds " the great *copper capstone* will again be placed in position, for the building will be " fitly framed together "!

A few months after the first atomic bombs were dropped on two crowded Japanese cities, a Bedouin shepherd boy was herding his goats along the western shores of the Dead Sea. He scrambled over bluffs that overlook the desert plain. In pursuit of a stray from his flock, he curiously tossed a rock into the mouth of one of the caves carved by the winds out of the white sandstone cliffs. Hearing the brittle sound of breakage, he ventured into the cave and found large earthen jars filled with ill-smelling oblong lumps that, months later, proved to be part of an ancient library of scrolls!

By 1951 many additional scrolls, along with thousands of scroll fragments, were unearthed in other caves in the area. The Dead Sea Scrolls not only include most of the Bible with other correlated documents and writing, but shed new light on the environment and religious thought of the young Jesus. The manuscripts identify Him, along with John the Baptist and John the Beloved, with the monastic order of the Essenes.

In addition to the recovery of original Biblical literature, another discovery was made on the desert plain between the bluffs where the scroll caves are located and the western shores of the Dead Sea. Ruins were uncovered here belonging to an ancient monastery which had been the headquarters of the Essenes. Their story throws a new and important light on Biblical studies and upon the status of modern Christianity, because it is now evident that the Essenes represent the most important influence that pervaded the New Testament witness!

The scrolls were first discovered in the early part of 1947—the same year that the " flying saucers " first made their presence known in the skies of earth to the general public! In 1947 the SECRET PLACES OF THE LION began to open!

Little has been reported to the people of the world on the scrolls because the finding of so much original material will obviously upset many present-day narrow theological beliefs and dogmas! Biblical scholars studying the scrolls are hesitant to release their findings because of the inevitable disturbances that will be created in the theological atmosphere!

The scrolls reveal that the Essenes called themselves the " Children of Light "; the " Sons of Light "; the " Sons of God "; the " Sons of Heaven." These, of course, refer to the " Goodly Company " serving Aton, the One God. The scrolls reveal that they were opposed by the " Sons of Darkness," the followers of the false god, Amun!

The scrolls speak of a future time when Christ will *divide* the earth and save the elect, who are called the people of the New Covenant. Other scrolls speak of the Essenes as the " Sons of the New Covenant."

There are references to the breaking of the *bread* and drinking of the *wine* as a symbol of " the sacred repast." The wine represents the " Holy Vine of David " and the bread " the life and knowledge of God." Those " Children of the Greater Light " who are descendants of the " Holy Vine of David " serve, through the " sacred repast," " the life and knowledge of God "!

What will the Christian world do with irrefutable evidence that Jesus' concepts grew out of a remarkable spiritual heritage to which many had contributed? How will narrow-minded theologians accept the indisputable fact that the Christian revelation did not come as a spectacular burst of spiritual nebula over the empty wilderness of Judea?

But that wilderness was not empty! It was filled with many " lights "; *lights* that were held bravely through the conflicts of many centuries by the Workers whose devotion to Aton, the One God of justice and mercy, in the midst of the universal idolatry of Amunism, marked them as special instruments of Divine Revelation.

Theologians once refused to accept the evidence that the world was round, although the ancient scientists had been saying and proving it for millennia! They refused to believe that there were other planetary systems with suns and moons besides our puny earth and its satellite! They screamed " heresy," and said that evil men were destroying " the foundations of the sacred faith." The " sacred faith " will not be destroyed if it is truly of God, but those who preach the " doctrines of men for the commandments of God " will be swept away in the new revelations about to burst forth upon the world of men!

The mists of the dark cloud of Amunism will be lifted and the Infinite Father will be revealed working in great and magnificent strokes; more compelling in terms of His Divine Love, more revealing in respect to the choice offered frail and wilful humanity, infinitely more convincing and real to sceptical mankind! Truth will no longer be shrouded in mystery!

" Now to him that is of power to establish you according to my gospel, and the preaching of Jesus Christ, according to the revelation of the mystery, which was kept secret since the world began, But now is made manifest, and by the scriptures of the prophets, according to the commandment of the everlasting God, made known to all nations for the obedience of faith . . . " (Romans xvi: 25–26).

The " mystery " will be completely revealed when the earth will be rent by earthquakes and the SECRET PLACES OF THE LION are secret no more.

The " mystery of mysteries " will be revealed at the sounding of the great trumpet. The earth will reap its reward because through countless ages the thoughts of evil men have created a vibration that must find expression now on a physical plane. The thoughts of those in the " Light " have created a frequency that will literally open the secret chambers and temples of remote antiquity! As the vibrations *sealed* and *protected* the tombs, they can also *open* the tombs in the " fullness of time "!

" . . . for there is nothing covered, that shall not be revealed; and hid, that shall not be known " (Matthew x: 26).

" And there were voices, and thunders, and lightnings; and there was a great earthquake, such as was not since men were upon the earth, so mighty an earthquake, and so great " (Revelation xvi: 18).

Nostradamus predicted a great earthquake that would reveal St.

Peter's tomb and destroy the Vatican! That which was discovered and called the Tomb of Simon Peter is not the true sepulchre of the Apostle! The "Seven Hills of Rome" will be torn asunder and tombs and truths, even as Joseph's tomb in Egypt was exposed on the night of the Final Exodus, will be revealed to a world bathed in the new vibrational radiance of the "Golden Dawn."

"He that hath an ear, let him hear. . . . To him that overcometh will I give to eat of the hidden manna, and will give him a white stone, and in the stone a new name written, which no man knoweth saving he that receiveth it" (Revelation ii: 17).

The *Harvest* gathered by the "angel messengers" will be small; they will eat of the "hidden manna"; they will be given a "white stone." In that "stone" there will be "a new name written."

The "hidden manna" is the frequency of the "Golden Dawn" the "white stone" is a purified planet; the "new name" is an entity lifted into another dimension of Time and Space!

When the SECRET PLACES OF THE LION open to man, he will find himself in the SECRET PLACES OF THE THUNDER, and the ancient knowledge of the SECRET PLACES OF THE STAIRS will be his once again after millions of years of seeking!

The earth will shake and tremble; the foundations of the hills will move and be shaken. The heavens will proclaim the *newness* and everlasting *oneness* of all things.

All this shall come to pass in this generation. Until the time of final Discovery, the Truth of the Greater Light is "Like a *lion* greedy of its prey . . . as it were a young lion lurking in *secret places*"!

EPILOGUE

"WHEN man again shall conquer the ocean, and fly in the air on wings like the birds, when he has learned to harness the lightning, then shall the time of warfare begin. Great shall the battle be twixt the forces, great the warfare of darkness and light. Nation shall rise against nation, using the dark forces to shatter the earth. Weapons of force shall wipe out the Earth-men, until half of the races of men shall be gone. Then shall come forth the Sons of the Morning, and give their edict to the children of men, saying: ' O men, cease from thy striving against thy brother, only thus can ye come to the Light. Cease from thy unbelief, O my brother, and follow the path and know ye are right ' " (The Emerald Tablets).

One great cycle of time is now ending—shortly a new cycle begins. The Christ knocks on the door of the heart of the world. Those that bid him enter shall be the " Children of the New Covenant."

Those who thought that perfection could be attained by eliminating and smothering all desire will learn a great universal truth: Man is never judged by the things that he does not do. He is judged by how he lives, what he thinks, says, and does; never by what he does not do!

Men are not accountable to anyone in matters of Spirit, except Jesus the Christ who rules this System! Therefore, the authority for this work lies in the fact that future discoveries will prove the information contained herein accurate! " The memory of man runneth not to the contrary."

Besides discoveries made *in* the earth, great finds will be made in the field of science *on* the earth. In the past man explored unknown continents; in the future, armed with curious instruments fashioned for the purpose, he will explore the unknown realms of light, colour, sound, and consciousness.

Now we are entering the " *twilight of the gods*," when the final destruction of the Old Age will take place and man and the gods will be regenerated and reunited! Man will have revealed unto him a true vision of his eternal heritage—that earthly things may show him the nature of his spirit!

" Out of the east come vast secrets: great conclaves of elders sit together, having loving designs on earth to men and women moving in earth. These conclaves of elders sit on earth and descry it for that which it containeth; verily do they see the treasure house of experience to be revealed, that now is covered. Great, great is the wealth so buried, so great that the mind of man conceiveth no idea as to its scope; civilizations once born and perished shall arise from out of the ruins of time; they shall manifest anew in substance; Great waters shall recede and bare their secrets . . . verily the work hath but begun " (Golden Scripts lxxxvi: 32–35).

" He that dwelleth in the *secret place* of the most High shall abide under the shadow of the Almighty " (Psalms xci: 1).

" Surely the Lord God will do nothing, but he revealeth his *secret* unto his servants the prophets. The *lion* hath roared, who will not fear? The Lord God hath spoken, who can but prophesy? " (Amos iii: 7–8.)

PAX VOBISCUM

APPENDIX

REINCARNATIONAL PATTERNS OF IDENTITIES

Aaron (see Tutankhamun).

Ahmose, ca. 1376 B.C., scribe under Akhnaton; *Levi, ca.* 1760 B.C., son of Jacob and Leah, and half-brother of Joseph; *Hur, ca.* 1323 B.C., brother-in-law of Moses, who held up Moses' hand along with Aaron; *Amos, ca.* 745 B.C., one of the Minor Prophets of Judea; *Mer,* one of the Three Wise Men; *Matthew* of Galilee, one of the Twelve Apostles; *St. Francis* of Assisi, A.D. 1181?–1226, Italian friar, founder of the Franciscan Order.

Ahmose I, 1580–1529 B.C., first Pharaoh of the Eighteenth Dynasty, Egypt; the *Ruling Prince* of Lemuria 12,000 years ago at the time of "Merk" and "Lady of the Sun"; *Amraphel* or *Hammurabi, ca.* 2000 B.C., contemporary with Abraham; *Joseph,* 1761 B.C., of the "coat of many colours"; *King David,* 1580–1540 B.C., of Israel; *Rekhmire, ca.* 1501–1447 B.C., Vizier under Thutmose III; *Maya,* 1428–1338 B.C., royal treasurer and prime minister from Amunhotep III to Horemheb; *Moses,* 1313–1193 B.C., Hebrew of Egypt who led the Children of Israel out of Egypt; *Ahmose II,* 569–525 B.C., of Egypt; *Daniel, ca.* 606–538 B.C., Babylonian captive, one of the Major Prophets of the Old Testament; *Joseph, ca.* 44 B.C., of Galilee, father of the Master Jesus; *Joseph Barnabas, ca.* A.D. 92, of Cyprus, who worked with Paul; *Merlin, ca.* A.D. 500, the magician of King Arthur's Court; Religious Leader at Mesa Verde, Indian who came from the south, A.D. 1200; *Montezuma ca.* A.D. 1500, Aztec of Mexico; *Joseph Smith,* A.D. 1805–1844, organizer of the Mormon Church.

Ahmose II (see Ahmose I).

Akhnaton or *Amunhotep IV,* 1370–1361 B.C., the so-called "heretic"; Pharaoh of Egypt; *Socrates,* 469–399 B.C., philosopher of Greece. *Simon Peter* (died A.D. 67), one of the Twelve Apostles; *Epictetus, ca.* A.D. 67–125, Roman Stoic philosopher; Saxon King; *William Lloyd Garrison,* A.D. 1805–1879, who established the *Liberator* at Boston to advocate emancipation of slaves.

Amenemopet (see Cato).

Amenophis, ca. 1412 B.C., architect and adviser of Amunhotep III, deified as God of Science and Medicine; *Thoth* of Atlantis; *Iemhotep, ca.* 3000

B.C., Third Dynasty, deified as God of Science and Medicine; *Baruch,*
ca. 586 B.C., of the Old Testament and Apocrypha; *Euclid, ca.* 300 B.C.,
geometrician; *Sir William Herschel,* A.D. 1738–1822, German-born
British astronomer.

Amos (see Ahmose).

Amraphel (see Ahmose I).

Amunhotep II, 1447–1420 B.C., grandfather of Amunhotep III; *Justin* the
Martyr, *ca.* A.D. 100–165.

Amunhotep III, 1412–1370 B.C. (died 1370 B.C.), father of Akhnaton, Smenkh-
kare, Tutankhamun, Meriten, Sinuhe; *Zoser, ca.* 3000 B.C., Third
Dynasty; *Apepa Aauserra* or *Apofis,* 177 B.C., Pharaoh of Joseph;
Jonathan, friend of David; *Ramses II,* 1300–1233 B.C., Pharaoh of the
" Greater Exodus "; *Plato,* 427–347 B.C., Greek philosopher; *Philip* of
Galilee, one of the Twelve Apostles; *King Arthur, ca.* A.D. 500, of the
Round Table, of England; *Emanuel Swedenborg,* A.D. 1688–1772,
Swedish scientist, philosopher, and mystic.

Amunhotep IV (see Akhnaton).

Ankhsenamun or *Ankhsenpaaton,* 1370–1348 B.C., Queen of Egypt, wife of
King Tutankhamun, and third daughter of Akhnaton and Nefretiti;
sister of Queen Tahpenes of Egypt, and wife of Hadad of Syria; first
wife of Aaron, one of the seven daughters of the Priest of Midian and
sister of Zipporah; *Claudia,* a Briton, wife of Mark the Evangelist;
Fortunata, A.D. 303, Christian martyr.

Ankhsenpaaton (see Ankhsenamun).

Anub-khper-re (see Seti).

Apepa Aauserra (see Amunhotep III).

Apofis (see Amunhotep III).

Aristotle (see Seti).

Arthur, King (see Amunhotep III).

Asenath (see Ilipaaton).

Atahualpa (see Tutankhamun).

Ay, 1350–1346 B.C., Pharaoh who succeeded Tutankhamun to the throne,
father of Queen Nefretiti; *Phammon,* the High Priest, in another incarnation; Phammon is now on Capella in the Constellation Auriga.

Barnabas (see Ahmose I).

Barsabas, one of the two candidates for the Apostleship succeeding Judas
Iscariot; Aton priest at the time of Akhnaton; *John Calvin,* A.D. 1509–
1564, French theologian.

Bartholomew (see Mahu).

Baruch (see Amenophis).

Bathsheba (see Ilipaaton).

Bathshua (see Ilipaaton).

Browne, Dr. Robert (see Tutankhamun).

Buddha, Gautama (see Jesus, the Christ).

Calvin, John (see Barsabas).

Cato, ca. 1376 B.C. (died 1338 B.C.), known as the greatest artist of Egypt,
father of the great artist Rahotep, who fashioned the Golden Mask of

King Tutankhamun; was thirteen Pharaohs throughout different
Egyptian periods; *Cheops* or *Khufu, ca.* 3100–2960 B.C., Fourth Dynasty;
Amenemopet, ca. 1020 B.C., the "New King" of the Delta of Egypt;
Confucius or *Kung-fu-tse* (Master Kong), 551–478 B.C., Grand Master
Mason and philosopher; teacher of Cambodia; artist in Ming Dynasty
(A.D. 1368–1644); in China; now *Lao Ming* of Peru, near Lake
Titicaca.
Cebes (see Genubath).
Cecilia, Saint (see Tantahpe).
Cheops (see Cato).
Claudia (see Ankhsenamun).
Clement, Saint (see Tutu).
Concordia (see Nefretiti).
Confucius (see Cato).
Cortes, Hernando (see Horemheb).
Daniel (see Ahmose I).
David, King (see Ahmose I).
Diocletian (see Horemheb).
Eddy, Mary Baker (see Nefretiti).
Eliezer (see Ra).
Elisabeth (see Ilipaaton).
Elisheba (see Ilipaaton).
Epictetus (see Akhnaton).
Euclid (see Amenophis).
Ezekiel (see Tutankhamun).
Fortunata (see Ankhsenamun).
Francis, Saint (see Ahmose).
Garrison, William Lloyd (see Akhnaton).
Genubath (born 1540 B.C.), son of Hadad and sister of Queen Tahpenes;
    prepared the body of *Ahmose I* so David could occupy it; child of
    Tutankhamun and Ankhsenamun; *Nadab,* son of Aaron and Elisheba;
    Cebes, ca. 469 B.C., companion of Simmias; *Marcus* (martyred A.D. 303),
    Roman tribune; *St. Hermagoras; Giovanni, ca.* A.D. 829, brother of
    Giustiniano Partecipazio.
George, Saint (see Tutankhamun).
Gershom (see Rahotep).
Giovanni (see Genubath).
Guinevere (see Tiyi).
Hadad (see Tutankhamun).
Hammurabi (see Ahmose I).
Hatshepsut (see Tiyi).
Hermagoras, Saint (see Genubath).
Herschel, Sir William (see Amenophis).
Hiram, King (see Ramses I).
Horemheb, 1346–1322 B.C., General and Egyptian Pharaoh; *Jeroboam, ca.*
    1501–1480 B.C., noted as the "man who made Israel to sin"; *Korah,*
    leader of the rebellion against Moses and Aaron; *Diocletian,* A.D.

284–305, Roman emperor; *Hernando Cortes,* A.D. 1485–1547, Spanish conqueror; English archaeologist in Egypt, A.D. 1873–1939.

Hur (see Ahmose).

Huya, ca. 1376 B.C., Major-domo for Queen Tiyi and Aton priest; *James the Less,* one of the Twelve Apostles.

Iemhotep (see Amenophis).

Ilipaamun (see Ilipaaton).

Ilipaaton or *Ilipaamun* (died 1338 B.C.), full sister of Amunhotep III and wife of Maya of Egypt; " *Lady of the Sun,*" historian of Lemuria 12,000 years ago who met the spaceman Merk, and interpreted his " footprints "; *Asenath, ca.* 1761 B.C., wife of Joseph of the " coat of many colours," Fifteenth Dynasty; *Bathsheba* or *Bathshua, ca.* 1580–1536 B.C., wife of David of Israel; *Queen Tahpenes, ca.* 1536–1529 B.C., wife of Ahmose I; *Elisheba,* second wife of Aaron; *Elisabeth, ca.* 16 B.C., of Judah, mother of *John the Baptist;* Indian from the south (male incarnation), A.D. 1200, who met the space craft, as did the same female entity previously during Lemurian times!

Isaiah (see Seti).

Ist-nofret (see Sitamun).

James the Less (see Huya).

Jeremiah (see Sinuhe).

Jeroboam (see Horemheb).

Jerome, Saint (see Rahotep).

Jesus, the Christ, 4 B.C.–A.D. 30, the Master Jesus, son of Mary and Joseph; *Melchizedek* or *Shem, ca.* 2000 B.C., son of Noah; *Gautama* (*Sakyamuni Siddhartha*) *Buddha,* 568–488 B.C.; *Zoroaster,* 660 B.C.

Joan of Arc (see Tiyi).

Joel (see John the Baptist).

John the Baptist (born 4 B.C.), of Judah; Hittite Ambassador to Egypt at the time of Akhnaton; *Joel, ca.* 720 B.C., Minor Prophet of the Old Testament; *Thomas,* the Doubter, one of the Twelve Apostles.

John the Beloved (see Seti).

Jonathan (see Amunhotep III).

Joseph of the " coat of many colours " (see Ahmose I).

Joseph, father of Jesus (see Ahmose I).

Joshua (see Tutu).

Judas Iscariot, who betrayed Jesus; Amun priest who administered the poison to Akhnaton, and was responsible for the death of Tutankhamun; not in the flesh at the present time.

Justin the Martyr (see Amunhotep II).

Justinian (see Ramses I).

Khaemweset (see Sinuhe).

Khufu (see Cato).

Kungfutse or *Kongfutse* (see Cato).

" *Lady of the Sun* " (see Ilipaaton).

Lao Ming (see Cato).

Levi (see Ahmose).

Linus (see Rahotep).

Luke (see Sinuhe).

Mahu, ca. 1376 B.C., chief of police under Akhnaton, and Aton priest; *Bartholomew* or *Nathanael,* one of the Twelve Apostles.

Maketaton, second daughter of Akhnaton and Nefretiti; *Zipporah,* wife of Moses and one of the seven daughters of the priest of Midian.

Mara, ca. 1420–1412 B.C., wife of Thutmose IV and mother of Amunhotep III and Ilipaamun; *Mary,* 17 B.C., mother of Jesus.

Marcus of Rome (see Genubath).

Mark (see Tutankhamun).

Mark and *Marcellianus,* martyred twins of Rome; twins who brought secret knowledge to Egypt in Tutankhamun period.

Martha (see Tantahpe).

Mary, mother of Jesus (see Mara).

Matthew (see Ahmose).

Maya (see Ahmose I).

Melchizedek (see Jesus, the Christ).

Meneptah, 1233–1223 B.C., thirteenth son of Ramses II; *Paul* of Tarsus (Saul), the Apostle; a founder of Unity.

Menkheperre-Seneb (see Tutankhamun).

Mer (see Ahmose).

Meritaton, ca. 1361–1360 B.C., wife of Smenkhkare and Queen of Egypt and first daughter of Akhnaton and Queen Nefretiti; child of King Tutankhamun and Queen Ankhsenamun; daughter of Seti I of Egypt who rescued Moses from the bulrushes and adopted him; wife of Lazarus or Lazar of Judea and sister-in-law of the Master Jesus.

Meriten, sister of Tutankhamun and Smenkhkare; *Lois,* grandmother of Timothy.

Merk (see Tutankhamun).

Merlin (see Ahmose I).

Miriam (see Tantahpe).

Montezuma (see Ahmose I).

Moses (see Ahmose I).

Nadab (see Genubath).

Nathan the Prophet (see Silas).

Nathanael (see Mahu).

Neb-kheperu-Re (see Tutankhamun).

Nefretari (see Tiyi).

Nefretiti, ca. 1376 B.C., wife of Akhnaton; *Concordia,* Peter's wife; *Theodora, ca.* A.D. 548, wife of Justinian, Roman Emperor.

Nichomachus (see Sitamun).

Partecipazio, Doge Giustiniano (see Tutankhamun).

Peter, Simon (see Akhnaton).

Paul of Tarsus (see Meneptah).

Phammon (see Ay).

Philip (see Amunhotep III).

Plato (see Amunhotep III).

Ra (Rahotep), *ca.* 1367–1360 B.C., son of Maya and Ilipaaton; Eliezer, son of Moses.

Rahotep, 1367–1350 B.C., great Egyptian artist, son of Cato, who fashioned the Golden Mask and throne chair of King Tutankhamun; *Solomon*, 1540–1501 B.C., son of David and Bathsheba; *Gershom*, eldest son of Moses; *Linus* of Antioch, artist who designed the Chalice of Antioch which held the Holy Grail; *St. Jerome, ca.* A.D. 340–420, maker of the Latin version of the Bible known as Vulgate; *Stauracius, ca.* A.D. 829, monk who was the custodian of the Church of Alexandria; *Brigham Young,* A.D. 1801–1877, Mormon leader and high priest.

Ramses I, 1322–1321 B.C., Pharaoh of Egypt; *Hiram, ca.* 1540–1501 B.C., King of Tyre and friend of Solomon; Head Aton priest, and brother of Maya; *Justinian,* A.D. 527–565, Roman Emperor; *Hyrum Smith, ca.* A.D. 1800–1844, brother of Joseph Smith of the Mormon Church.

Ramses II (see Amunhotep III).

Rehoboam (see Smenkhkare).

Rekhmire (see Ahmose I).

Ricardo, Father (see Tutankhamun).

Senti-Khaem (see Sinuhe).

Seti I (see Smenkhkare).

Seti or *Anub-khper-re, ca.* 1292 B.C., ninth son of Ramses II, surviving crown prince, killed during the Exodus; *Isaiah*, 765 B.C., Major Prophet of the Old Testament; *Aristotle*, 384–322 B.C., Greek philosopher; *John the Beloved* of Galilee, one of the Twelve Apostles; *Leonardo da Vinci,* A.D. 1452–1519, Italian artist.

Setne-Khaem (see Sinuhe).

Setymeramun (see Sinuhe).

Sheba, Queen of (see Tiyi).

Shem (see Jesus, the Christ).

Shishak (see Thutmose III).

Silas or *Silvanus,* friend of Paul; *Nathan* the Prophet at the time of David; Aton priest at the time of Akhnaton.

Simmias (see Tutankhamun).

Sinuhe or *Setymeramun, ca.* 1376–1356 B.C., court physician at the time of Akhnaton and was for one month Pharaoh of Egypt—reigned 1346–1346 B.C. as *King Setymeramun; Khaemweset* or *Setne-Khaem* (known to his father as *Senti-Khaem*), *ca.* 1292 B.C., fourth son of Ramses II, the wizard prince; *Jeremiah, ca.* 612–550 B.C., of Judah, Major Prophet of the Old Testament; *Luke,* the physician of Antioch

Sitamun, ca. 1412 B.C., half-sister and wife of Amunhotep III; prepared the body of *Tahpenes* so Bathshua or Bathsheba could take over; *Ist-nofret* wife of Ramses II; *Nicomachus* (male incarnation), *ca.* 100 B.C., Neo-Pythagoran philosopher.

Smenkhkare, 1361–1360 B.C.—nine months Pharaoh of Egypt (born 1390 B.C.), son of Amunhotep III and Sitamun; *Rehoboam, ca.* 1501 B.C., son of Solomon; *Seti I,* 1321–1300 B.C., Pharaoh of Egypt whose daughter rescued Moses from the bulrushes, and father of Ramses II; *Timothy* of Asia Minor, favourite disciple of Paul.

Smith, Hyrum (see Ramses I).

Smith, Joseph (see Amhose I).

Socrates (see Akhnaton).

Solomon (see Rahotep).

Stauracius (see Rahotep).

Swedenborg, Emanuel (see Amunhotep III).

Sylvanus (see Silas).

Tahpenes, Queen (see Ilipaaton).

Tantahpe (died 1338 B.C.), daughter of Maya and Ilipaaton, who played the sistrum as priestess of Isis; *Miriam,* 1323–1193 B.C., sister of Moses and wife of Hur, who led the feminine group of the Exodus with music and dancing; *Martha,* favourite sister of the Master Jesus; *St. Cecilia* (martyred A.D. 230), native of Rome, regarded as patroness of church music.

Theodora (see Nefretiti).

Thomas (see John the Baptist).

Thoth (see Amenophis).

Thutmose III or *Shishak,* 1501–1447 B.C., of the Eighteenth Dynasty; *Pythagoras,* 590–500 B.C., Greek philosopher; now *Koot Hoomi Lal Singh* (Master K. H.) of Shigatse, in Tibet.

Timothy (see Smenkhkare).

Tiyi, Queen, ca. 1412–1370 B.C., favourite wife of Amunhotep III and mother of Akhnaton; *Hatshepsut* or *Queen of Sheba, ca.* 1514–1480 B.C., wife of Thutmose II and III and co-regent with both; *Nefretari, ca.* 1300 B.C., wife of Ramses II; *Guinevere, ca.* A.D. 500, wife of King Arthut; *Joan of Arc,* A.D. 1412–1431, French patriot—"Maid of Orleans."

Tutankhamun or *Tutankhaton* or *Neb-kheperu-Re,* ("Ratut"), 1360–1350 B.C. (born 1370 B.C.), boy king of the Eighteenth Dynasty, son of Amunhotep III and Sitamun; *Merk,* space visitor from Hesperus (Venus) who came to Lemuria 12,000 years ago and brought "footprints"; waif on the Nile at the time of Joseph and Asenath—Fifteenth Dynasty; *Hadad* (born 1565 B.C.) of Syria, contemporary with David and Solomon; *Menkheperre-Seneb, ca.* 1501 B.C., High Priest of Egypt under Thutmose III; *Aaron* (born 1316 B.C.), brother of Moses; *Ezekiel, ca.* 606–538 B.C., of Judah, Major Prophet of the Old Testament; *Simmias,* 480 B.C., student of Phylos (Philolaus), contemporary with Socrates and Plato; *Zacharias* or *Zechariah* of Judah, father of John the Baptist; *Mark* (born A.D. 18), the Evangelist; *St. George* (martyred A.D. 303), Roman tribune; *Doge Giustiniano Partecipazio, ca.* A.D. 829, of Venice; *Father Ricardo* during the Spanish Inquisition; *Atahualpa,* A.D. 1532, Inca assassinated by Pizarro; *Dr. Robert Browne,* A.D. 1550–1633, of England, father of Congregationalism.

Tutankhaton (see Tutankhamun).

Tutu, ca. 1376 B.C., minister of foreign affairs for Akhnaton; *Uriah* the Hittite, *ca.* 1580 B.C., husband of Bathsheba before David took her;

Joshua, who led the Israelites into the " Promised Land "; *St. Clement*,
A.D. 91–100, Bishop of Rome.
Uriah (see Tutu).
Vinci, Leonardo da (see Seti).
Young, Brigham (see Rahotep).
Zacharias or *Zechariah* (see Tutankhamun).
Zipporah (see Maketaton).
Zoroaster (see Jesus the Christ).
Zoser (see Amunhotep III).

NEW CHRONOLOGICAL ARRANGEMENT OF DATES ACCORDING TO ANCIENT MANUSCRIPTS

DATE	ISRAEL	EGYPT
1580 B.C.	David becomes King of Judah, with his capital at Hebron. He is thirty years old.	Ahmose I becomes King of Egypt. He is twenty years old.
1573 B.C.	David becomes King of all Israel.	
1560 B.C.	David and Joab in Edom. Hadad (five years old) flees to Egypt.	Ahmose I now co-regent with Amunhotep I.
1545 B.C.	Hadad (twenty years old), marries sister (fifteen years old) of Queen Tahpenes.	Ahmose I (fifty-five years old); Queen Tahpenes (forty years old). Death of Amunhotep I. Ahmose I now co-regent with Thutmose I.
1540 B.C.	David dies at seventy. Solomon king. Hadad now 25; his wife now 20. Genubath born.	Ahmose I (60) has seizure, but recovers. (David takes body of Ahmose I and Ahmose I incarnates as Genubath.)
1539 B.C.	Hadad hears of David's death. Genubath now one year old. Hadad returns to his native Edom.	Ahmose I (David) now 61. (Bathsheba dies a few years later and takes the body of Queen Tahpenes who expires in Egypt.)

NEW CHRONOLOGICAL ARRANGEMENT OF DATES
ACCORDING TO ANCIENT MANUSCRIPTS
(continued)

DATE	ISRAEL	EGYPT
1536 B.C.	Solomon starts to build Temple.	
1529 B.C.	Solomon completes erection of Temple of God in Jerusalem.	Ahmose I (David) dies at seventy-one years. Tahpenes (Bathsheba) dies at fifty-six years. Thutmose I now only King of Egypt.
1514 B.C.		Thutmose II becomes King of Egypt. (Hatshepsut, daughter of Thutmose I, co-regent with her husband Thutmose II.)
1501 B.C.	Genubath now 39, and vassal King of Edom. Solomon dies. Rehoboam King of Judah. Jeroboam King of Israel.	Thutmose III becomes King of Egypt. (Hatshepsut co-regent with her half-brother until 1480 B.C.)
1497 B.C.		Thutmose III moves northward to invade Palestine.
1480 B.C.	Death of Jeroboam.	Death of Hatshepsut.

ACCEPTED ISRAEL BIBLICAL CHRONOLOGY	CORRECTED CHRONOLOGY	ACCEPTED EGYPTIAN CHRONOLOGY

DAVID
1010 B.C.
    40 years.
970 B.C.
	DAVID
	1580 B.C.
	    40 years.
	1540 B.C.
		AHMOSE I
		1580 B.C.
		    22 years.
		1558 B.C.

SOLOMON
970 B.C.
    39 years.
931 B.C.
	SOLOMON
	1540 B.C.
	    39 years.
	1501 B.C.
		AMUNHOTEP I
		1558 B.C.
		    13 years.
		1545 B.C.

REHOBOAM (South-Judah)
931 B.C.
    17 years.
914 B.C.
	REHOBOAM (South-Judah)
	1501 B.C.
	    17 years.
	1484 B.C.
		THUTMOSE I
		1545 B.C.
		    31 years.
		1514 B.C.

JEROBOAM (North-Israel)
931 B.C.
    21 years.
910 B.C.
	JEROBOAM (North-Israel)
	1501 B.C.
	    21 years.
	1480 B.C.
		THUTMOSE II
		1514 B.C.
		    13 years.
		1501 B.C.

		HATSHEPSUT 1514 B.C. 34 years. 1480 B.C.
		THUTMOSE III 1501 B.C. 54 years. 1447 B.C.

PERIODS OF PHARAONIC REIGN

CORRECTED CHRONOLOGY OF EGYPT

Eighteenth Dynasty

AHMOSE I—1580–1529 B.C. (1560 B.C. Ahmose I co-regent with Amunhotep I.)

AMUNHOTEP I—1560–1545 B.C. (Amunhotep I died in 1545 B.C.)

THUTMOSE I—1545–1514 B.C. (1529 B.C. Thutmose I now only King of Egypt.)

THUTMOSE II—1514–1480 B.C. (Hatshepsut co-regent with Thutmose II and III until 1480 B.C., when she died.)

THUTMOSE III—1501–1447 B.C.

AMUNHOTEP II—1447–1420 B.C.

THUTMOSE IV—1420–1412 B.C.

AMUNHOTEP III—1412–1370 B.C. (Died spring of 1370 B.C.)

AKHNATON (AMUNHOTEP IV)—1370–1361 B.C. (Born 1408 B.C., son of Amunhotep III and Queen Tiyi; married Nefretiti, daughter of Priest Ay, in 1387 B.C.; co-regent with his father in 1382 B.C.; City of Akhetaton begun in 1378 B.C.; Akhnaton quarrelled with Nefretiti in 1362 B.C.; Akhnaton died in 1361 B.C. at the age of 47.)

SMENKHKARE—1361–1360 B.C.—9 months. (Born 1390 B.C., son of Amunhotep III and his second wife, Sitamun; co-regent with Akhnaton from 1362–1361 B.C. Married the oldest daughter of Akhnaton and Queen Nefretiti, Meritaton. Murdered with his wife in a royal chariot by the Amun priesthood.)

TUTANKHAMUN—1360–1350 B.C.—9 years. (Born December 9; 1370 B.C.; also known as " Neb-kheperu-Re " and preferred the name " Ratut." Was ten years of age when he ascended the throne, and died in the spring of 1350 B.C., April 23, at the age of nineteen; youngest son of Amunhotep III and Sitamun.)

AY—1350–1346 B.C. (Father of Nefretiti.)

SETYMERAMUN—1346–1346 B.C. (The physician, Sinuhe, was one month Pharaoh of Egypt; reigned as King Setymeramun.)

HOREMHEB—1346–1322 B.C. ("Pharaoh of the Oppression " and last Pharaoh of the Eighteenth Dynasty; married Princess Beketamun, daughter of Amunhotep III and Tiyi.)

HOUSE OF AMUNHOTEP
EIGHTEENTH DYNASTY EGYPT

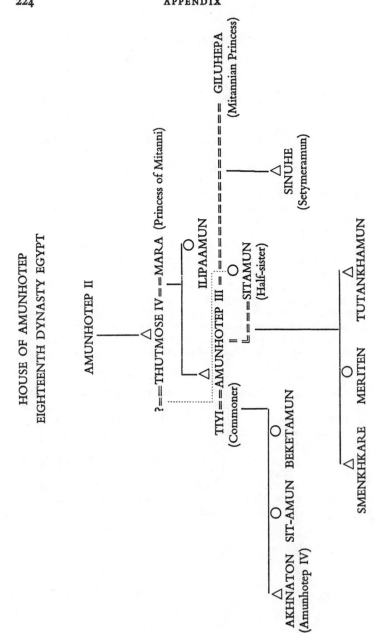

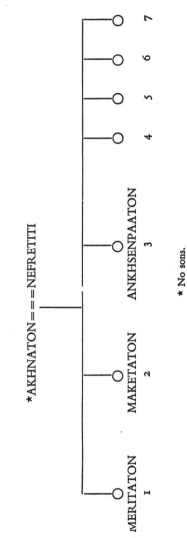

FAMILY OF AKHNATON
EIGHTEENTH DYNASTY EGYPT

*AKHNATON===NEFRETITI

MERITATON
1

MAKETATON
2

ANKHSENPAATON
3

4

5

6

7

* No sons.

COURT OFFICIALS AT AKHETATON
EIGHTEENTH DYNASTY EGYPT

AY======TYI	AMENOPHIS	MAYA======ILPAAMUN
(Governor of Thebes)	(Architect)	(Royal Treasurer)
NEFRETITI		TANTAHPE — RA
MAHU	AHMOSE	CATO=====?
(Chief of Police)	(Scribe)	(Artist)
		THOTMES BEK AUTA RAHOTEP
TUTU	HUYA	SINUHE (Setymeramun)
(Foreign Minister)	(Major-Domo for Tiyi)	(Physician)

PERIODS OF PHARAONIC REIGN

CORRECTED CHRONOLOGY OF EGYPT

Nineteenth Dynasty

RAMSES I—1322–1321 B.C.

SETI I—1321–1300 B.C. (Father of the Princess who rescued Moses from the bulrushes. Moses was born 1313 B.C. during eighth year of reign of Seti I; Aaron was born 1316 B.C.)

RAMSES II—1300–1233 B.C. ("Pharaoh of the *Greater* Exodus." Moses went to Midian 1273 B.C. when he was forty years old; Aaron was forty-three. Final EXODUS was April 6–7, *Midnight,* 1233 B.C.; Moses was eighty years old; Aaron was eighty-three.)

MENEPTAH—1233–1223 B.C. ("Pharaoh of the Post-Exodus period in Egypt.")

AMUNMOSE—1223–1220 B.C.

SIPTAH—1220–1214 B.C.

SETI II—1214–1210 B.C.

ARISU (Aarsu)—1210–1200 B.C. (A Syrian usurper.)

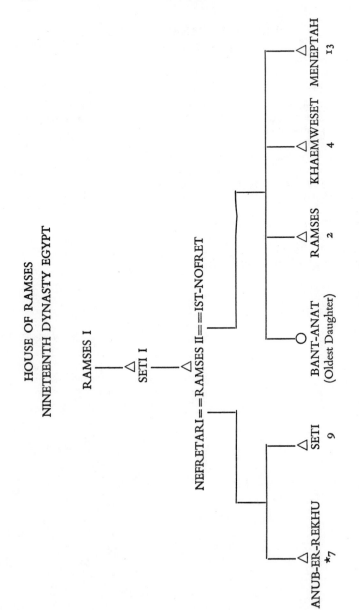

HOUSE OF RAMSES
NINETEENTH DYNASTY EGYPT

RAMSES I

SETI I

NEFRETARI==RAMSES II==IST-NOFRET

ANUB-ER-REKHU
*7

SETI
9

BANT-ANAT
(Oldest Daughter)

RAMSES
2

KHAEMWESET
4

MENEPTAH
13

* Numbers indicate order of birth of sons of Ramses II.

PHARAOHS OF THE EXODUS

AKHNATON . . . . "Pharaoh of the *Lesser* Exodus."
SMENKHKARE ⎫
TUTANKHAMUN ⎬ . . . . . . (Pharaohs when successive waves of small groups
AY ⎪ of Israelites left Egypt.)
SETYMERAMUN ⎭
HOREMHEB . . . . "Pharaoh of the Oppression."
RAMSES I ⎫ . . . . (Pharaohs when successive waves of small groups
SETI I ⎭ of Israelites left Egypt.)
RAMSES II . . . . "Pharaoh of the *Greater* Exodus."
MENEPTAH . . . . "Pharaoh of the Post-Exodus period in Egypt."

WHY CHRIST WAS BORN FOUR YEARS "BEFORE CHRIST"

When Christ was born time was reckoned in the Roman Empire from the founding of the city of Rome. When Christianity became the universal religion over what had been the Roman world, a monk named Dionysius Exiguus, at the request of the Emperor Justinian, made a calendar, A.D. 526, reckoning time from the Birth of Christ, to supersede the Roman Calendar.

Long after the Christian Calendar had replaced the Roman Calendar it was found that Dionysius had made a mistake in placing the Birth of Christ in the year 753 A U C (from the founding of Rome). It should have been 749 or a year or two earlier. Therefore, we say that Christ was born 4 B.C. merely because the maker of the Christian Calendar made a mistake of four or five years in co-ordinating it with the Roman Calendar, which it replaced.

CHRONOLOGY OF EVENTS CONNECTED WITH THE CUP
OF THE LAST SUPPER (HOLY GRAIL)

A.D. 30	Mark (twelve years old) picks it up from the Table of the Last Supper in the Upper Room of his mother's home, Mary of Jerusalem. It was the only *clay cup* served with twelve others which were made of *silver*.
A.D. 44	Mark (twenty-six years old) takes it with him to Antioch when he leaves Jerusalem with Barnabas and Paul.
A.D. 50	Peter brings it from Antioch to Jerusalem. He leaves his own silver cup he had used at the Last Supper in its place. Linus, the Greek artist, had just completed the silver chalice to hold the clay cup. Then Peter replaced it with his own silver one which was the same size. The silver cup now inside the chalice was Peter's.
A.D. 63	Clay cup Peter had returned to Jerusalem taken by Joseph of Arimathea when he journeyed to Britain. Philip, who had the Spear which had been used to pierce Jesus' side, gave this object to Joseph, and told him to take both the Spear and Cup with him to England and the site of the later Glastonbury Abbey. The Cup was kept in a secret place in a hidden crypt beneath the Abbey. A chalice was again made for it, and later it disappeared. But it was *not* stolen or destroyed. It was translated to another dimension of Time and Space. It shall make its appearance on earth again in the years ahead!
A.D. ?	Cup, or "Holy Grail," restored and returned to the earth.